SAPPORO ⚽ ✈

⚽ MIYAGI

P A C I F I C

O C E A N

⚽ IBARAKI

AMA

002

## DANCING TO GLORY – THE WORLD'S GREAT PLAYMAKERS

David Beckham, Luis Figo and Francesco Totti can class themselves as signed-up members of the footballing superstars club, but until they have made their mark on the biggest stage of all, their life membership remains a tantalising target.

**4**

## THE WORLD'S TOP TEN STRIKERS

Who are going to be the Golden Boot contenders at the 2002 World Cup Finals? We pick a likely top ten.

**12**

## A GUIDE TO EVERY FINALIST

A country-by-country guide to the squads, likely formations, the men that matter, roads to qualification, every country's low down, and history at the World Cup.

**15**

A Last Chance Saloon Production.
Edited by Chris Hunt & Jon Hayden
Design by Suzanne Johns and Mark Church at
Richard Rowe and Partners with special thanks to Darryl Tooth
Contributors Nick Gibbs & Luke Nicoli
All photographs supplied by Action Images
Special thanks to Tony Warner at Paradigm-ICT

First published in Great Britain in 2002 by Hayden Publishing Limited.
Copyright © Hayden Publishing.

Colour Origination by PDQ Digital Media Solutions Ltd.
Printed and bound in Italy by LEGO, Vicenza.
ISBN 1 90363 509 8

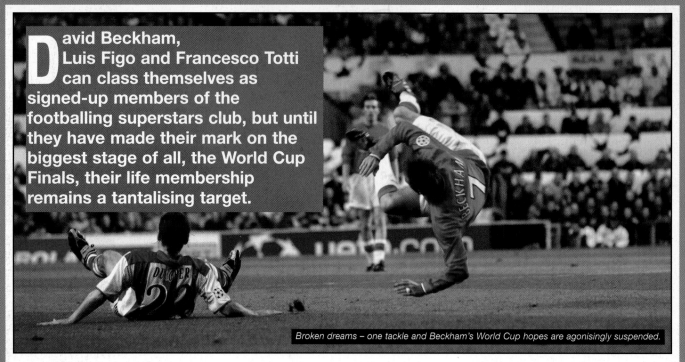

**D**avid Beckham, Luis Figo and Francesco Totti can class themselves as signed-up members of the footballing superstars club, but until they have made their mark on the biggest stage of all, the World Cup Finals, their life membership remains a tantalising target.

*Broken dreams – one tackle and Beckham's World Cup hopes are agonisingly suspended.*

Those already enshrined in the history of the beautiful game, thanks to their historic contributions to the Finals of yesteryear, include the greats Pelé and Maradona, Dutch master Johan Cruyff, England's Geoff Hurst and the Italian Paolo Rossi, but as this summer's finals approach on the horizon, who will be the next name to join such esteemed company?

Of all the runners and riders, our very own Becks was hotly tipped to take the tournament by storm following a bitter-sweet induction four years ago. His omission from England's starting line-up for the opening two games at France '98 caused more of a stir than the actual results, yet when he was finally unleashed by Glenn Hoddle, Becks delivered in the grandest manner. A trademark free-kick against Colombia booked a place in the second round as his star began

to rise to the very top. The media lavished the pin-up with praise, while his critics were told 'do believe the hype'. Yet he would soon discover that every silver lining has a cloud.

As England squared up against old foes Argentina in what was one of the best matches of the tournament, a petulant flick on the calf of Diego Simeone signalled Becks's premature exit from the game. Just four days after his national hero status had been projected, he was a traitor who had cost his nation the chance of further progress.

To suggest back then that England would plan to go into their next World Cup mission with Beckham as captain would have brought cries of derision, but he has done so much more than merely rebuild a reputation that had been so savagely shattered.

As runner-up in FIFA's World Player of the Year award this year, he has won every honour possible with Manchester United and risen to the challenge as England captain. "I've enjoyed the responsibility of the job," says the quietly spoken Londoner, whose dramatic late goal against Greece booked his country's passage to the finals.

"When I was asked to be England captain I didn't have to think twice about accepting it and I have been pleased with the way it's gone since I've had the arm band."

"The team has picked up well and after a bad start to our qualifying campaign, we did well to come back and finish top of our group. I have had so much success with United over the years, but what is missing is to win something with England. Hopefully that can happen at this World Cup."

Then an incident in Manchester United's April Champions League quarter-final clash with Deportivo La Coruña changed everything.

Already bruised by Diago Tristan's tackle a week earlier, a 16th minute late lunge by Pedro Duscher seems

He may not be fit enough to play, but Captain Beckham will still lift his team-mates in Japan/Korea.

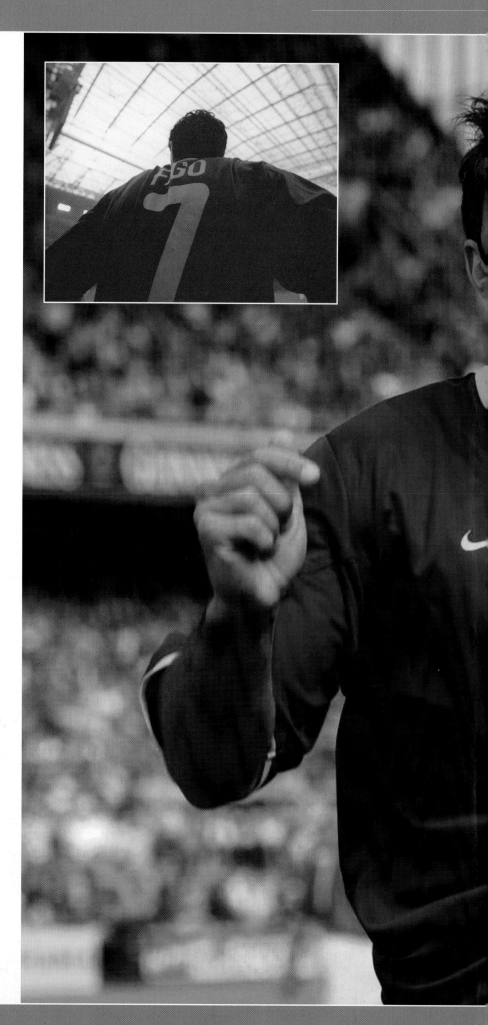

to have destroyed Beckham's (and possibly England's) World Cup dreams. It's a strange and bitter irony that the blow, which has broken a bone in Beck's left foot, should have been delivered by an Argentine boot.

Beckham had every hope of avenging England's defeat to Argentina at France 98 and take his place among the pantheon of footballing World Cup greats. Everything now depends on whether he recovers full fitness in time for the Finals and, at the time of writing, that's reckoned to be no more than a 50/50 possibilty.

Fit or not, Beckham will almost certainly travel to Japan/Korea, where is presence will act as a considerable boost to his team-mates. England fans can only wait and hope.

Nothing less than brilliance will do for masterly Portuguese midfielder Luis Figo, the man who claimed that same World Player of the Year award a couple of months back. At £37.5m, he was the world's costliest player when he made a highly controversial move from Barcelona to Real Madrid in 2000, but what a bargain he has proved to be.

Whether it's from the right flank or in the centre of midfield, Figo is one of the greatest players to have pulled on that colourful Portugal shirt, yet still has some way to go to eclipse the best.

That mantle is still held by the great Eusebio and the reason why he is held in such esteem is the fact that his finest hour occurred in a World Cup finals. The 1966 tournament in England may have been won by the hosts, yet Eusebio was its greatest star.

After failing to qualify in 1994 and 1998, this is Figo's first chance to show his worth on the highest stage and there is every reason to believe he can deliver. Captain of a national team whose inconsistency is as bewildering as their brilliance on the ball, they have been handed an enticing opening group and that should ensure their brilliant No.10 has plenty of time to pull the strings as he makes his mark.

"I have done so much in the game, but playing in a World Cup is the ultimate achievement for any player,"

says Figo. "I go there believing Portugal can win the tournament. We have the players to beat anyone in the world and now we have to go out and prove it. I know there is high expectation on me, but that is what I like."

Figo has replaced Zinedine Zidane as the world's number one player. For the mercurial Frenchman, who shone like a beacon as his country won the World Cup four years ago, this tournament will be all about confirming that he has it all.

Unlike Beckham, the balding Real Madrid playmaker doesn't have the looks to go with his genius, but Zidane is the best all-round midfielder and has the one medal they all want safely packed into his overflowing trophy cabinet. "Both personally and as a team, it's going to be harder for us this time," he warns.

"The emotion of winning the World Cup in front of our own fans is something that can never be beaten, but the team has the ability in every area, so we can do it again."

"But to reach such peaks fills you with the desire to do it again. You don't get many chances, maybe just two if you are lucky, so I know this could be my last chance on such a platform."

Zidane scored twice in that 1998 World Cup Final against Brazil, which was billed as a duo between himself and Brazilian superstar Ronaldo. Unfortunately, the Inter Milan striker's knee injury scuppered his performance that day and he's been suffering ever since. However, it appears the greatest non-playing footballer the game has ever seen

may be on the verge of making a dramatic return in time for this summer's tournament.

After playing his first game for Brazil in some two-and-a-half years a few weeks ago, coach Luis Felipe Scolari will doubtless be under pressure to include him if he can get anywhere close to full fitness. Yet even a half-fit Ronaldo is worth a gamble. He possesses such grace and skill on the ball that when he is running at goal, there is not a single defender in the world who can stop him within the laws of the game.

He did enough in the game against Yugoslavia to suggest that

he can still sparkle at the highest level and prove to the world that he has the ability to fill the legendary number 10 shirt. Certainly it

remains his dream to board a plane to Japan and Korea this summer.

"I have learnt not to take anything for granted, but I believe the World Cup is my destiny," he says. "The team has done very well without me but I deserve some good fortune. Of course the final decision rests with the coach, but I would like to declare myself ready for the greatest show on earth."

Certainly, success in the number ten shirt goes hand-in-glove with the World Cup and the task for Ronaldo and company must be to match the achievements of Maradona, the greatest World Cup hero of them all. He is the only player who can claim to have single-handedly won the trophy as he danced his way to glory with Argentina in Mexico 86. And as his nation has been installed as tournament favourites this time, the footy-mad Argentine fans will be looking for another hero to take on the baton.

Whether that will be Lazio striker Hernan Crespo or Manchester United midfielder Juan Sebastian Veron remains to be seen. Both have the ability to make this tournament their own and for Veron, it will be the chance to prove his doubters wrong after a difficult first – and possibly last – season at Old Trafford.

At £28m, he became English football's most expensive signing by some distance last summer, but the towering playmaker has struggled to find his feet in the Premiership and fit into United's system this season. Indeed, the likes of Beckham, Ryan Giggs and Ruud Van Nistelrooy have comfortably overshadowed a player who rarely

That man is likely to be Roma's Francesco Totti. A scorer of brilliant goals each week in Serie A, he also has the brains to go with his ability. As an out-and-out striker or a player that drops deep, he can unlock the most miserly of defences and with a team that thinks defence before attack, the hopes of a nation will rest on his shoulders this summer. "I can deal with the pressure," he said prior to his country's friendly victory against England recently.

"To play for Italy you need to be more than just a footballer because the expectations are so high. If people see me as a major player, then I see that as an honour rather than a problem. There is still bitterness of losing the Euro 2000 final to France, so if I can play my part in helping Italy do better this time, then I will be a very happy man."

Whatever happens this summer, the World Cup Finals will become a tournament of star players rather than star teams. Those who shine brightest will play a big part in shaping their country's destiny while at the same time etching their own place in football folklore. Now, let the fun begin.

has a bad game for his country and the talk remains strong that he may return to Lazio after the World Cup.

Yet his importance to Argentina cannot be underestimated and although Crespo and Gabriel Batistuta remain the golden boys who score all the goals, the supply line always harps back to Veron, and success this summer is largely dependent on a series of stunning displays from the United man. If he pulls it off, those tough times in his club career will be quickly forgotten and his transfer value will no doubt hit new heights, so his club cannot really lose.

Crespo, incidentally, is joint-favourite with Thierry Henry to join the esteemed company of Frenchman Just Fontaine, Germany's Gerd Muller, Mario Kempes of Argentina and England's Gary Lineker to finish as a World Cup Finals top-scorer and when the winners medals are handed out in Yokohama on June 30, it's a safe bet that the side with the most potent goalscorer in the tournament will be on hand.

Italy boasted such a player when Paolo Rossi shot the Azzurri to success in 1982 and for history to repeat that triumph of 20 years ago, they will need one of their potent strikers to come to the fore this time.

## HENRY

## OWEN

**NAME:** *Thierry Henry.* **AGE:** *24.*
**COUNTRY:** *France.* **CLUB:** *Arsenal.*

### SO WHERE'S HE SPRUNG FROM THEN?
Thierry set out on the road to fame and fortune as a winger at the French FA's football academy at Clairefontaine alongside his great friends Nicolas Anelka and David Trezeguet. His tricks and turn of pace prompted the then Monaco coach Arsene Wenger to sign him in 1994, but it wasn't until his £10million switch to Italian giants Juventus four years later that he emerged as a real star in the making. Unfortunately, his dream move turned into a nightmare when he made just 16 appearances and scored three goals in his one season in Turin. He was reunited with Wenger at Arsenal for the start of the 1999-2000 season and he hasn't looked back since.

### AND WHAT'S SO GOOD ABOUT HIM?
In a word, it's that pace. Henry would give Atto Bolden a run for his money when it comes to sprinting. Then, when you add skill to the equation and an uncanny knack of scoring breathtaking goals, you have a player who's got the lot. As soon as Tel arrived at the Marble Halls, Wily Ool Wenger took all these ingredients and converted him from winger to striker, instantly transforming him as a player. With almost 60 league goals in three seasons, he is now a Gunners legend.

### BUT WOULD YOU SAY HE'S A BORN WINNER?
Well, he picked up a winner's medal at the World Cup four years ago, and repeated the feat two years later at the European Championships in Holland and Belgium, so you'd have to say yes. On the domestic level, Thierry has been top-scorer for The Gunners in each of his three seasons at the club and could well break his duck on the trophy trail too this season as Wenger's side is still in the hunt for FA Cup and Premiership glory.

### FINALLY, A WORLD CUP RATING
With the likes of Zidane and Pires providing the ammunition, there's every chance that Henry will score the goals to fire France to their second successive World Cup Final success.

**NAME:** *Michael Owen.* **AGE:** *22.*
**COUNTRY:** *England.* **CLUB:** *Liverpool.*

### SO WHERE'S HE SPRUNG FROM THEN?
Michael burst onto the scene at Anfield as a fresh-faced 17-year-old in 1997 and has since emerged as the best striker to wear the England shirt since the halcyon days of Jimmy Greaves and Bobby Charlton. And who are we to argue? Michael's statistics speak for themselves: 63 league goals in just 121 league games for Liverpool has already earnt him God-like status among the Kop faithful, while his wonder goal against Argentina in the 1998 tournament quickly elevated him onto the world stage. Although his career has since been hampered with hamstring problems, Michael remains a feared opponent whenever he slips on the white shirt and he'll be keen to add to his 14 international goals from 32 appearances, which included that hat-trick against Germany in the qualifying campaign.

### AND WHAT'S SO GOOD ABOUT HIM?
Again, it's the pace that separates Michael from his striking counterparts. He might not be the strongest of players, but what he lacks in muscle he more than makes up for in speed. In full flow, most defenders are left trailing in his wake and rumours around Anfield suggest that he can run 100 metres in 11 seconds. But we're doing Mike a huge injustice here; he can also score goals, goals, goals from anywhere around the 18-yard box and with either foot, to boot!

### BUT WOULD YOU SAY HE'S A BORN WINNER?
Well he hasn't done too badly so far. Michael's goals last season helped Gerard Houllier's side to an unprecedented treble of League Cup, FA Cup and UEFA Cup success, while his goals this season in the Champions League continue to elevate his form to another level. Two late goals in the FA Cup Final success against Arsenal last season also suggest he has the strength of character to perform under the most intense pressure.

### FINALLY, A WORLD CUP RATING
Michael will be a marked man whenever he steps onto the pitch this summer, but much will depend on the supply line to him. If the England midfield create the chances, then you can count on him to finish the job off.

## TOTTI

## CRESPO

**NAME:** *Francesco Totti.* **AGE:** *25.*
**COUNTRY:** *Italy.* **CLUB:** *Roma.*

**NAME:** *Hernan Crespo.* **AGE:** *26.*
**COUNTRY:** *Argentina.* **CLUB:** *Lazio.*

### SO WHERE'S HE SPRUNG FROM THEN?

Francesco is one of that rare breed of footballers who has stayed with the same club, namely AS Roma, for his entire career. He made his Seria A debut at the age of 16 against Brescia, but in his first five seasons in the first-team remained something of a peripheral figure. However, he sprung to life in the 1997–98 season when he scored 13 times in a Roma side that started to show real Scudetta ambitions. His form was rewarded with an international call-up against Switzerland and he is now looked upon as a talismanic figure for both club and country. As captain of Roma, he will forever be remembered as the man that led the club to the title last year.

### AND WHAT'S SO GOOD ABOUT HIM?

Totti can best be described as the Italian version of Peter Beardsley, but with much better looks! He is a wizard on the ball and a goalmaker as well as a goaltaker. He seems to prefer playing behind the front two and that is when he is at his most dangerous; a really difficult player for defenders to mark. He finds it hard to fit into the 4-4-2 formation, which Italian sides are always built on, unless he plays alongside his friend Alessandro Del Piero. But wherever he plays, Italy are not the same team unless Totti is in it.

### BUT WOULD YOU SAY HE'S A BORN WINNER?

He will always be regarded as a winner following his success at Roma, but Totti is a big name for the big occasion. Like many of the current squad, he was a member of the Italian under-21 side that won the European Championships in 1996 and was widely regarded as Man-of-the-Match during his country's Euro 2000 Final appearance against France. He also scored in the penalty shoot-out against Holland at the semi-final stage, proving his nerve in the most pressured of situations.

### FINALLY, A WORLD CUP RATING

He might not grab the headlines like Del Piero, but Totti can hold the key to Italy's success. Now in the peak of form, much will be expected from his magical feet.

### SO WHERE'S HE SPRUNG FROM THEN?

Hernan started his career back home in Argentina with leading club River Plate and such was his presence, even at the tender age of 18, that he was handed the nickname 'Valdanito' because of his similarities with former superstar Jorge Valdano. With 24 goals to his name in three seasons, he was soon attracting the attention of the big Serie A clubs and it was Parma who took the plunge with a cool £10million bid in 1996. A fee of this size was thought a huge gamble for a club not known for its excessive expenditure, yet he repaid the faith with a goal every two games in his four seasons at the club. As the most wanted man in Italy, the big guns were lining up to sign him, and in 2000 he moved to Lazio on a five-year contract for an initial £80,000 a week in a £20 million deal.

### AND WHAT'S SO GOOD ABOUT HIM?

In terms of goalscoring, there's just one word for the guy: prolific. He's in the prime of his career, not only for club but also for country. With 17 goals in 36 appearances for Argentina, Hernan strikes fear into every defender he faces and having coped with the pressures of scoring for Lazio, he's now a stronger player mentally than he was before his arrival at the Stadio Olympico. If he gets a chance, he doesn't need an Andy Cole-number of chances to put the ball away and he's also as good with his head as he is with his feet. In fact, he's the ultimate striker.

### BUT WOULD YOU SAY HE'S A BORN WINNER?

Individually, there are few strikers in world football as good, but if we're talking success, then it's only started to fall into place these past couple of years. His 26 goals in 32 league appearances in his first season at Lazio went a long way in making his name, while Argentina are many people's favourites to lift the World Cup this summer. Having played just once in France '98, he is keen to make more of an impact and add to the Olympic silver medal he picked up in Atlanta in 1996.

### FINALLY, A WORLD CUP RATING

Hernan will be a fantastic success, no question, but much depends on Gabriel Batistuta. Coach Marcelo Bielsa feels the pair cannot work together, so if Crespo gets the nod, then the world is his oyster.

## LARSSON

## SUKUR

## OKOCHA

**NAME:** *Henrik Larsson.* **AGE:** *30.*
**COUNTRY:** *Sweden.* **CLUB:** *Celtic.*

### SO WHERE'S HE SPRUNG FROM THEN?
Although a big star back home in Sweden, Henrik really made a name for himself following his £5million arrival at Parkhead in the summer of 1997. In four years with Dutch First Division side Feyenoord, he had netted just 26 league goals, but that was to change in Scotland as he became a one-man goal machine and the scourge of defenders everywhere. His first two seasons were marked with 45 league goals and although his career was interrupted with a double leg fracture at Lyon in October 1999, he bounced back to win the European Golden Boot with 35 league goals as Celtic took the title last season.

### AND WHAT'S SO GOOD ABOUT HIM?
A very intelligent player, Larsson appears ghost-like in the box and is very difficult to pin down. Although he's not particularly tall, he scores plenty of goals with his head, making him the perfect goalscoring machine.

### BUT WOULD YOU SAY HE'S A BORN WINNER?
A late winner, more like.

### FINALLY, A WORLD CUP RATING
Although a star in his own right, Henrik can only be as good as the players around him, namely his strike partner Marcus Allback. And if the Heerenveen man is on top of his game then he'll make the space for Larsson to weave his undoubted magic.

**NAME:** *Hakan Sukur.* **AGE:** *30.*
**COUNTRY:** *Turkey.* **CLUB:** *Parma.*

### SO WHERE'S HE SPRUNG FROM THEN?
Hakan has almost single-handedly put Turkey on the football map. They have now emerged as a nation to be feared and much of this success can be found at the feet of 'The Bull of the Bosphorus'. With 35 international goals in 70 appearances, he is regarded as the best-ever Turkish striker. He joined Serie A giants Inter Milan, but five league goals in his first season saw him shipped off to Parma last August where he has finally found his feet again.

### AND WHAT'S SO GOOD ABOUT HIM?
Like an old-fashioned English centre forward, Hakan is a real handful for any defender. Tall, awkward and uncompromising, he also has good touch for a big man and leads the line very well. Yet it would be wrong to label him a targetman; Sukur creates chances too, and there are few strikers as good in the air. A danger man in every respect.

### BUT WOULD YOU SAY HE'S A BORN WINNER?
A championship winner in all his top-flight seasons with Galatasaray, the hysteria surrounding him remains at David Beckham-sized proportions. However, Hakan has been pilloried following his move to Italy and will be looking to the World Cup to show us all that he still remains a deadly striker.

### FINALLY, A WORLD CUP RATING
Many of Sukur's goals come from good wing play but, with Sergen Yalcin struggling with a knee injury and Emre Belozoglu stuck on the bench at Inter, there could be a ring-rustiness to his supply line.

**NAME:** *Augustine 'Jay-Jay' Okocha.* **AGE:** *28.*
**COUNTRY:** *Nigeria.* **CLUB:** *Paris St Germain.*

### SO WHERE'S HE SPRUNG FROM THEN?
Having started his career with Nigerian side Rangers, Jay-Jay's career in Europe started with German Fourth Division side Neunkirchen and by the end of the 1995-6 season he'd moved to Turkish club Fenerbahçe for £1 million, where he and his new side immediately won the Turkish league championship. In just two seasons in the Turkish First Division, Okocha's value rocketed. Paris St Germain paid Fenerbahçe an astonishing £10million for his services in the summer of 1998.

### AND WHAT'S SO GOOD ABOUT HIM?
You can always expect the unexpected - one minute he'll let fly from 30 yards, the next he'll be dribbling past six players before shooting! Very much like Italy's Totti, Okocha prefers to play behind the front two, where he can let his silky skills and breathtaking juggling confuse even the most hardened of defenders. The only criticism? – sometimes his laidback attitude on the pitch has been interpreted as laziness.

### BUT WOULD YOU SAY HE'S A BORN WINNER?
Well, success was forthcoming at international level in the early days. Jay-Jay was a member of the side that won the 1994 African Cup of Nations and repeated the feat two years later as a member of the side that won Olympic gold at the Atlanta Games, but was only a bit-part player at the 1994 finals, scoring just the one goal for Nigeria.

### FINALLY, A WORLD CUP RATING
He is to his country what Teddy Sheringham is to England - intelligent, has great vision and is often seen with a dodgy barnet!

 ★★

 ★★

 ★

# GOMES

*NAME: Nuno Gomes.  AGE: 25.*
*COUNTRY: Portugal.  CLUB: Fiorentina.*

### SO WHERE'S HE SPRUNG FROM THEN?
Nuno started his professional career at Boavista and inspired the club to the Portuguese Cup in 1997, having scored 60 goals in three seasons. His prolific form attracted the attention of the country's biggest clubs and Benfica soon came calling. He took some time to settle, but regular Champions League football took his career to another level and his potential as an international player was realised at Euro 2000 where he was a star in a Portugal side that reached the semi-finals. With four goals to his credit, including one in the semi-final against France, he joined Fiorentina for £12million, where he has taken over from Argentinean Gabriel Batistuta as the club's superstar.

### AND WHAT'S SO GOOD ABOUT HIM?
His skill and agility are just as impressive as his eye for goal. England fans won't need reminding of his ability as he was the man who, having seen his country battle back from 2-0 down, scored the all-important third goal during the first round of Euro 2000.

### BUT WOULD YOU SAY HE'S A BORN WINNER?
Not so much a born winner, but a player born with attitude! If you cast your minds back to Euro 2000, Gomes was one of the players who lost his head following Zinedine Zidane's Golden Goal penalty winner at the semi-final stage.

### FINALLY, A WORLD CUP RATING
Technically, a superb striker and that is why he makes our top ten. He won't get a hatful of goals, but when he does score it'll turn heads.

# RONALDINHO

*NAME: Ronaldinho.  AGE: 21.*
*COUNTRY: Brazil.  CLUB: Paris St Germain.*

### SO WHERE'S HE SPRUNG FROM THEN?
Forget Ronaldo, Ronaldinho Gaucho is the new star of Brazilian football. Having scored 15 goals in 14 matches for his club side Gremio, he burst onto the scene with the national team at the Copa America in 1999 where he scored an amazing goal against Venezuela that was reminiscent of Pelé's wonderful goal in the 1958 World Cup Final. Now he has been recalled, his ten goals from 22 appearances makes him a star to keep an eye on this summer.

### AND WHAT'S SO GOOD ABOUT HIM?
Frightening pace and skill. He admits that he learnt his dribbling skills by running rings around his dog in the back yard of his home in the run-down town of Oporto Alegre. With a build on a par with that of Ronaldo, he is the perfect foil for the less agile but equally skilful Romario and the prospect of the pair of them working in tandem this summer is enough to frighten all their opponents.

### BUT WOULD YOU SAY HE'S A BORN WINNER?
Well if you're widely regarded as the new Ronaldo, then you can't be doing too badly! So far, he's won the Player of the Tournament award at the World Youth Cup in 1997, finished top scorer at the Confederations Cup in 2000 with six goals and also top scored for his country in qualifying for the Sydney Olympics.

### FINALLY, A WORLD CUP RATING
Ronaldinho is the golden boy of Brazilian football and, when given his chance, is tipped to become the star of the tournament.

# RAUL

*NAME: Raul Gonzalez.  AGE: 24.*
*COUNTRY: Spain.  CLUB: Real Madrid.*

### SO WHERE'S HE SPRUNG FROM THEN?
Raul Gonzalez Blanco started out as a youth team player with Atletico Madrid but his prolific form soon had Real Madrid keen. Raul was always going to become a star in Spain and as a fresh-faced 17-year-old, scored a respectable nine league goals in his first 28 appearances. Raul has since bagged well over 100 goals in La Liga, netting 25 goals in 36 appearances last season.

### AND WHAT'S SO GOOD ABOUT HIM?
Confident with both feet, Raul's game is about outfoxing his opponents rather than using sheer pace or brute force. He has an uncanny knack of ghosting into the right position at the right time, and can also call on his array of tricks to beat the attention of his markers.

### BUT WOULD YOU SAY HE'S A BORN WINNER?
There's no denying that in the glorious colours of Real Madrid, Raul is a born superstar. He is the golden boy of the side, the goal-getter and the perfect foil for the craftsmanship of Zinedine Zidane. However, his career in a Spanish shirt has been chequered to say the least. He failed to make the Euro 96 squad, and never shone at either France 98 or Euro 2000, despite scoring 11 goals in eight qualifying matches on the way to the finals in Holland and Belgium.

### FINALLY, A WORLD CUP RATING
There is no doubting Raul's ability inside and outside the box, but much will depend on how well his partnership with Deportivo's Diego Tristan forms.

# GROUP F

| OPPONENT | DATE | UK TIME | VENUE |
|----------|------|---------|-------|
| Nigeria | **2 June** | 06.30 | **Ibaraki, Japan** |
| England | **7 June** | 12.30 | **Sapporo, Japan** |
| Sweden | **12 June** | 07.30 | **Miyagi, Japan** |

## "*the tournament's hot favourites*"

# ARGENTINA

Argentina are the red-hot favourites to win the first World Cup of the new millennium with a team oozing world-class quality in not only their first choice players, but in an outstanding squad. A quick look at their awe-inspiring attacking force demonstrates just what the rest of the finalists are up against. Hernan Crespo topped the South American goalscoring charts with nine goals in 12 appearances establishing him as first choice striker since replacing Gabriel Batistuta as sub in the 3-1 win away to Colombia. It's not certain that Batistuta, Argentina's all-time top goalscorer with 55 goals – his 55th netted in the 2-2 draw in Paraguay – will be selected for the finals, but in pairing Crespo with Claudio Lopez, Argentina has a formidable striking partnership. Waiting in the wings is Javier Saviola who helped Argentina win the 2001 World Youth Cup. Saviola was the tournament's leading scorer with 11 goals and voted the competition's Most Valuable Player. This led the youngster to a £19 million move from River Plate to Barcelona – making him the world's most expensive teenager in the process.

Even the loss of Diego Simeone, their captain and most capped player – with 104 international appearances – failed to undermine Argentina's faultless path through the qualifiers. Simeone suffered a cruciate ligament injury and is not certain to be fit for the Finals. His last appearance for Argentina was the 2-0 victory in Ecuador that clinched Argentina's place in the Finals – with four games to spare! Argentina dominated the South American group from the kick off. An opening 4-1 win over Chile put them to the top of the table and thereafter they never relinquished pole position. Coach Marcelo Bielsa used only 28 players during qualifying (compared to Brazil's staggering 62!), most of whom play club football with top European sides. Only Ariel Ortega and Juan Roman Riquelme play in Argentina's debt-ridden domestic league, while the tenacious Juan Pablo Sorin plays across the border in the bizarre world of Brazilian soccer.

Argentina, up to the end of qualification, had suffered just one defeat in their previous 24 games (away to Brazil) and in that time failed to score just once, against Kevin Keegan's England side at Wembley in February 2000. England will face Argentina in Japan with still painful memories of their last World Cup encounter, which ended in an Argentine victory after a dramatic second-round penalty shoot out.

Twelve years earlier England and Argentina had met in the quarter-finals of the Mexico World Cup when Diego Maradona scored his infamous "hand of god" goal, following it a few minutes later with a moment of sublime footballing genius, scoring, arguably, one of the competition's best ever goals. England were beaten 2-1 and Argentina marched on to win the World Cup. In recognition of Maradona's contribution to the national team, the country has retired his number 10 shirt, so no Argentine player at the 2002 tournament will be allocated that squad number.

Frankly, it won't matter what shirt numbers Argentina's quality side wear. They are the favourites – the team that everyone must beat to win the World Cup.

---

## ★ THE LOWDOWN

**Population:** 37.3 million

**Capital:** Buenos Aires

**Leader:** Fernando De La Rua

**Life Expectancy:** Male: 72 yrs Female: 79 yrs

>> Warning for vegetarians visiting Argentina; beef dominates the restaurant menus and every part of the animal is eaten, including the intestines and udders!

>> Argentina leads the world in setting voluntary greenhouse gas targets.

>> In 1995 the Argentine Foreign Minister offered to buy the Falkland Islands from the Islanders; 2000 islanders were offered 800 dollars each, it was not successful.

★ **ASSOCIATION:** Asociaion de Futbol Argentino

★ **JOINED FIFA:** 1912

★ **JOINED CONMEBOL:** 1916

★ **PLAYERS:** 306,400

★ **CLUBS:** 3,035

★ **WEBSITE:** www.afa.org.ar

★ **HONOURS:** World Cup – 1978, 1986; Copa America – 1910/21/25/27/29/37/41/45/46/47/55/57/59/91/93.

*Argentina's all-time top goalscorer.*

## ★ ROAD TO QUALIFICATION

Mar 00 **Chile** (h) > (w) **4-1**
Batistuta 10, Veron 34, 71 pen, Lopez,C 88

Apr 00 **Venezuela** (a) > (w) 0-**4**
Crespo 1, Ortega 4, 76, Ayala 8

Jun 00 **Bolivia** (h) > (w) **1-0** Lopez,C 82

Jun 00 **Colombia** (a) > (w) 1-**3**
Batistuta 24, 45, Crespo 75

Jul 00 **Ecuador** (h) > (w) **2-0**
Crespo 24, Lopez,C 51

Jul 00 **Brazil** (a) > (l) 3-**1** Almeyda 45

Aug 00 **Paraguay** (h) > (d) **1-1** Aimar 67

Sep 00 **Peru** (a) > (w) 1-**2**
Crespo 27, Veron 38

Oct 00 **Uruguay** (h) > (w) **2-1**
Gallardo 28, Batistuta 42

Nov 00 **Chile** (a) > (w) 0-**2**
Ortega 26, Husain 90

Mar 01 **Venezuela** (h) > (w) **5-0**
Crespo 13, Sorin 31, Veron 51, Gallardo 60, Samuel 85

Apr 01 **Bolivia** (a) > (d) 3-**3**
Crespo 43, 88, Sorin 89

Jun 01 **Colombia** (h) > (w) **3-0**
Kily Gonzalez 22, Lopez,C 35, Crespo 38

Aug 01 **Ecuador** (a) > (w) 0-**2**
Veron 19, Crespo 34 pen

Sep 01 **Brazil** (h) > (w) **2-1**
Gallardo 76, Cris 84 og

Oct 01 **Paraguay** (a) > (d) 2-**2**
Pocchettino 67, Batistuta 73

Nov 01 **Peru** (h) > (w) **2-0**
Samuel 46, Lopez,C 85

Nov 01 **Uruguay** (a) > (d) 1-**1** Lopez,C 44

## ★ FINAL GROUP TABLE

| Team | P | W | D | L | F | A | Pts |
|---|---|---|---|---|---|---|---|
| **Argentina** | **18** | **13** | **4** | **1** | **42** | **15** | **43** |
| Ecuador | 18 | 9 | 4 | 5 | 23 | 20 | 31 |
| Brazil | 18 | 9 | 3 | 6 | 31 | 17 | 30 |
| Paraguay | 18 | 9 | 3 | 6 | 29 | 23 | 30 |
| Uruguay | 18 | 7 | 6 | 5 | 19 | 13 | 27 |
| Colombia | 18 | 7 | 6 | 5 | 20 | 15 | 27 |
| Bolivia | 18 | 4 | 6 | 8 | 21 | 33 | 18 |
| Peru | 18 | 4 | 4 | 10 | 14 | 25 | 16 |
| Venezuela | 18 | 5 | 1 | 12 | 18 | 44 | 16 |
| Chile | 18 | 3 | 3 | 12 | 15 | 27 | 12 |

## ★ RECENT RESULTS

Feb 02 **Wales** (a) > 1-**1** (d) Cruz 62

Mar 02 **Cameroon** (n) > 2-2 (d)
Veron 18 pen, Aimar 62

Coach Marcelo Bielsa's 3-3-1-3 formation is designed to be adaptable and allows Argentina's flair players to shine. German Burgos has established himself as the number one goalkeeper behind a three-man defence of the experienced Nestor Sensini, Roberto Ayala and Walter Samuel. If injuries should rule out any of the trio, Argentina can call on Mauricio Pochettino, Nelson Vivas or even Javier Zanetti. Under Bielsa's system Zanetti is pushed forward on the right of a three-man midfield with either Juan Pablo Sorin or Kily Gonzalez on the left. The crucial central role is held by Matias Almeyda alongside pivotal playmaker Juan Sebastian Veron, who has a free role linking midfield to a three-man attack. Up front Hernan Crespo and Claudio Lopez combines well with Gabriel Batistuta, Argentina's top scorer, adding to their firepower.

# PROBABLE FORMATION 3-3-1-3

BURGOS

SENSINI · SAMUEL

AYALA

ZANETTI · ALMEYDA · SORIN

VERON

BATISTUTA · C LOPEZ · CRESPO

## ★ MEN THAT MATTER!

### HERNAN CRESPO

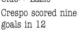

Age>> 26
Club>> Lazio

Crespo scored nine goals in 12 appearances during the qualifiers where he linked well with Gabriel Batistuta and Claudio Lopez. Cost Lazio £37 million in 2000 and playing his second World Cup.

### ARIEL ORTEGA

Age>> 28
Club>> River Plate

Finished the last World Cup in shame with a red card for head-butting an opponent. Influential midfielder playing his third World Cup and was also a silver medallist at the 1996 Olympics.

### JUAN SEBASTIAN VERON

Age>> 27
Club>> Man U.

The pulse of the Argentine midfield and likewise with Lazio until passport scandal opened the way for a move to England. Playing in his second World Cup and only missed two qualifiers.

## ★ PROBABLE SQUAD ★ QUALIFICATION RECORD

| NAME | POSITION | CLUB | APS/GOALS | GAMES | MINS | Y/C | R/C | GOALS |
|---|---|---|---|---|---|---|---|---|
| Roberto Bonano | Goalkeeper | Barcelona, Spain | 12/0 | 9 | 736 | 2 | 0 | 0 |
| German Burgos | Goalkeeper | Atletico Madrid, Spain | 34/0 | 8 | 704 | 2 | 0 | 0 |
| Pablo Cavallero | Goalkeeper | Celta Vigo, Spain | 6/0 | 2 | 180 | 1 | 0 | 0 |
| Roberto Ayala | Defender | Valencia, Spain | 74/3 | 17 | 1530 | 2 | 0 | 1 |
| Mauricio Pochettino | Defender | Paris Saint-Germain, France | 15/2 | 6 | 540 | 3 | 0 | 1 |
| Walter Samuel | Defender | Roma, Italy | 31/3 | 17 | 1530 | 4 | 0 | 2 |
| Roberto Sensini | Defender | Parma, Italy | 60/0 | 8 | 636 | 1 | 0 | 0 |
| Nelson Vivas | Defender | Internazionale, Italy | 37/1 | 9 | 664 | 2 | 0 | 0 |
| Pablo Aimar | Midfielder | Valencia, Spain | 18/1 | 12 | 587 | 2 | 0 | 1 |
| Matias Almeyda | Midfielder | Parma, Italy | 31/1 | 8 | 439 | 3 | 0 | 1 |
| Marcelo Gallardo | Midfielder | Monaco, France | 41/14 | 6 | 233 | 0 | 0 | 3 |
| Kily Gonzalez | Midfielder | Valencia, Spain | 30/4 | 13 | 1014 | 1 | 0 | 1 |
| Claudio Husain | Midfielder | Napoli, Italy | 12/1 | 3 | 198 | 0 | 0 | 1 |
| Gustavo Lopez | Midfielder | Celta Vigo, Spain | 29/4 | 10 | 246 | 0 | 0 | 0 |
| Ariel Ortega | Midfielder | River Plate, Argentina | 81/17 | 16 | 1113 | 1 | 0 | 3 |
| Diego Simeone | Midfielder | Lazio, Italy | 104/11 | 14 | 1203 | 3 | 0 | 0 |
| Juan Sorin | Midfielder | Cruzeiro, Brazil | 33/5 | 14 | 971 | 1 | 0 | 2 |
| Juan Sebastian Veron | Midfielder | Manchester United, England | 46/7 | 16 | 1372 | 2 | 0 | 5 |
| Javier Zanetti | Midfielder | Internazionale, Italy | 64/3 | 14 | 1101 | 1 | 0 | 0 |
| Gabriel Batistuta | Forward | Roma, Italy | 75/55 | 5 | 427 | 0 | 0 | 5 |
| Claudio Lopez | Forward | Lazio, Italy | 47/10 | 16 | 1063 | 3 | 0 | 6 |
| Hernan Crespo | Forward | Lazio, Italy | 33/17 | 12 | 839 | 0 | 0 | 9 |
| Javier Saviola | Forward | Barcelona, Spain | 1/0 | 1 | 15 | 0 | 0 | 0 |

KEY: APPS/GOALS = International Appearances/Goals; GAMES=Qualification Games played; MINS=Minutes played; Y/C= Yellow cards R/C=Red cards

# HISTORY AT THE WORLD CUP

**1930 1934 1938 1950 1954 1958 1962 1966 1970 1974 1978 1982 1986 1990 1994 1998**

**1930 >** Argentina's Guillermo Stabile finishes top scorer with 8 goals in the first World Cup tournament.

**1950 >** Argentina enter and then withdraw from the 1950 World Cup.

**1966 >** Bad-tempered Argentina, dubbed 'Animals' by Alf Ramsey, have captain Antonio Rattin sent off against England.

**1978 >** Argentina, featuring Ossie Ardiles, Ricky Villa and Mario Kempes, win the World Cup.

**1994 >** Former hero Diego Maradona fails a routine drug test and is thrown out of the World Cup.

**1986 >** Diego Maradona-inspired Argentina win the World Cup beating West Germany 3-2 in the Final.

**1990 >** Monzon and Dezotti are sent off in the World Cup Final against West Germany.

**1958 >** Argentina's best players, Angelillo, Maschio and Sivori, are snatched up by Italian clubs and play for Italy at World Cup.

**1934 >** Argentina lose Monti, Orsi and Guaita to Italian team and send a third string in response.

**1938 >** Argentina lose out to France to host 1938 Tournament and refuse to enter for another 20 years.

**1970 >** Argentina, denied hosting the 1970 tournament, finish bottom of their qualifying group.

**1998 >** Ariel Ortega is sent off as Argentina lose to Holland to a late Bergkamp goal.

## ★ WORLD CUP HISTORY

| | | | |
|---|---|---|---|
| 1930 >> Runners-Up | | 1970 >> Did Not Qualify | |
| 1934 >> First Round | | 1974 >> Second Round | |
| 1938 >> Did Not Enter | | 1978 >> Winners | |
| 1950 >> Withdrew | | 1982 >> Second Round | |
| 1954 >> Did Not Enter | | 1986 >> Winners | |
| 1958 >> First Round | | 1990 >> Runners-Up | |
| 1962 >> First Round | | 1994 >> Second Round | |
| 1966 >> Quarter-Final | | 1998 >> Quarter-Finals | |

## ★ WORLD CUP RECORDS, STORIES AND WEIRDNESS

**MOST GOALS IN A TOURNAMENT** >> Guillermo Stábile scored 8 in the 1930 tournament.

**GREATEST WORLD CUP GOAL** >> Diego Maradona unquestionably scored the greatest ever goal seen at a World Cup Finals. Against England in 1986, and just minutes after the infamous "Hand of God" goal, Maradona ran from his own half beating English player after player then slipped it past a bemused and helpless Peter Shilton. Argentina won 2-0.

# GROUP H

| OPPONENT | DATE | UK TIME | VENUE |
|----------|------|---------|-------|
| Japan | **4 June** | 10.00 | **Saitama, Japan** |
| Tunisia | **10 June** | 10.00 | **Oita, Japan** |
| Russia | **14 June** | 07.30 | **Shizuoka, Japan** |

## ★ THE LOWDOWN

**Population:** 10.2 million

**Capital:** Brussels

**Leader:** Guy Verhofstadt

**Life Expectancy:** Male: 74 yrs Female: 81 yrs

>> Belgium only became independent from the Netherlands in 1830.

>> Besides being famous for sprouts, chocolate and good lager, the Belgians also claim to have "invented" fish & chips. Mmm, what a healthy, well-balanced diet!

>> Brussels is the seat of both the European Union and NATO.

## "will it be an early bath for the Belgiques?"

# BELGIUM

Six successive successful qualifications for the Finals (without hosting the tournament along the way) make Belgium something of a World Cup fixture. But they rarely cut the mustard, departing on the early flight home. In France, they drew all three of their group games against Holland (0-0), Mexico (2-2) and South Korea (1-1) and that was that.

Their best performance was at Mexico 86 where, defying the form book, they reached the semi-finals only to be beaten by Argentina and then lose a thrilling third place play-off to France, 4-2 after extra-time.

Nobody would accuse the current Belgium side of possessing abundant flair, but they are a solid, reliable outfit who know their capabilities and play to them. Belgium finished second in their qualifying group with an impressive tally of 25 goals in eight games. However, 14 of those were against minnows San Marino including a 10-1 thrashing in which 59th minute substitute Bob Peeters scored the 8th, 9th and 10th goal for an unlikely hat-trick.

Crucially in the group, they got the better of Scotland over two matches. In Glasgow, the Belgians salvaged a point after trailing 2-0 and having right-back Eric Deflandre sent off. Marc Wilmots halved the deficit in the 58th minute and Daniel Van Buyten scored the crucial equaliser in stoppage time. Van Buyten, incidentally, has not played for Belgium since that game.

The return fixture in Brussels saw Belgium go ahead after 28 minutes. Playmaker Johan Walem hit a superb measured pass for Wesley Sonck to set up left back Nico Van Kerckhoven, as he ran unmarked into the box. A Bart Goor goal in the last minute saw Belgium run out 2-0 winners.

Against Croatia however, a goalless draw at home in their opening game and a 1-0 defeat away sent Belgium to the play-offs against the Czech Republic.

Striker Gert Verheyen proved crucial to the outcome of both games. In Brussels, Verheyen scored his eighth international goal giving Belgium a 1-0 victory. In Prague, Belgium had to do some solid defending to hold on to their slender aggregate lead, but in the 85th minute Verheyen was fouled in the area. Up stepped captain Marc Wilmots to convert the penalty for his eighth goal of the qualifiers and book Belgium's place in the Finals.

What Belgium will achieve in Japan and Korea is difficult to assess. They are capable of finishing in the top half of their Group, but they're just as likely to all fall down. They begin against a much-improved Japanese side then face tough African outfit Tunisia. However, the crucial match will be the last group outing in Shizuoka against Russia, a European team of equal ability.

★ **ASSOCIATION:** Union Royale des Societes de
Football Association

★ **JOINED FIFA:** 1904

★ **JOINED UEFA:** 1954

★ **PLAYERS:** 390,500

★ **CLUBS:** 2,120

★ **WEBSITE:** www.footbel.com

★ **HONOURS:** Olympics – 1920.

*Glen De Boeck auditions for Riverdance during a quiet moment in a match.*

## ★ ROAD TO QUALIFICATION

Sep 00 **Croatia** (h) > (d) 0-0

Oct 00 **Latvia** (a) > (w) 0-**4**
Wilmots 4, Peeters 12, Cavens 81,
Verheyen 90

Feb 01 **San Marino** (h) > (w) **10**-1
Vanderhaeghe 10, 50, Mpenza, E 13, Goor
25, 62, Baseggio 65, Wilmots 71, Peeters,
B 75, 83, 88

Mar 01 **Scotland** (a) > (d) 2-2
Wilmots 58, Van Buyton 90

Jun 01 **Latvia** (h) > (w) **3**-1
Wilmots 2, Mpenza, E 12, Zemlinskis 50 og

Jun 01 **San Marino** (a) > (w) 1-**4**
Wilmots 10, 89 pen, Verheyen 60,
Sonck 68

Sep 01 **Scotland** (h) > (w) **2**-0
Van Kerckhoven 28, Goor 90

Oct 01 **Croatia** (a) > (l) 1-**0**

## ★ FINAL GROUP TABLE

| Team | P | W | D | L | F | A | Pts |
|---|---|---|---|---|---|---|---|
| Croatia | 8 | 5 | 3 | 0 | 15 | 2 | 18 |
| **Belgium** | **8** | **5** | **2** | **1** | **25** | **6** | **17** |
| Scotland | 8 | 4 | 3 | 1 | 12 | 6 | 15 |
| Latvia | 8 | 1 | 1 | 6 | 5 | 16 | 4 |
| San Marino | 8 | 0 | 1 | 7 | 3 | 30 | 1 |

## ★ RECENT RESULTS

Feb 02 **Norway** (h) > (w) **1**-0 Tanghe 82

Mar 02 **Greece** (a) > (l) 3-**2**
Goor 28, Sonck 54

## DID YOU KNOW?

**Midfielder Sven Vermant made his international debut against Armenia in October 1995 but had to wait a further three years for his second appearance.**

While Robert Waseige remains a steadfast advocate of the 4-4-2 system, his rigid approach has made Belgium a team less than exciting to watch. Waseige believes in attacking football but the current side lacks any real flair. Defensively, keeper Geert De Vlieger plays behind a central partnership of Glen De Boeck and Joos Valgaeren with Eric Van Meir an alternative. Right back Eric Deflandre and Nico Van Kerckhoven on the left are encouraged to get forwards. Johan Walem has developed into a playmaker and should perfectly complement the hard-working team captain, Marc Wilmots, who sits alongside him. Bart Goor is firmly established on the left of midfield although the right side is still a problem – Sven Vermant will probably get the nod ahead of Timmy Simons. In attack, Wesley Sonck has been a revelation alongside the in form Gert Verheyen. The tall Bob Peeters and the tenacious Emile Mpenza provide attacking alternatives.

## PROBABLE FORMATION  4-4-2

DE VLEIGER

DEFLANDRE

VAN KERCKHOVEN

VALGAEREN   DE BOECK

VERMANT   WILMOTS   WALEM   GOOR

SONCK   VERHEYEN

## ★ MEN THAT MATTER!

### WESLEY SONCK

Age>> 23

Club>> Genk

This young striker, blessed with extraordinary pace, was the discovery of the qualifiers for Belgium. He has the makings of becoming Belgian's Michael Owen injecting creativity into a side that needs it.

### MARC WILMOTS

Age>> 33

Club>> Schalke

Influential captain travelling to his fourth World Cup. He scored eight goals in qualifying including the decisive penalty in the play off against the Czech Republic. Takes penalties and free kicks.

### BART GOOR

Age>> 29

Club>> Hertha Berlin

Ever-present on the left of midfield throughout the qualifiers who will be making his World Cup debut. He scored twice in Belgium's 10-1 thrashing of San Marino. Played at Euro 2000.

## ★ PROBABLE SQUAD                    ★ QUALIFICATION RECORD

| NAME | POSITION | CLUB | APS/GOALS | GAMES | MINS | Y/C | R/C | GOALS |
|---|---|---|---|---|---|---|---|---|
| **Geert De Vlieger** | Goalkeeper | Willem II, Holland | 21 /0 | 10 | 900 | 0 | 0 | 0 |
| **Ronny Gaspercic** | Goalkeeper | Real Betis, Spain | 8 /0 | 0 | 0 | 0 | 0 | 0 |
| **Frederic Herpoel** | Goalkeeper | Ghent, Belgium | 2 /0 | 0 | 0 | 0 | 0 | 0 |
| **Philippe Clement** | Defender | Brugge, Belgium | 14 /0 | 2 | 180 | 1 | 0 | 0 |
| **Bertrand Crasson** | Defender | Anderlecht, Belgium | 26 /1 | 2 | 114 | 1 | 0 | 0 |
| **Glen De Boeck** | Defender | Anderlecht, Belgium | 30 /0 | 5 | 404 | 0 | 0 | 0 |
| **Eric Deflandre** | Defender | Lyon, France | 36 /0 | 9 | 786 | 1 | 1 | 0 |
| **Marc Hendrikx** | Defender | Anderlecht, Belgium | 15 /0 | 3 | 57 | 0 | 0 | 0 |
| **Joos Valgaeren** | Defender | Celtic, Scotland | 13 /0 | 5 | 418 | 0 | 0 | 0 |
| **Daniel Van Buyton** | Defender | Marseille, France | 3 /1 | 2 | 122 | 0 | 0 | 1 |
| **Nico Van Kerckhoven** | Defender | Schalke, Germany | 35 /3 | 6 | 529 | 0 | 0 | 1 |
| **Eric Van Meir** | Defender | Standard Liege, Belgium | 28 /1 | 8 | 676 | 2 | 0 | 0 |
| **Walter Baseggio** | Midfielder | Anderlecht, Belgium | 8 /1 | 3 | 246 | 1 | 0 | 1 |
| **Danny Boffin** | Midfielder | St Truiden, Belgium | 49 /1 | 3 | 38 | 0 | 0 | 0 |
| **Bart Goor** | Midfielder | Hertha Berlin, Germany | 32 /7 | 10 | 852 | 0 | 0 | 3 |
| **Timmy Simons** | Midfielder | Brugge, Belgium | 6 /0 | 4 | 273 | 0 | 0 | 0 |
| **Sven Vermant** | Midfielder | Schalke, Germany | 9 /0 | 6 | 225 | 0 | 0 | 0 |
| **Johan Walem** | Midfielder | Standard Liege, Belgium | 29 /1 | 6 | 525 | 2 | 0 | 0 |
| **Marc Wilmots** | Midfielder | Schalke, Germany | 62 /24 | 9 | 719 | 0 | 0 | 7 |
| **Emile Mpenza** | Forward | Schalke, Germany | 35 /12 | 5 | 424 | 1 | 0 | 2 |
| **Bob Peeters** | Forward | Vitesse Arnhem, Holland | 12 /4 | 7 | 247 | 1 | 0 | 3 |
| **Wesley Sonck** | Forward | Genk, Belgium | 7 /1 | 6 | 291 | 1 | 0 | 1 |
| **Gert Verheyen** | Forward | Brugge, Belgium | 42 /10 | 8 | 720 | 0 | 0 | 3 |

**KEY:** APPS/GOALS = International Appearances/Goals; GAMES=Qualification Games played; MINS=Minutes played; Y/C= Yellow cards R/C=Red cards

# HISTORY AT THE WORLD CUP

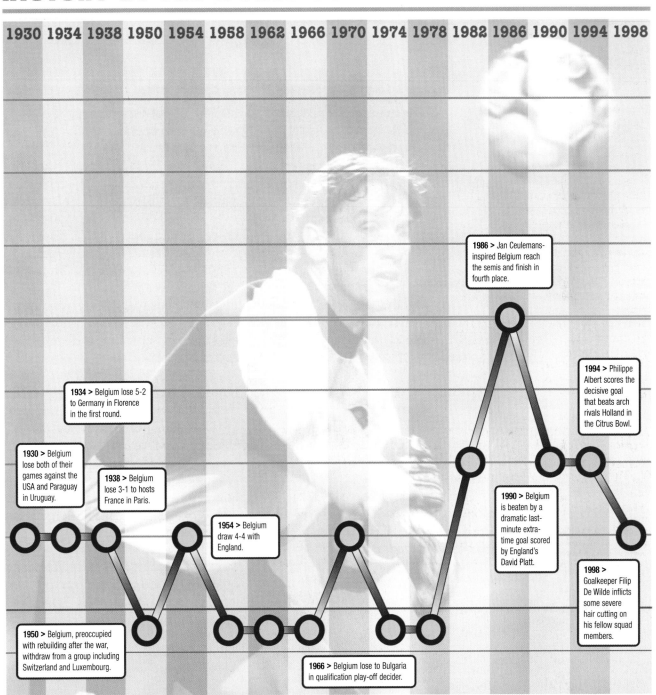

**1930 1934 1938 1950 1954 1958 1962 1966 1970 1974 1978 1982 1986 1990 1994 1998**

**1986 >** Jan Ceulemans-inspired Belgium reach the semis and finish in fourth place.

**1994 >** Philippe Albert scores the decisive goal that beats arch rivals Holland in the Citrus Bowl.

**1934 >** Belgium lose 5-2 to Germany in Florence in the first round.

**1930 >** Belgium lose both of their games against the USA and Paraguay in Uruguay.

**1938 >** Belgium lose 3-1 to hosts France in Paris.

**1954 >** Belgium draw 4-4 with England.

**1990 >** Belgium is beaten by a dramatic last-minute extra-time goal scored by England's David Platt.

**1998 >** Goalkeeper Filip De Wilde inflicts some severe hair cutting on his fellow squad members.

**1950 >** Belgium, preoccupied with rebuilding after the war, withdraw from a group including Switzerland and Luxembourg.

**1966 >** Belgium lose to Bulgaria in qualification play-off decider.

## ★ WORLD CUP HISTORY

| 1930 | >> First Round | 1970 | >> First Round |
|------|------|------|------|
| 1934 | >> First Round | 1974 | >> Did Not Qualify |
| 1938 | >> First Round | 1978 | >> Did Not Qualify |
| 1950 | >> Withdrew | 1982 | >> Second Round |
| 1954 | >> First Round | 1986 | >> Fourth Place |
| 1958 | >> Did Not Qualify | 1990 | >> Second Round |
| 1962 | >> Did Not Qualify | 1994 | >> Second Round |
| 1966 | >> Did Not Qualify | 1998 | >> First Round |

## ★ WORLD CUP RECORDS, STORIES AND WEIRDNESS

**LATEST GOAL** >> England's David Platt put the winning goal past Belgium in the 119th minute of a second round match at Italy '90.

# GROUP C

| OPPONENT | DATE | UK TIME | VENUE |
|---|---|---|---|
| Turkey | **3 June** | 10.00 | **Ulsan, Japan** |
| China | **8 June** | 12.30 | **Seogwipo, Korea** |
| Costa Rica | **13 June** | 07.30 | **Suwon, Korea** |

## "they put the 'beautiful' into the beautiful game"

# BRAZIL

Historically speaking, Brazil are the World Cup's most successful team. They've won the competition on an unprecedented four occasions and are the only team to have appeared in every tournament since 1930. In the past their glorious one touch passing game put the 'beautiful' into the beautiful game.

But that was then and this is now. The Brazilian national side is currently in a mess. From the start of the South American qualifying tournament in March 2000 to the time they finally booked their place in the Finals, with their last match at home to Venezuela in November 2001, Brazil suffered no fewer than six defeats. An amazing record when you realise Brazil had only previously suffered one defeat in qualifying throughout their entire history!

During qualifying Brazil had four (yes four!) different coaches, none of whom had any real affinity for the beautiful game. Wanderley Luxemburgo had been in charge since France 98 and, to his credit, masterminded a 3-1 victory over South American rivals Argentina, but that was sandwiched between defeats by Paraguay (2-1) and Chile (3-0). He met his personal Waterloo at the Sydney Olympics. Brazil, hot favourites to win gold, were knocked out at the quarter-final stage by a nine-man Cameroon. Before he boarded the plane home Luxemburgo was told he was sacked.

Candido was put in caretaker charge for a trip to Venezuela, arguably South America's worst team. Candido selected Romario – who had been recalled by Luxemburgo and had

scored a hat-trick against Bolivia – who again responded with a four-goal haul in a 6-0 win.

Emerson Leon took over for the next ten games during which he used a staggering 62 players. He presided over a 1-0 World Cup qualifying defeat by Ecuador and a disastrous Confederations Cup. Although sanctioned by the Brazilian FA to take an experimental squad to the Cup, they were less than happy when Brazil drew games with Canada and Japan and were ignominiously defeated by Australia.

Luiz Felipe Scolari was the choice of both fans and media alike, but he too didn't start well, suffering a 1-0 defeat in Uruguay. Another experimental Brazil squad suffered defeats by Mexico and Honduras at the Copa America. Back on the World Cup trail, home wins over Paraguay and Chile were offset by away defeats in Argentina and Bolivia.

Brazil, Uruguay and Colombia were by now vying for the fourth automatic qualifying place and the play-off spot in the last round of matches. Fortunately, Brazil had the easier task – at home to Venezuela, against whom they had never lost. This time they didn't fail and picked up the points for qualification.

Scolari's Brazil had done what they needed to do. The World Cup is Brazil's favourite arena. And with their glorious history and a squad of experienced players, it's not too much to hope that, once the horrors of the last couple of years are forgotten, Brazil will once more be the football masters everyone longs to see....

### ★ THE LOWDOWN

**Population:** 174.4 million

**Capital:** Brasilia

**Leader:** Fernando Cardoso

**Life Expectancy:** Male: 59 yrs
Female: 68 yrs

>> Brazil is the largest South American country. It shares common boundaries with every other South American country except Chile and Ecuador.

>> Besides coffee, Brazil has exported to the rest of the world some of the most well known dances of the last century. These include the Samba, the Bossa Nova and the Lambada. Unless you have grace, stamina, and a bottom shaped like two tennis balls in a sock, stick to the coffee.

>> The most famous Brazilian festival is "Carnaval".

- ★ **ASSOCIATION:** Confederacao Brasileira de Futebol
- ★ **JOINED FIFA:** 1923
- ★ **JOINED CONMEBOL:** 1916
- ★ **PLAYERS:** 552,000
- ★ **CLUBS:** 13,987
- ★ **WEBSITE:** www.brasilfutebol.com
- ★ **HONOURS:** World Cup – 1958, 1962, 1970, 1994; Copa America – 1919, 1922, 1949, 1989, 1997, 1999.

## ★ ROAD TO QUALIFICATION

Mar 00 **Colombia** (a) > (d) 0-**0**

Apr 00 **Ecuador** (h) > (w) **3**-2
Rivaldo 17, 52, Roberto Carlos 43

Jun 00 **Peru** (a) > (w) 0-**1** Carlos, A 35

Jun 00 **Uruguay** (h) > (d) 1-1
Rivaldo 85 pen

Jul 00 **Paraguay** (a) > (l) 2-**1** Rivaldo 74

Jul 00 **Argentina** (h) > (w) **3**-1
Alex 5, Vampeta 45, 51

Aug 00 **Chile** (a) > (l) 3-0

Sep 00 **Bolivia** (h) > (w) **5**-0
Romario 12, 77, 81, Rivaldo 47 Marques 88

Oct 00 **Venezuela** (a) > (w) 0-**6**
Euller 21, Juninho 29, Romario 31, 36, 39 pen, 64

Nov 00 **Colombia** (h) > (w) **1**-0
Roque Junior 90

Mar 01 **Ecuador** (a) > (l) 1-**0**

Apr 01 **Peru** (h) > (d) 1-1 Romario 65

Jun 01 **Uruguay** (a) > (l) 1-**0**

Aug 01 **Paraguay** (h) > (w) **2**-0
Marcelinho 4, Rivaldo 69

Sep 01 **Argentina** (a) > (l) 2-**1** Ayala 2 og

Oct 01 **Chile** (h) > (w) **2**-0
Edilson 52, Rivaldo 63

Nov 01 **Bolivia** (a) > (l) 3-**1** Edilson 26

Nov 01 **Venezuela** (h) > (w) **3**-0
Luizao 12, 19, Rivaldo 34

## ★ FINAL GROUP TABLE

| Team | P | W | D | L | F | A | Pts |
|---|---|---|---|---|---|---|---|
| Argentina | 18 | 13 | 4 | 1 | 42 | 15 | 43 |
| Ecuador | 18 | 9 | 4 | 5 | 23 | 20 | 31 |
| **Brazil** | **18** | **9** | **3** | **6** | **31** | **17** | **30** |
| Paraguay | 18 | 9 | 3 | 6 | 29 | 23 | 30 |
| Uruguay | 18 | 7 | 6 | 5 | 19 | 13 | 27 |
| Colombia | 18 | 7 | 6 | 5 | 20 | 15 | 27 |
| Bolivia | 18 | 4 | 6 | 8 | 21 | 33 | 18 |
| Peru | 18 | 4 | 4 | 10 | 14 | 25 | 16 |
| Venezuela | 18 | 5 | 1 | 12 | 18 | 44 | 16 |
| Chile | 18 | 3 | 3 | 12 | 15 | 27 | 12 |

## ★ RECENT RESULTS

Feb 02 **Saudi Arabia** (a) > (w) 0-**1**
Djalminha 72

Mar 02 **Iceland** (h) > (w) **6**-1
Anderson Polga 4, 73, Kleberson 19, Kaka 46, Gilberto Silva 51, Edilson 63

Mar 02 **Yugoslavia** (h) > (w) **1**-0 Luizao 71

*Roberto Carlos, all poise and skill.*

## DID YOU KNOW?

**Garrincha scored and was sent-off in the 1962 semi-final against Chile but FIFA gave him the all-clear to play in the Final.**

Brazil's summer line-up is still unpredictable and will depend on the recovery of Ronaldo and whether Romario, at 36, is even selected for the squad. Brazil have played so many games and used so many players (62 in the qualifiers) in the last eighteen months that there has been no settled line-up from one match to the next. In defence, Cafu and Roberto Carlos are certain to play with Antonio Carlos and Roque Junior probably the centre backs in front of goalkeeper Marcos. Juninho Paulista is a major creative force in midfield, although Rivaldo, alongside him, should be too – but seems to lack that spark that would take him from reliable to the special. Vampeta and Ze Roberto should play the wide midfield roles, but coach Scolari may opt for the destructive (and cynical) prowess of Emerson Ferreira. The attack, if Romario or Ronaldo are not immediately available, will fall to Flamengo's controversial Edilson alongside Bayern Munich's Giovane Elber. Luizao and Marcelinho are also front men contenders.

## PROBABLE FORMATION 4-4-2

## ★ MEN THAT MATTER!

### RIVALDO

Age>> 30

Club>> Barcelona

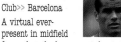

A virtual ever-present in midfield from where he has averaged a goal every two games including eight in the qualifiers. His popularity is on the wane with the fans demanding better performances.

### JUNINHO PAULISTA

Age>> 28

Club>> Vasco Da Gama/Atletico Madrid (loan)

Injury ruled him out of France 98 but he is currently in excellent form for both club and country. Made his debut in February 1995 and later had spells with Middlesbrough and Atletico Madrid.

### ROMARIO

Age>> 36

Club>> Vasco Da Gama

FIFA Golden Ball winner as the tournament's best player in Brazil's 1994 World Cup-winning team. This is his fourth World Cup, recalled during the qualifiers and continues to show sharp form inside the box.

## ★ PROBABLE SQUAD     ★ QUALIFICATION RECORD

| NAME | POSITION | CLUB | APS/GOALS | GAMES | MINS | Y/C | R/C | GOALS |
|---|---|---|---|---|---|---|---|---|
| **Dida** | Goalkeeper | Corinthians, Brazil | 40/0 | 7 | 630 | 0 | 0 | 0 |
| **Marcos** | Goalkeeper | Palmeiras, Brazil | 11/0 | 6 | 540 | 0 | 0 | 0 |
| **Rogerio Ceni** | Goalkeeper | Sao Paulo, Brazil | 13/0 | 5 | 450 | 0 | 0 | 0 |
| **Antonio Carlos** | Defender | Roma, Italy | 10/1 | 9 | 794 | 3 | 0 | 1 |
| **Cafu** | Defender | Roma, Italy | 102/5 | 11 | 990 | 3 | 1 | 0 |
| **Cris** | Defender | Cruzeiro, Brazil | 8/0 | 3 | 270 | 0 | 0 | 0 |
| **Edmilson** | Defender | Lyon, France | 12/0 | 8 | 675 | 3 | 0 | 0 |
| **Juan** | Defender | Flamengo, Brazil | 7/0 | 3 | 254 | 0 | 0 | 0 |
| **Lucio** | Defender | Bayer Leverkusen, Germany | 13/0 | 7 | 630 | 1 | 0 | 0 |
| **Roberto Carlos** | Defender | Real Madrid, Spain | 83/6 | 12 | 1050 | 1 | 0 | 1 |
| **Roque Junior** | Defender | Milan, Italy | 9/1 | 8 | 720 | 4 | 0 | 1 |
| **Denilson** | Midfielder | Real Betis, Spain | 51/7 | 6 | 165 | 0 | 0 | 0 |
| **Djalminha** | Midfielder | Deportivo Coruna, Spain | 4/0 | 2 | 100 | 0 | 0 | 0 |
| **Emerson Ferreira** | Midfielder | Roma, Italy | 41/5 | 10 | 900 | 5 | 0 | 0 |
| **Juninho Paulista** | Midfielder | Vasco da Gama, Brazil | 32/4 | 11 | 595 | 0 | 0 | 2 |
| **Rivaldo** | Midfielder | Barcelona, Spain | 57/28 | 15 | 1319 | 1 | 0 | 8 |
| **Vampeta** | Midfielder | Corinthians, Brazil | 40/2 | 15 | 972 | 2 | 0 | 2 |
| **Ze Roberto** | Midfielder | Bayer Leverkusen, Germany | 42/3 | 8 | 386 | 0 | 0 | 0 |
| **Edilson** | Forward | Flamengo, Brazil | 11/4 | 4 | 321 | 1 | 0 | 2 |
| **Luizao** | Forward | Corinthians, Brazil | 5/3 | 3 | 125 | 0 | 0 | 2 |
| **Romario** | Forward | Vasco da Gama, Brazil | 69/54 | 5 | 450 | 0 | 0 | 8 |
| **Ronaldinho Gaucho** | Forward | Paris Saint-Germain, France | 23/10 | 6 | 308 | 2 | 0 | 0 |
| **Ronaldo** | Forward | Internazionale, Italy | 54/36 | 0 | 0 | 0 | 0 | 0 |

**KEY:** APPS/GOALS = International Appearances/Goals; GAMES=Qualification Games played; MINS=Minutes played; Y/C= Yellow cards R/C=Red cards

# HISTORY AT THE WORLD CUP

**1930 1934 1938 1950 1954 1958 1962 1966 1970 1974 1978 1982 1986 1990 1994 1998**

**1950 >** Brazil host the first post-war World Cup tournament.

**1950 >** Ademier Menezes, including four against Sweden, tops the 1950 World Cup goal charts with nine goals.

**1938 >** Brazil's 'Black Diamond' Leonidas scores four goals as they beat Poland 6-5 after extra-time.

**1958 >** Brazil, inspired by Vava (2), Pelé (2) and Zagalo, beat hosts Sweden 5-2 in a thrilling Final.

**1962 >** Amarildo, Zito and Vava are all on target as Brazil beat Czechoslovakia to retain the World Cup.

**1954 >** Brazil is involved in the 'Battle of Berne' with Hungary. A vicious match that includes three sending-offs.

**1966 >** Pelé, cynically treated by opponents, is injured and the unhappy Brazilians are knocked out.

**1970 >** Brazil beat Italy 4-1 with goals from Pelé, Gerson, Jairzinho and Carlos Alberto in the Final.

**1974 >** Brazil perform poorly trying to play to a 'European' style but still reach the semis.

**1978 >** Brazil finish in third place but are 'robbed' by Argentina of a place in the Final.

**1982 >** Zico is stretchered off after a dangerous foul by Argentina's Maradona.

**1986 >** Zico misses a penalty against France then Julio Cesar does likewise in the later shoot out.

**1990 >** Brazil is stunned by a 1-0 defeat by ten-man Argentina in the second round.

**1994 >** A record fourth World Cup win for Brazil, featuring Romario, beating Italy on penalties.

**1998 >** Ronaldo off then on the team sheet as Brazil lose the Final to France 3-0.

## ★ WORLD CUP HISTORY

| | |
|---|---|
| 1930 >> First Round | 1970 >> Winners |
| 1934 >> First Round | 1974 >> Fourth Place |
| 1938 >> Third Place | 1978 >> Third Place |
| 1950 >> Runners-Up | 1982 >> Second Round |
| 1954 >> Quarter-Final | 1986 >> Quarter-Final |
| 1958 >> Winners | 1990 >> Second Round |
| 1962 >> Winners | 1994 >> Winners |
| 1966 >> First Round | 1998 >> Runners-Up |

## ★ WORLD CUP RECORDS, STORIES AND WEIRDNESS

**MOST GOALS** >> Pele has achieved more than any other player in World Cup history. Surprisingly, he hasn't topscored in any of the four World Cups in which he's appeared, but he occupies third place on the all-time topscorers table with 12 goals. He is, however, the only player to have won three World Cups.

**MOST GOALS IN A TOURNAMENT** >> Ademir totalled 9 for Brazil in Brazil in 1950, including 4 against Sweden.

**GREATEST TEAM EVER** >> The World Cup Brazilian side of 1970 has often been described as the best football team of all time. Its list of world class players included Pelé, Jairzinho, Tostao and Rivelino. They won all six games in the 1970 competition.

## "Indomitable Lions carry African hopes"

# CAMEROON

Cameroon, reigning African champions, have qualified for a fifth World Cup Finals, a record number of appearances in the Finals for an African country. The whole world still remembers how at Italia 90 Roger Milla, with his exuberant goal celebrations and his charismatic Cameroon team mates, endeared themselves to a worldwide football-loving audience. Now, with their fourth successive appearance at the Finals, there is every hope and expectation that while carrying the hopes of African football they will better their previous quarter-final appearance, which is the furthest any African nation has progressed at the tournament.

A somewhat unanticipated success at the Sydney Olympics, where the Cameroon Under-23s took the gold medal, has meant that a good number of the current squad has already tasted international success and we can expect that several of the Cameroon players, including current African Footballer of the Year Patrick Mboma, his strike partner Samuel Eto'o and winger Lauren Etame Mayer, will be found among the real entertainers in Japan/Korea.

Qualification for the Finals proved to be relatively painless. 50 teams entered the Confederation Africaine de Football (CAF) competition; all teams playing a knock-out preliminary round with home/away legs. The 25 winners of the preliminary round then went through to the second phase, which contained five groups with five teams in each group. The five group winners would qualify for the World Cup Finals.

After seeing off Somalia in the preliminary round, Cameroon dominated Group 1, a group that also included Angola, Zambia, Togo and Libya – none of whom had ever reached the Finals – winning six of their eight matches and losing only one, away to nearest rivals Angola. Cameroon took 19 points; Angola finished runner up on 13.

Patrick Mboma finished top scorer on 6, including a hat-trick at the away leg against Libya, and Samuel Eto'o and Marc-Vivien Foe chipped in with three each. A 2-2 draw away to World Cup favourites Argentina in a friendly in March this year has set them up nicely for Japan/Korea.

The Indomitable Lions they may be on the pitch, but off it they've done well not to be utterly subdued by last year's coaching turmoil. With only months to go to the start of the tournament, German-born coach Winfried Schäfer has taken on the managerial role after Frenchman Pierre Lechantre had given way to Olympic coach Paul Akono and then returned, following Akono's resignation, only to lead the team to a disappointing Confederations Cup where he became a managerial casualty yet again.

## ★ THE LOWDOWN

**Population:** 15.8 million

**Capital:** Yaounde

**Leader:** Peter Musonge

**Life Expectancy:** Male: 53 yrs Female: 55 yrs

>> There are four times as many radios as TVs in Cameroon, which will account for the immense popularity of the BBC's World Service during the World Cup.

>> Cameroon has the highest mountain in sub-Saharan West Africa, and yes, it's called Mount Cameroon!

>> The modern state was formed in 1961 from French Cameroon and part of British Cameroon.

★ **ASSOCIATION:** Federation Camerounaise de Football
★ **JOINED FIFA:** 1962
★ **JOINED CAF:** 1963
★ **PLAYERS:** 9,400
★ **CLUBS:** 200
★ **WEBSITE:** None.
★ **HONOURS:** African Nations Cup – 1984, 1988, 2000, 2002; Olympics – 2000.

*Jacques Songo'o gives crystal clear instructions to Cameroon's three-man defence.*

## ★ ROAD TO QUALIFICATION

Apr 00 **Somalia** (a) > (w) 0-**3**
Mboma 26, Foe 31, Eto'o 37

Apr 00 **Somalia** (h) > (w) **3**-0 (agg **6**-0)
Jama 15, 27, Olembe 48

Jun 00 **Libya** (a) > (w) 0-**3**
Mboma 35, 67, 88 pen

Jul 00 **Angola** (h) > (w) **3**-0
Abanda 20, Tchoutang 68, 74

Jan 01 **Togo** (a) > (w) 0-**2**
Eto'o 57, Mboma 75

Feb 01 **Zambia** (h) > (w) **1**-0 Mboma 22

Apr 01 **Libya** (h) > (w) **1**-0 Lauren 78

May 01 **Angola** (a) > (l) 2-**0**

Jul 01 **Togo** (h) > (w) **2**-0 Eto'o 27, Foe 49

Jul 01 **Zambia** (a) > (d) 2-2
Foe 52, N'diefi 64

## ★ FINAL GROUP TABLE

| Team | P | W | D | L | F | A | Pts |
|---|---|---|---|---|---|---|---|
| Cameroon | 8 | 6 | 1 | 1 | 14 | 4 | 19 |
| Angola | 8 | 3 | 4 | 1 | 11 | 9 | 13 |
| Zambia | 8 | 3 | 2 | 3 | 14 | 11 | 11 |
| Togo | 8 | 2 | 3 | 3 | 10 | 13 | 9 |
| Libya | 8 | 0 | 2 | 6 | 7 | 19 | 2 |

## ★ RECENT RESULTS

Mar 02 **Argentina** (a) > (d) 2-2
Eto'o 19, Suffo 86

## DID YOU KNOW?

Roger Milla, who changed his name from Miller to sound more African, is the oldest man to score in the final stages of a World Cup. He was 42 when he scored against Russia in the 1994 World Cup.

Cameroon's fourth coach in a year, Winfried Schafer, has stuck with the familiar 3-5-2 formation which has served the Indomitable Lions so well in recent years. Raymond Kalla, Rigobert Song, the captain, and Bill Tchato form a formidable back three in front of goalkeeper Boukar Alioum and have been automatic choices for much of the last two years. The five-man midfield is given width by Geremi Njitap and Pierre Wome on the right and left respectively. In midfield, Marc-Vivien Foe is the central playmaker with Lauren Etame-Mayer to his right and the impressive Salomon Olembe on his left. All in all, an attack minded midfield that has no cause to fear amyone. The striking partnership pitches together the goal machine and star of African football Patrick Mboma with the young and pacy Samuel Eto'o. Nicolas Alnoudji could earn a place in midfield while Pius N'Diefi is a likely alternative up front.

## PROBABLE FORMATION  3-5-2

ALIOUM

KALLA    TCHATO

SONG

NJITAP    ETAME-MAYER    OLEMBE    WOME

FOE

ETO'O    MBOMA

## ★ MEN THAT MATTER!

### PATRICK MBOMA

Age>> 31
Club>> Parma
Missed the 2002 African Nations Cup Final through injury but won it in 2000 along with the Olympic Gold. Turned down Cameroon at USA 94 but played at France 98. He is the team's top scorer.

### SAMUEL ETO'O

Age>> 21
Club>> Mallorca
Only 21 but already a medal winner at the African Nations Cup and the Olympics. He made a brief 24-minute appearance against Italy at France 98 for only his fourth cap.

### RIGOBERT SONG

Age>> 25
Club>> Koln
Cameroon's captain with four African Nations Cup and two World Cups under his belt. Regarded as one of Africa's best defenders with club experience in France, Italy, England and Germany.

## ★ PROBABLE SQUAD  ★ QUALIFICATION RECORD

| NAME | POSITION | CLUB | APS/GOALS | GAMES | MINS | Y/C | R/C | GOALS |
|---|---|---|---|---|---|---|---|---|
| Boukar Alioum | Goalkeeper | Samsunspor, Turkey | 38/0 | 7 | 630 | 0 | 0 | 0 |
| Idriss Carlos Kameni | Goalkeeper | Le Havre, France | 1/0 | 0 | 0 | 0 | 0 | 0 |
| Jacques Songo'o | Goalkeeper | Metz, France | 66/0 | 0 | 0 | 0 | 0 | 0 |
| Raymond Kalla | Defender | Extremadura, Spain | 47/2 | 5 | 450 | 0 | 0 | 0 |
| Pierre Njanka | Defender | Strasbourg, France | 12/0 | 7 | 629 | 2 | 1 | 0 |
| Geremi Njitap | Defender | Real Madrid, Spain | 38/0 | 6 | 540 | 0 | 0 | 0 |
| Rigobert Song | Defender | Koln, Germany | 59/2 | 6 | 540 | 0 | 0 | 0 |
| Bill Tchato | Defender | Montpellier, France | 12/1 | 7 | 485 | 0 | 0 | 0 |
| Jerry-C'tn Tchuisse | Defender | Moscow Spartak, Russia | 2/0 | 2 | 118 | 0 | 0 | 0 |
| Pierre Wome | Defender | Bologna, Italy | 46/1 | 2 | 160 | 0 | 0 | 0 |
| Nicolas Alnoudji | Midfielder | Caykur Rizespor, Turkey | 15/0 | 7 | 474 | 1 | 0 | 0 |
| Serge Branco | Midfielder | Eintracht Frankfurt, Germany | 1/0 | 1 | 1 | 0 | 0 | 0 |
| Jean Dika | Midfielder | Uniao Lamas, Portugal | 4/0 | 2 | 180 | 0 | 0 | 0 |
| Joel Epalle | Midfielder | Panahaiki, Greece | 22/2 | 6 | 420 | 0 | 0 | 0 |
| Lauren Etame-Mayer | Midfielder | Arsenal, England | 15/1 | 3 | 270 | 2 | 0 | 1 |
| Marc-Vivien Foe | Midfielder | Lyon, France | 47/6 | 5 | 411 | 1 | 0 | 2 |
| Salomon Olembe | Midfielder | Nantes, France | 39/3 | 5 | 379 | 0 | 0 | 0 |
| Bernard Tchoutang | Midfielder | Roda JC, Holland | 35/6 | 4 | 222 | 0 | 0 | 2 |
| Samuel Eto'o | Forward | Mallorca, Spain | 27/7 | 4 | 339 | 0 | 0 | 0 |
| Joseph-Desire Job | Forward | Middlesbrough, England | 34/5 | 3 | 133 | 0 | 0 | 0 |
| Patrick Mboma | Forward | Sunderland, England | 42/23 | 5 | 424 | 0 | 0 | 2 |
| Pius N'diefi | Forward | Sedan, France | 13/3 | 4 | 198 | 0 | 0 | 1 |
| Patrick Suffo | Forward | Sheffield United, England | 18/2 | 3 | 69 | 0 | 0 | 0 |

**KEY:** APPS/GOALS = International Appearances/Goals; GAMES=Qualification Games played; MINS=Minutes played; Y/C= Yellow cards R/C=Red cards

# HISTORY AT THE WORLD CUP

**1930 1934 1938 1950 1954 1958 1962 1966 1970 1974 1978 1982 1986 1990 1994 1998**

**1998 >** Accusations of anti-African bias as Francois Omam Biyik's second disallowed goal against Chile means Cameroon are out.

**1990 >** Roger Milla becomes the star of Italia 90 with his five World Cup goals and much more besides.

**1982 >** Cameroon secure draws with Peru, Poland and Italy but fail to progress by one goal.

**1994 >** Rigobert Song is sent off against Brazil, a feat he would repeat against Chile in '98.

**1974 >** Cameroon lose a second round play off with Zaire in Kinshasa.

**1986 >** Cameroon suffer 5-2 aggregate defeat by Zambia in the second round of qualifying.

## ★ WORLD CUP HISTORY

| | |
|---|---|
| **1930** >> Did Not Enter | **1970** >> Did Not Qualify |
| **1934** >> Did Not Enter | **1974** >> Did Not Qualify |
| **1938** >> Did Not Enter | **1978** >> Did Not Qualify |
| **1950** >> Did Not Enter | **1982** >> Second Round |
| **1954** >> Did Not Enter | **1986** >> Did Not Qualify |
| **1958** >> Did Not Enter | **1990** >> Quarter-Final |
| **1962** >> Did Not Enter | **1994** >> First Round |
| **1966** >> Did Not Enter | **1998** >> First Round |

## ★ WORLD CUP RECORDS, STORIES AND WEIRDNESS

**RED CARDS** >> Cameroon share second place with Uruguay, after Brazil and Argentina, for being shown the most red cards (6) in all World Cup Finals.

**BEST MATCH** >> Cameroon against Argentina 1990 ended this match with nine men and managed to keep the defending champions at bay, securing a famous victory in the opening game of the 1990 World Cup.

# GROUP C

| OPPONENT | DATE | UK TIME | VENUE |
|----------|------|---------|-------|
| Costa Rica | **4 June** | 07.30 | **Gwangiu, Korea** |
| Brazil | **8 June** | 12.30 | **Seogwipo, Korea** |
| Turkey | **13 June** | 07.30 | **Seoul, Korea** |

*"oriental debutantes"*

# CHINA

## ★ THE LOWDOWN

**Population:** 1.3 billion

**Capital:** Beijing

**Leader:** Zhu Rongji

**Life Expectancy:** Male: 69 yrs
Female: 73 yrs

>> China is the third largest country in the world after Canada and Russia, but contains the highest population

>> It has 52.5 million students in junior middle schools, the same number of people as the entire population of England.

>> China has over 5000 family names, the most common are Zhang, Wang, Li and Zhao.

>> 2002 is the Chinese year of the horse.

Yu Genwei made history with his first international goal against Oman in Shenyang, scoring the goal that takes China to their first ever World Cup Finals. The midfielder normally sits on the substitutes' bench and is called on late in the game to replace the established players Yang Cheng or Ma Mingyu. In the absence of creative Qi Hong, who scored the winner for a massively pressurised China in the previous game against the United Arab Emirates, Yu Genwei started a World Cup qualifier for the first time. After 36 minutes he scored the goal Chinese soccer had been waiting for, for 40 years.

China has been attempting to qualify for the Finals since 1982 despite having 7.5 million registered footballers, although its professional league, dominated by the Dalian Shide club, only came into existence in 1994.

Progress has been made at junior levels and in women's football as the respective sides have all qualified for international tournaments.

The appointment of Serb coach Bora Milutinovic, combined with a modicum of good luck plus undoubted determination, has been responsible for China booking their place in Japan/Korea. A more open Chinese society has meant that Chinese players have also benefited from overseas experience. Defenders Fan Zhiyi, Sun Jihai and midfielder Zhang Enhua have played in Britain, while forwards Xie Hui and Yang Chen play in Germany. Sun Jihai is reputed to be under scrutiny by several Italian sides and the influential Li Tie of Liaoning, China's Player of the Year, is in line for a move to Holland.

The qualifying journey began with the easiest of first round groups where they collected maximum points, scoring 25 goals including a 10-1 thrashing of the Maldives in their opening match (a hat-trick for Xie Hui). The team's first piece of good fortune came with the news that the Asian Confederation decided to seed the United Arab Emirates instead of the in form Iran. The subsequent draw meant China would avoid the main Asian football powerhouses of Iran and Saudi Arabia.

Luck stayed with them when the loss of key midfielder Zhang Enhua through injury led to the unearthing of a bright new talent in Li Weifeng, who combined superbly with the driving Li Tie, to dominate games from midfield. After opening with a 3-0 home win over the seeded United Arab Emirates, they faced a testing tie away to Oman. The Chinese survived a first-half missed penalty, then broke the deadlock in the 70th minute through Qi Hong. Fan Zhiyi's penalty six minutes from time sealed the victory.

A trip to Qatar nearly undid the good work done. With defeat looming, Li Weifeng's scored a dramatic last minute equaliser. Uzbekistan were despatched 2-0 despite China losing Wu Chengying, sent off in the 74th minute. The United Arab Emirates presented them with a must win tie, but China produced a resolute winning performance which left a celebratory victory over Oman taking China to the first Asian World Cup Finals.

China's aims will be modest in South Korea and, if their luck continues, hope to reach the second round, which means defeating Costa Rica – a former Milutinovic team.

★ **ASSOCIATION:** Football Association of the People's Republic of China

★ **JOINED FIFA:** 1979

★ **JOINED AFC:** 1974

★ **PLAYERS:** 2,250,000

★ **CLUBS:** 1,045

★ **WEBSITE:** www.fa.org.cn

★ **HONOURS:** None.

*It maybe the year of the horse, but Wu Chengying takes things a bit far trying to climb on his invisible dobbin.*

## ★ ROAD TO QUALIFICATION

Apr 01 **Maldives** (h) > (w) **10-1**
Xu Yan 13, 45, Wu 17, Xie 42, 49, 62, Zhiyi 51, 75, Yeng 59, Lin 90

Apr 01 **Maldives** (a) > (w) 0-**1** Xie 44

May 01 **Cambodia** (a) > (w) 0-**4**
Li, J 5, 63, Qu 43, Ma 58

May 01 **Indonesia** (h) > (w) **5-1**
Li, W 51, Yeng 60, Xie 70, 90, Qi 79

May 01 **Cambodia** (h) > (w) **3-1**
Ma 6, Xu Yan 21, Li, B 87

May 01 **Indonesia** (a) > (w) 0-**2**
Xie 44, Wu 70

Aug 01 **UAE** (h) > (w) **3-0**
Li Xiao 3, Qi 20, Hao 34

Aug 01 **Oman** (a) > (w) 0-**2** Qi 71, Zhiyi 84

Sep 01 **Qatar** (a) > (d) 1-**1** Li, W 89

Sep 01 **Uzbekistan** (h) > (w) **2-0**
Li, W 63, Zhiyi 75

Sep 01 **UAE** (a) > (w) 0-**1** Qi 43

Oct 01 **Oman** (h) > (w) **1-0** Yu 36

Oct 01 **Qatar** (h) > (w) **3-0**
Su 11, Qu 29, Hao 56

Oct 01 **Uzbekistan** (a) > (l) 1-0

## ★ 2ND RND GROUP TABLE

| Team | P | W | D | L | F | A | Pts |
|---|---|---|---|---|---|---|---|
| China PR | 8 | 6 | 1 | 1 | 13 | 2 | 19 |
| UAE | 8 | 3 | 2 | 3 | 10 | 11 | 11 |
| Uzbekistan | 8 | 3 | 1 | 4 | 13 | 14 | 10 |
| Qatar | 8 | 2 | 3 | 3 | 10 | 10 | 9 |
| Oman | 8 | 1 | 3 | 4 | 7 | 16 | 6 |

## ★ 1ST RND GROUP TABLE

| Team | P | W | D | L | F | A | Pts |
|---|---|---|---|---|---|---|---|
| China PR | 6 | 6 | 0 | 0 | 25 | 3 | 18 |
| Indonesia | 6 | 4 | 0 | 2 | 16 | 7 | 12 |
| Maldives Rep. | 6 | 1 | 1 | 4 | 8 | 19 | 4 |
| Cambodia | 6 | 0 | 1 | 5 | 2 | 22 | 1 |

## ★ RECENT RESULTS

Feb 02 **Hong Kong** (a) > (d) 1-**1** Yu 64
*(Hong Kong won 5-4 on pens)*

Feb 02 **Slovenia** (n) > (d) **0-0**
*(Slovenia won 4-3 on pens)*

**DID YOU KNOW?**

In the mid-seventies China played a friendly against West Bromwich Albion, the second half of which was televised live on BBC2.

China will have the tallest goalkeeper at the World Cup in the 6ft 7in and agile Jiang Jin – something of a comfort to their back four led by Fan Zhiyi. Li Weifeng, who replaced the established Zhang Enhua in qualification, has formed a useful defensive partnership with Fan Zhiyi and both are dangerous at set pieces. In attack, China has one of Asia's finest strikers in Hao Haidong who is partnered by the tall Su Maozhen. However, midfield is China's real problem. Qi Hong is the creative force while Li Tie provides the drive, but overall China's midfield is too lightweight and will soon be overrun, especially by top class European opposition. In Ma Minygu China have a useful free kick specialist and a player who likes to shoot from distance, while Li Ming on the right is another positive-minded player.

## PROBABLE FORMATION 4-4-2

JIANG JIN

SUN JIHAI — WU CHENGYING

LI WEIFENG — FAN ZHIYI

LI MING — LI TIE — MA MINGYU — QI HONG

HAO HAIDONG — SU MAOZHEN

## ★ MEN THAT MATTER!

### FAN ZHIYI

Age>> 32

Club>> Dundee

Defender/midfielder who has been the star of Chinese football in recent years largely thanks to his exploits abroad. He will captain China at their first World Cup.

### QI HONG

Age>> 25

Club>> Shanghai Shenhua

China's most important midfield player. Creative and robust, he has the spark to make surprising things happen as well as scoring the occasional goal himself.

### SU MAOZHEN

Age>> 29

Club>> Shandong

Su Maozhen is China's big target man who regularly scored goals for China under Milutinovic. Injury ruled him out for all but three qualifiers but is likely to return to the team for the World Cup.

## ★ PROBABLE SQUAD

## ★ QUALIFICATION RECORD

| NAME | POSITION | CLUB | APS/GOALS | GAMES | MINS | Y/C | R/C | GOALS |
|---|---|---|---|---|---|---|---|---|
| Jiang Jin | Goalkeeper | Tianjin Taida, China | 34/0 | 10 | 879 | 0 | 0 | 0 |
| Ou Chuliang | Goalkeeper | Yunnan Hongta, China | 3/0 | 1 | 70 | 0 | 0 | 0 |
| Qi An | Goalkeeper | Dalian Shide, China | 5/0 | 4 | 282 | 0 | 0 | 0 |
| Du Wei | Defender | Shanghai Shenhua SVA, China | 3/0 | 2 | 180 | 0 | 0 | 0 |
| Fan Zhiyi | Defender | Dundee, Scotland | 25/6 | 12 | 1061 | 1 | 0 | 4 |
| Gang Chen Jin | Defender | Qingdao Yizhong, China | 2/0 | 1 | 9 | 0 | 0 | 0 |
| Li Weifeng | Defender | Shenzhen Ping'an, China | 41/9 | 12 | 1080 | 0 | 0 | 3 |
| Pu Yang | Defender | Beijing Guo'an, China | 9/0 | 6 | 229 | 1 | 0 | 0 |
| Sun Jihai | Defender | Manchester City, England | 14/0 | 9 | 645 | 2 | 0 | 0 |
| Wu Chengying | Defender | Shanghai Shenhua SVA, China | 40/4 | 6 | 525 | 3 | 1 | 0 |
| Zhang Enhua | Defender | Dalian Shide, China | 6/0 | 2 | 100 | 0 | 0 | 0 |
| Li Ming | Midfielder | Dalian Shide, China | 18/2 | 8 | 523 | 0 | 0 | 0 |
| Li Tie | Midfielder | Liaoning Bird, China | 40/3 | 12 | 1080 | 1 | 0 | 0 |
| Li Xiaopeng | Midfielder | Shandong Luneng, China | 22/1 | 10 | 813 | 1 | 0 | 1 |
| Ma Mingyu | Midfielder | Sichuan Dahe, China | 31/7 | 13 | 966 | 0 | 0 | 2 |
| Shao Yi Jia | Midfielder | Beijing Guo'an, China | 10/9 | 4 | 63 | 0 | 0 | 0 |
| Shen Si | Midfielder | Shanghai Zhongyuan Huili, China | 31/4 | 9 | 667 | 0 | 0 | 0 |
| Qi Hong | Midfielder | Shanghai Shenhua SVA, China | 28/10 | 9 | 710 | 0 | 0 | 4 |
| Hao Haidong | Forward | Dalian Shide, China | 12/9 | 6 | 453 | 1 | 0 | 2 |
| Qu Bo | Forward | Qingdao Yizhong, China | 13/4 | 5 | 341 | 1 | 0 | 2 |
| Su Maozhen | Forward | Shandong Luneng, China | 22/13 | 3 | 181 | 0 | 0 | 1 |
| Xie Hui | Forward | Shanghai Shenhua SVA, China | 15/14 | 2 | 119 | 0 | 0 | 0 |
| Yu Genwei | Forward | Tianjin Taida, China | 9/1 | 5 | 169 | 1 | 0 | 1 |

**KEY:** APPS/GOALS = International Appearances/Goals; GAMES=Qualification Games played; MINS=Minutes played; Y/C= Yellow cards R/C=Red cards

# HISTORY AT THE WORLD CUP

1930 1934 1938 1950 1954 1958 1962 1966 1970 1974 1978 1982 1986 1990 1994 1998

**1986 >** China score 23 goals in six games in qualifying but still manage to finish behind Hong Kong.

**1990 >** China finish fourth in the six-team World Cup Asian Qualifying Tournament in Singapore.

**1994 >** Finish second to Iraq by a point in Asian Group A.

**1998 >** Finish third behind Saudi Arabi and Iran in Asian Second Qualifying Round.

**1982 >** China lose 2-1 to New Zealand in Asia/Oceania play-off in Singapore.

## ★ WORLD CUP HISTORY

| | |
|---|---|
| **1930** >> Did Not Enter | **1970** >> Did Not Enter |
| **1934** >> Did Not Enter | **1974** >> Did Not Enter |
| **1938** >> Did Not Enter | **1978** >> Did Not Enter |
| **1950** >> Did Not Enter | **1982** >> Did Not Qualify |
| **1954** >> Did Not Enter | **1986** >> Did Not Qualify |
| **1958** >> Did Not Enter | **1990** >> Did Not Qualify |
| **1962** >> Did Not Enter | **1994** >> Did Not Qualify |
| **1966** >> Did Not Enter | **1998** >> Did Not Qualify |

## ★ WORLD CUP RECORDS, STORIES AND WEIRDNESS

**FIRST SPONSOR** >> The first sponsor of the Chinese national team was the Qixin pharmaceutical factory in Guangzhou in 1989.

**SMALLEST CROWD** >> In the 1988 Asia Cup Finals, China played Bahrain in front of a crowd of just 200 in Qatar.

# GROUP C

| OPPONENT | DATE | UK TIME | VENUE |
|---|---|---|---|
| China | **4 June** | 07.30 | **Gwangiu, Korea** |
| Turkey | **9 June** | 10.00 | **Incheon, Korea** |
| Brazil | **13 June** | 07.30 | **Suwon, Korea** |

## ★ THE LOWDOWN

**Population:** 3.7 million

**Capital:** San Jose

**Leader:** Miguel Rodriguez

**Life Expectancy:** Male: 73 yrs
Female: 78 yrs

>> Tourism is the main industry in Costa Rica.

>> There is no summer or winter as such, just a rainy season from May to November and a dry season from December to April.

>> Costa Rica is part of the Pacific "Rim of Fire", which is not what the male botty region feels like after 14 pints and a vindaloo, but has 7 of the area's 42 active volcanoes and is prone to large and unexpected eruptions. Actually, it sounds exactly like a man's pant area after a good night out!

## "the 'Ticos' will test even the best"

# COSTA RICA

Costa Rica qualified for the World Cup Finals as North/ Central American group winners – a successful qualification programme that owed much to their tenacity and a disconcerting habit of snatching results from the jaws of defeat in the dying seconds of games.

It had not started well with the appointment of new Brazilian coach Gilson Nunez, who admitted he knew nothing about Costa Rican football. And it showed. Costa Rica were beaten in their opening semi-final group game by Barbados. They recovered to beat the USA 2-1 in controversial circumstances when they were awarded a penalty, which Hernan Medford converted, four minutes into injury time.

Home wins over Guatemala and Barbados followed plus a draw in the USA. Next up Guatemala, and they were within two minutes of qualifying for the next stage when Guatemala's Carlos Ruiz scored to make it 2-1, forcing not only a play-off but the resignation of Nunez. Nunez's assistant Alexandre Guimaraes took over and in the play-off (held in neutral Miami) Costa Rica thrashed Guatemala 5-2 with Manchester City's Paulo Wanchope and Rolando Fonseca among the scorers.

The final group of six teams now competed for three World Cup Final places. Once again Costa Rica started poorly, struggling to salvage a point from their home tie with Honduras. Twice Costa Rica had to come back from behind before the determined Rodrigo Cordero finally netted the second equaliser in injury time.

The turning point in the campaign came at the Guillermo Caneda stadium in Mexico City with an astonishing 2-1 victory over Mexico. Mexico had never been beaten in a competitive game in the stadium that in 30 years had witnessed 54 World Cup games. Fonseca cancelled out Mexico's seventh minute lead with a stunning 25-yard free kick and the winner came just three minutes from time from Hernan Medford, who played in Costa Rica's only previous World Cup appearance in 1990. Wins over Jamaica, Honduras, Trinidad & Tobago and the USA followed, but it was a goalless home draw with Mexico that clinched Costa Rica's place in the Finals.

They will be considered one of the outsiders at the Finals – as they were at Italia 90. But then Costa Rica, featuring Alexandre Guimares, surprised everyone by beating both Scotland and Sweden to reach the Second Round. In Paulo Wanchope they have a regular goalscorer who last year scored five goals in four Copa America ties and another seven in the qualifiers. And then there is the "Ticos" main striker Rolando Fonseca, who at 27 is the country's all-time top goalscorer with 39 goals (in 75 games) including ten during qualifying.

Costa Rica can draw on plenty of recent tournament experience. Apart from the 2001 Copa America, Costa Rica were runners-up at both the 2001 UNCAF Cup and the 2002 Gold Cup.

★ **ASSOCIATION:** Federacion Costarricense de Futbol

★ **JOINED FIFA:** 1921

★ **JOINED FOOTBALL CONFEDERATION:** 1962

★ **PLAYERS:** 12,500

★ **CLUBS:** 431

★ **WEBSITE:** www.intnet.co.cr/sports/fedefutbol/fede.html

★ HONOURS: CCCF/CONCACAF Gold Cup – 1941, 1946, 1948, 1953, 1955, 1960, 1961, 1963, 1969, 1989.

*High scoring Paulo Wanchope.*

## ★ ROAD TO QUALIFICATION

**Jul 00 Barbados** (a) > (l) 2-**1**  Madrigal 47

**Jul 00 United States** (h) > (w) **2**-1
Fonseca, R 10, Medford 90 pen

**Aug 00 Guatemala** (h) > (w) **2**-1
Wanchope 33, 58

**Sep 00 Barbados** (h) > (w) **3**-0
Soto 36, Fonseca, R 41, Meford 54

**Oct 00 United States** (a) > (d) 0-**0**

**Nov 00 Guatemala** (a) > (l) 2-**1**
Fonseca, R 71

**Jan 01 Guatemala** (n) > (w) **5**-2
Wanchope 6, Fonseca, R 43, 59, Parks 58,
Soto 87

**Feb 01 Honduras** (h) > (d) **2**-2
Fonseca, R 65, Lopez 90

**Mar 01 Trinidad & Tobago** (h) > (w) **3**-0
Bryce 46, Wanchope 80, 89

**Apr 01 United States** (a) > (l) 1-**0**

**Jun 01 Mexico** (a) > (w) 1-**2**
Fonseca, R 72, Medford 86

**Jun 01 Jamaica** (h) > (w) **2**-1
Marin 4, Wanchope 38

**Jun 01 Honduras** (a) > (w) 2-**3**
Wanchope 9, Fonseca, R 13, Solis 83

**Sep 01 Trinidad & Tobago** (a) > (w) 0-**2**
Gomez 4, 35

**Sep 01 United States** (h) > (w) **2**-0
Fonseca, R 39, 68

**Oct 01 Mexico** (h) > (d) **0**-0

**Nov 01 Jamaica** (a) > (w) 0-**1** Sunsing 5

## ★ FINAL GROUP TABLE

| Team | P | W | D | L | F | A | Pts |
|---|---|---|---|---|---|---|---|
| Costa Rica | 10 | 7 | 2 | 1 | 17 | 7 | 23 |
| Mexico | 10 | 5 | 2 | 3 | 16 | 9 | 17 |
| United States | 10 | 5 | 2 | 3 | 11 | 8 | 17 |
| Honduras | 10 | 4 | 2 | 4 | 17 | 17 | 14 |
| Jamaica | 10 | 2 | 2 | 6 | 7 | 14 | 8 |
| Trinidad & Tob | 10 | 1 | 2 | 7 | 5 | 18 | 5 |

## ★ SEMI-FINAL GROUP TABLE

| Team | P | W | D | L | F | A | Pts |
|---|---|---|---|---|---|---|---|
| United States | 6 | 3 | 2 | 1 | 14 | 3 | 11 |
| Costa Rica | 6 | 3 | 1 | 2 | 9 | 6 | 10 |
| Guatemala | 6 | 3 | 1 | 2 | 9 | 6 | 10 |
| Barbados | 6 | 1 | 0 | 5 | 3 | 20 | 3 |

## ★ RECENT RESULTS

**Jan 02 South Korea** (a) > (w) 1-**3**
Gomez 44, Wanchope 77, 82

**Feb 02 United States** (a) > (l) 2-**0**

**Mar 02 Morocco** (h) > (l) **0**-1

## DID YOU KNOW?

**Coach Alexandre Guimaraes was a member of Costa Rica's 1990 World Cup Squad making three substitute appearances against Brazil, Sweden and Czechoslovakia.**

Club football in Costa Rica is usually played to 3-5-2 and so will the national team. At the back Luis Marin is first choice sweeper alongside Saprissa team players Reynaldo Parks, an excellent man-marker, and the hard-working Gilberto Martinez. In midfield, Mauricio Solis handles the defensive duties while possession-loving Walter Centeno is the playmaker. Jervis Drummond, a former track athlete, provides blistering pace on the right with, at left wing back, Carlos Castro in a role suited to his close control skills. Rolando Fonseca, Costa Rica's all-time top goalscorer, is allowed to roam just behind the front two and link up play down the middle. Veteran Hernan Medford and Costa Rica's best known player Paulo Wanchope are the two-pronged attack. The three – Fonseca, Medford and Wanchope – can all switch their roles in the attack. Wilmer Lopez can provide another creative outlet in midfield, but any further changes to the side and the quality will evaporate.

## PROBABLE FORMATION  3-5-2

LONNIS

PARKS   MARTINEZ

MARIN

DRUMMOND   CENTENO   M SOLIS   C CASTRO

FONSECA

MEDFORD   WANCHOPE

## ★ MEN THAT MATTER!

### ROLANDO FONSECA

Age>> 27
Club>> La Piedad
Costa Rica's all-time top goalscorer with an increasing tally to his name. He scored ten goals during qualification from open play and directly from free kicks. A real danger to defences.

### PAULO WANCHOPE

Age>> 25
Club>> Manchester City
Hot on the heels of Fonseca in the all-time goal stakes with a vastly superior scoring rate. Despite their rivalry, the high-profile Wanchope combines well with Fonseca.

### HERNAN MEDFORD

Age>> 34
Club>> Saprissa
A survivor from Italia 90 where he scored the winner against Sweden that took Costa Rica into the Second Round. Medford played in all 17 qualifiers including six as a sub.

## ★ PROBABLE SQUAD   ★ QUALIFICATION RECORD

| NAME | POSITION | CLUB | APS/GOALS | GAMES | MINS | Y/C | R/C | GOALS |
|---|---|---|---|---|---|---|---|---|
| Ricardo Gonzalez | Goalkeeper | Alajuelense, Costa Rica | 5/0 | 0 | 0 | 0 | 0 | 0 |
| Erick Lonnis | Goalkeeper | Saprissa, Costa Rica | 71/0 | 9 | 810 | 0 | 0 | 0 |
| Alvaro Mesen | Goalkeeper | Alajuelense, Costa Rica | 13/0 | 8 | 720 | 0 | 0 | 0 |
| Juan B Esquivel | Defender | Saprissa, Costa Rica | 2/0 | 0 | 0 | 0 | 0 | 0 |
| Austin Berry | Defender | Herediano, Costa Rica | 65/6 | 6 | 464 | 3 | 0 | 0 |
| Carlos Castro | Defender | Alajuelense, Costa Rica | 16/0 | 10 | 788 | 1 | 0 | 0 |
| Jervis Drummond | Defender | Saprissa, Costa Rica | 36/1 | 12 | 1066 | 3 | 0 | 0 |
| Alexander Madrigal | Defender | La Piedad, Mexico | 9/1 | 6 | 530 | 0 | 0 | 1 |
| Luis Marin | Defender | Alajuelense, Costa Rica | 71/3 | 6 | 540 | 2 | 0 | 1 |
| Gilberto Martinez | Defender | Saprissa, Costa Rica | 18/0 | 10 | 900 | 2 | 0 | 0 |
| Reynaldo Parks | Defender | Saprissa, Costa Rica | 47/1 | 17 | 1513 | 1 | 0 | 1 |
| Harrold Wallace | Defender | Alajuelense, Costa Rica | 53/1 | 10 | 764 | 0 | 0 | 0 |
| Steven Bryce | Midfielder | Alajuelense, Costa Rica | 24/4 | 11 | 581 | 1 | 0 | 1 |
| Walter Centeno | Midfielder | Saprissa, Costa Rica | 45/6 | 10 | 741 | 1 | 0 | 0 |
| Rodrigo Cordero | Midfielder | Herediano, Costa Rica | 24/1 | 15 | 1037 | 2 | 0 | 0 |
| Ronald Gomez | Midfielder | OFI Crete, Greece | 50/17 | 6 | 390 | 1 | 0 | 2 |
| Wilmer Lopez | Midfielder | Alajuelense, Costa Rica | 63/6 | 10 | 641 | 0 | 1 | 1 |
| Mauricio Solis | Midfielder | Alajuelense, Costa Rica | 80/5 | 12 | 655 | 1 | 0 | 1 |
| William Sunsing | Midfielder | New England Revolution, USA | 17/1 | 10 | 236 | 0 | 0 | 1 |
| Rolando Fonseca | Forward | La Piedad, Mexico | 75/38 | 16 | 1150 | 2 | 0 | 8 |
| Hernan Medford | Forward | Saprissa, Costa Rica | 86/19 | 17 | 966 | 1 | 0 | 3 |
| Paulo Wanchope | Forward | Manchester City, England | 47/34 | 13 | 1080 | 4 | 0 | 7 |
| Oscar Rojas | Forward | La Piedad, Mexico | 3/0 | 1 | 90 | 0 | 0 | 0 |

**KEY:** APPS/GOALS = International Appearances/Goals; GAMES=Qualification Games played; MINS=Minutes played; Y/C= Yellow cards R/C=Red cards

# HISTORY AT THE WORLD CUP

1930 1934 1938 1950 1954 1958 1962 1966 1970 1974 1978 1982 1986 1990 1994 1998

**1958 >** Costa Rica lose 3-1 on aggregate to Mexico in deciding fixtures for place in Finals.

**1990 >** Juan Arnoldo Cayasso scores the goal that beats Scotland in Costa Rica's first World Cup match.

**1962 >** Costa Rica play first qualifier beating Guatemala in San Jose.

**1954 >** Costa Rica refused entry into the World Cup because their application was on the wrong form.

## ★ WORLD CUP HISTORY

| | | | |
|---|---|---|---|
| **1930** >> Did Not Enter | | **1970** >> Did Not Qualify | |
| **1934** >> Did Not Enter | | **1974** >> Did Not Qualify | |
| **1938** >> Did Not Enter | | **1978** >> Did Not Qualify | |
| **1950** >> Did Not Enter | | **1982** >> Did Not Qualify | |
| **1954** >> Did Not Enter | | **1986** >> Did Not Qualify | |
| **1958** >> Did Not Qualify | | **1990** >> Second Round | |
| **1962** >> Did Not Qualify | | **1994** >> Did Not Qualify | |
| **1966** >> Did Not Qualify | | **1998** >> Did Not Qualify | |

## ★ WORLD CUP RECORDS, STORIES AND WEIRDNESS

**MOST GOALS** >> Yugoslavian Bora Milutinovic has coached a World Cup record number (4) of teams, including Costa Rica, taking all of them past the first round.

| OPPONENT | DATE | UK TIME | VENUE |
|---|---|---|---|
| Mexico | **3 June** | 07.30 | **Niigata, Japan** |
| Italy | **8 June** | 10.00 | **Ibaraki, Japan** |
| Ecuador | **13 June** | 12.30 | **Yokohama, Japan** |

## *"old hands bolster a struggling side"*

# CROATIA

### ★ THE LOWDOWN

**Population:** 4.3 million

**Capital:** Zagreb

**Leader:** Ivica Racan

**Life Expectancy:** Male: 70 yrs Female: 78 yrs

>> Croatia declared its independence in 1991 following the break-up of Yugoslavia.

>> The Croatian territory encompasses 1,185 islands, islets and reefs, including 67 inhabited islands.

>> Croatia controls most land routes from Western Europe to the Aegean Sea and Turkish Straits.

Four years ago Croatia made a sensational World Cup debut, reaching the semi-finals before losing to eventual winners France. After qualifying via the play-offs, they beat Jamaica and Japan to finish as group runners-up to Argentina. That earned them a second-round clash with Romania, which was decided by a Davor Suker penalty.

In the last eight, Croatia gave a magnificent performance defeating Germany 3-0. The Croatians' aggressive approach rattled the Germans who had Christian Worns sent off five minutes before the break. Robert Jarni put Croatia ahead on the stroke of half time with Vlaovic and Davor Suker scoring late on for a comprehensive victory.

Croatia's World Cup fairy tale ended when they came up against the superior French side who had a player sent off and had to come from behind to win 2-1. As consolation Croatia won the third place play-off beating Holland 2-1 with the winning goal scored by Suker – his sixth of the tournament – making him top scorer at France 98.

Croatia will have to do well if they are to come close to equalling their performance of four years ago. They missed out on Euro 2000 and have been trying to rebuild their ageing team ever since. Even so, coach Mirko Jozic has had to lure back several long-serving players who had opted for international retirement. Alen Boksic, Robert Prosinecki and Igor Stimac have all

been persuaded to put back on the red and white checked shirt and add their experience to a team in the midst of a tough qualifying campaign.

Croatia were drawn in a tight group alongside Belgium and Scotland, with Latvia and San Marino making up the numbers. A 0-0 draw in Belgium was an ideal start to their campaign, but the 1-1 home draw against Scotland was not. Coach Miroslav Blazevic stood down and in came Jozic to try and rectify a run of one win in the previous nine games.

Jozic did get Croatia winning again. A first half Bosko Balaban hat-trick helped Croatia to a 4-1 home win against Latvia. Four more goals were netted against San Marino while Balaban scored the only goal in a 1-0 victory in Riga over Latvia.

A goalless draw away to Scotland, combined with their superior goal difference, put Croatia within touching distance of qualification and, boosted by another four-goal haul in San Marino, Croatia knew all they had to do was to beat Belgium in their last game to book their place at the World Cup Finals.

Two years earlier Croatia had failed to qualify for Euro 2000, and it looked, for a while, as if it was going to be *déjà vu* all over again. A lacklustre performance was looking far worse after Prosinecki missed a first half penalty, but with 15 minutes remaining, the deadlock was broken as Boksic swept in Balaban's cross for the winning goal.

★ **ASSOCIATION:** Croatian Football Association

★ **JOINED FIFA:** 1992

★ **JOINED UEFA:** 1992

★ **PLAYERS:** 78,200

★ **CLUBS:** 1,221

★ **WEBSITE:** www.hns-cff.hr

★ **HONOURS:** None

*Astute midfielder Zvonimir Soldo.*

## ★ ROAD TO QUALIFICATION

Sep 00 **Belgium** (a) > (d) 0-**0**

Oct 00 **Scotland** (h) > (d) **1**-1 Boksic 15

Mar 01 **Latvia** (h) > (w) **4**-1
Balaban 8, 42, 45, Vuguric 89

Jun 01 **San Marino** (h) > (w) **4**-0
Vlaovic 3, Balaban 30, Suker 55 pen,
Vugrinec 61

Jun 01 **Latvia** (a) > (w) 0-**1** Balaban 39

Sep 01 **Scotland** (a) > (d) 0-**0**

Sep 01 **San Marino** (a) > (w) 0-**4**
Kovac, N 40, Prosinecki 48, 90, Soldo 77

Oct 01 **Belgium** (h) > (w) **1**-0 Boksic 75

## ★ FINAL GROUP TABLE

| Team | P | W | D | L | F | A | Pts |
|------|---|---|---|---|---|---|-----|
| Croatia | 8 | 5 | 3 | 0 | 15 | 2 | 18 |
| Belgium | 8 | 5 | 2 | 1 | 25 | 6 | 17 |
| Scotland | 8 | 4 | 3 | 1 | 12 | 6 | 15 |
| Latvia | 8 | 1 | 1 | 6 | 5 | 16 | 4 |
| San Marino | 8 | 0 | 1 | 7 | 3 | 30 | 1 |

## ★ RECENT RESULTS

Feb 02 **Bulgaria** (h) > (d) 0-**0**

Mar 02 **Slovenia** (h) > (d) **0**-0

## DID YOU KNOW?

Coach Mirko Jozic has already guided a team to World Cup success at Under-20 level when Yugoslavia won the World Youth Cup in 1987.

Croatia's 3-5-2 formation is organised, primarily, for defence. In front of keeper Stipe Pletikosa are a back three of man-marker Dario Simic, the uncompromising Robert Kovac and sweeper Igor Tudor – widely regarded as one of Croatia's best players, The five-man midfield is geared to stifling their opponents' play. Stjepan Tomas is a sweeper turned defensive midfielder and is anchored alongside the astute Zvonimir Soldo. Boris Zivkovic is another defender converted into a right (or left) wing-back position, while Robert Jarni, at 33, usually provides crosses and long passes from the left, although he's sometimes invited to play as a third forward. Croatia's most talented and experienced player, Robert Prosinecki, is their only genuinely attacking midfielder providing the link to the England-based pair of Bosko Balaban and Alen Boksic. The old guard of Davor Suker and Goran Vlaovic will act as cover for the striker's slot.

## PROBABLE FORMATION 3-5-2

PLETIKOSA

D SIMIC · R KOVAC

TUDOR

ZIVKOVIC · TOMAS · SOLDO · JARNI

PROSINECKI

BALABAN · BOKSIC

## ★ MEN THAT MATTER!

### BOSKO BALABAN

Age>> 23
Club>> A. Villa
Balaban came to the fore during qualifying scoring five of Croatia's 15 goals including a hat-trick against Latvia. It was his cross that set up the decisive goal against Belgium.

### IGOR TUDOR

Age>> 24
Club>> Juventus
Outstanding in qualifying, Tudor is an excellent defender. He causes opponents real problems at corners and free kicks. Played just 13 minutes in three sub appearances at France 98.

### ROBERT PROSINECKI

Age>> 31
Club>> Portsmouth
Has the distinction of scoring at two World Cups with different countries – Yugoslavia in 1990 and Croatia in 1998. Attacking midfielder who can still turn a game at international level.

## ★ PROBABLE SQUAD                                           ★ QUALIFICATION RECORD

| NAME | POSITION | CLUB | APS/GOALS | GAMES | MINS | Y/C | R/C | GOALS |
|------|----------|------|-----------|-------|------|-----|-----|-------|
| Tomislav Butina | Goalkeeper | Dinamo Zagreb, Croatia | 3/0 | 1 | 90 | 0 | 0 | 0 |
| Stipe Pletikosa | Goalkeeper | Hajduk Split, Croatia | 16/0 | 6 | 540 | 0 | 0 | 0 |
| Zeljko Pavlovic | Goalkeeper | Anderlecht Belgium | 7/0 | 1 | 90 | 0 | 0 | 0 |
| Mario Cvitanovic | Defender | Venezia, Italy | 27/4 | 1 | 44 | 1 | 0 | 0 |
| Robert Kovac | Defender | Bayern Munich, Germany | 17/0 | 6 | 528 | 2 | 0 | 0 |
| Dario Simic | Defender | Internazionale, Italy | 47/1 | 7 | 630 | 1 | 0 | 0 |
| Igor Stimac | Defender | Hajduk Split, Croatia | 53/2 | 4 | 360 | 0 | 0 | 0 |
| Stjepan Tomas | Defender | Vicenza, Italy | 15/1 | 3 | 267 | 0 | 0 | 0 |
| Igor Tudor | Defender | Juventus, Italy | 25/0 | 6 | 450 | 2 | 0 | 0 |
| Boris Zivkovic | Defender | Bayer Leverkusen, Germany | 13/1 | 5 | 405 | 0 | 0 | 0 |
| Igor Biscan | Midfielder | Liverpool, England | 15/1 | 4 | 104 | 1 | 0 | 0 |
| Robert Jarni | Midfielder | Las Palmas, Spain | 75/1 | 8 | 675 | 0 | 0 | 0 |
| Niko Kovac | Midfielder | Bayern Munich, Germany | 18/2 | 5 | 424 | 3 | 0 | 1 |
| Robert Prosinecki | Midfielder | Portsmouth, England | 45/10 | 7 | 578 | 1 | 0 | 2 |
| Milan Rapajic | Midfielder | Fenerbahce, Turkey | 20/1 | 2 | 94 | 0 | 0 | 0 |
| Danijel Seric | Midfielder | Panathinaikos, Greece | 24/0 | 2 | 115 | 0 | 0 | 0 |
| Zvonimir Soldo | Midfielder | Stuttgart, Germany | 58/3 | 5 | 386 | 1 | 0 | 1 |
| Mario Stanic | Midfielder | Chelsea, England | 42/7 | 3 | 195 | 1 | 0 | 0 |
| Bosko Balaban | Forward | Aston Villa, England | 13/6 | 8 | 523 | 1 | 0 | 5 |
| Alen Boksic | Forward | Middlesbrough, England | 35/10 | 2 | 165 | 0 | 0 | 2 |
| Davor Suker | Forward | 1860 Munich, Germany | 66/44 | 5 | 333 | 1 | 0 | 1 |
| Goran Vlaovic | Forward | Panathinaikos, Greece | 49/15 | 4 | 243 | 0 | 0 | 1 |
| Davor Vugrinec | Forward | Lecce, Italy | 18/7 | 7 | 320 | 1 | 0 | 2 |

KEY: APPS/GOALS = International Appearances/Goals; GAMES=Qualification Games played; MINS=Minutes played; Y/C= Yellow cards R/C=Red cards

# HISTORY AT THE WORLD CUP

**1930 1934 1938 1950 1954 1958 1962 1966 1970 1974 1978 1982 1986 1990 1994 1998**

**1998 >** Robert Prosinecki scores a World Cup goal for Croatia against Jamaica on the way to the semis.

**1990 >** Robert Prosinecki scores a World Cup goal for Yugoslavia against the United Arab Emirates.

## ★ WORLD CUP HISTORY

| | |
|---|---|
| 1930 >> Did Not Enter | 1970 >> Did Not Enter |
| 1934 >> Did Not Enter | 1974 >> Did Not Enter |
| 1938 >> Did Not Enter | 1978 >> Did Not Enter |
| 1950 >> Did Not Enter | 1982 >> Did Not Enter |
| 1954 >> Did Not Enter | 1986 >> Did Not Enter |
| 1958 >> Did Not Enter | 1990 >> Did Not Enter |
| 1962 >> Did Not Enter | 1994 >> Did Not Enter |
| 1966 >> Did Not Enter | 1998 >> Third Place |

## ★ WORLD CUP RECORDS, STORIES AND WEIRDNESS

**MOST GOALS IN A TOURNAMENT** >> Davor Suker in France 98 with 6.

**UNIQUE SCORING RECORD** >> Robert Prosinecki is the only player to have scored for two different countries. He represented Yugoslavia in 1990, scoring against the United Arab Emirates and then Croatia in 1998, scoring against Jamaica.

# GROUP A

| OPPONENT | DATE | UK TIME | VENUE |
|----------|------|---------|-------|
| Uruguay | **1 June** | 10.00 | **Ulsan, Korea** |
| Senegal | **6 June** | 07.30 | **Daegu, Korea** |
| France | **11 June** | 07.30 | **Incheon, Korea** |

## "will they bring home the bacon?"

# DENMARK

**D**enmark reached the 1998 World Cup quarter-finals before bowing out to Brazil 3-2 in one of the tournament's most thrilling games. An exciting and positive Danish side almost forced extra-time when Marc Reiper's header crashed against the crossbar in the 89th minute. That slender defeat marked the international retirement of Michael Laudrup, who is now assistant coach of the national side. Two years later at Euro 2000 Denmark looked a pale shadow of their World Cup team. No goals, no wins, no draws and no points.

New coach, and former Danish player, Morten Olsen had to make changes after the Euro 2000 debacle, promoting youngsters such as Claus Jensen and Dennis Rommedahl. Even so, Denmark did not make a promising start to their World Cup qualifying group. Although a 2-1 win over Iceland in Reykjavik was a welcome opening result, successive 1-1 draws with Northern Ireland – where Rommedahl scored his first goal – and Bulgaria weakened the Danes' chances of qualifying.

Added to Danish woes was the retirement from international football of legendary goalkeeper Peter Schmeichel after 128 appearances (he later earned a 129th in a friendly against Slovenia). His successor was Sunderland goalkeeper Thomas Sorenson who had previously made just one appearance for the national side.

The morale boosting 2-1 win over Germany in a friendly proved a turning point for Olsen. It was the Danes' first victory over the Germans since the 1992 European Championship Final and Rommedahl's two goals was the first time a Dane had scored twice against the Germans since 1930. Confidence boosted, the Danes blasted Malta 5-0 (including a

hat-trick from Denmark's leading marksman Ebbe Sand). A magnificent goalless draw against the Czech Republic, in which goalkeeper Sorenson was excellent, put their qualification efforts back on track.

Two late goals in successive matches against the Czech Republic and Malta put by now unbeaten Denmark at the top of the table. With three games left, it was a three-horse race between Bulgaria, the Czech Republic and Denmark for the automatic and play-off qualification places. It was going to go down to the wire.

A Danish win over Iceland in their last game would assure qualification irrespective of the outcome between Bulgaria and the Czech Republic. Olsen's men were up for it and stormed to a 4-0 lead by the 35th minute with Rommedahl, Sand and Thomas Gravesen (twice) scoring. Sand and Jan Michaelsen added further goals for a 6-0 win. Denmark were going to the World Cup Finals for only the third time in their history.

Morten Olsen's Denmark will be realistically looking to progress beyond the group stage. The side is studded with top internationals, most of whom play outside Denmark. The British-based contingent includes Thomas Gravesen of Everton and Thomas Sorensen, who has performed well in goal and has comfortably emerged from the enormous shadow cast by the legendary Peter Schmeichel. Thomas Gravesen and Stig Tofting have developed a good partnership with Jesper Gronkjaer, Martin Jorgensen or Dennis Rommedahl providing the width. Ebbe Sand is the team's main striker, his nine goals in ten qualifying appearances justifying his selection, with Jon Dahl Tomasson in the withdrawn striker's role.

## ★ THE LOWDOWN

**Population:** 5.3 million

**Capital:** Copenhagen

**Leader:** Poul Rasmussen

**Life Expectancy:** Male: 74 yrs
Female: 79 yrs

>> Until 1976 the Danish Football Rulers, the DFU, banned professional footballers from playing in the national team.

>> Danes are renowned for their good environmental attitude; the Danish countryside is full of wind turbines, providing clean energy.

>> They are less inventive when it comes to surnames; nearly 8% of the population is called Jensen. Who'd be a Danish postman??!!

★ **ASSOCIATION:** Dansk Boldspil Union

★ **JOINED FIFA:** 1904

★ **JOINED UEFA:** 1954

★ **PLAYERS:** 268,600

★ **CLUBS:** 1,555

★ **WEBSITE:** www.vbu.dk

★ **HONOURS:** European Championship – 1992.

## ★ ROAD TO QUALIFICATION

**Sep 00 Iceland** (a) > (w) 1-**2**
Tomasson 26, Bisgaard 48

**Oct 00 Northern Ireland** (a) > (d) 1-**1**
Rommedahl 60

**Oct 00 Bulgaria** (h) > (d) **1**-1 Sand 72

**Mar 01 Malta** (a) > (w) 0-**5**
Sand 8, 63, 79, Heitz 51, Jensen 76

**Mar 01 Czech Republic** (a) > (d) 0-**0**

**Jun 01 Czech Republic** (a) > (w) **2**-1
Sand 5, Tomasson 81

**Jun 01 Malta** (h) > (w) **2**-1 Sand 43, 83

**Sep 01 Northern Ireland** (h) > (d) **1**-1
Rommedahl 3

**Sep 01 Bulgaria** (a) > (w) 0-**2**
Tomasson 47, 90

**Oct 01 Iceland** (h) > (w) **6**-0
Rommedahl 12, Sand 14, 65, Gravesen 31, 35, Michaelsen 90

## ★ FINAL GROUP TABLE

| Team | P | W | D | L | F | A | Pts |
|---|---|---|---|---|---|---|---|
| **Denmark** | **10** | **6** | **4** | **0** | **22** | **6** | **22** |
| Czech Republic | 10 | 6 | 2 | 2 | 20 | 8 | 20 |
| Bulgaria | 10 | 5 | 2 | 3 | 14 | 15 | 17 |
| Iceland | 10 | 4 | 1 | 5 | 14 | 20 | 13 |
| N. Ireland | 10 | 3 | 2 | 5 | 11 | 12 | 11 |
| Malta | 10 | 0 | 1 | 9 | 4 | 24 | 1 |

## ★ RECENT RESULTS

**Feb 02 Saudi Arabia** (a) > (w) 0-**1** Sand 17

**Mar 02 Rep of Ireland** (a) > (l) 3-**0**

*Martin Laursen is surprised by the sudden appearance of a round white thing.*

## DID YOU KNOW?

It was not until 1976 that the Danish national team allowed professional players to be considered for the team.

Denmark, undefeated throughout the World Cup qualifiers, scored goals freely and conceded few. This owes much to Morten Olsen's adaptable 4-4-1-1 formation that can quickly pack the defence or flow forward in numbers in attack. Goalkeeper Thomas Sorenson is well protected by the superb central defensive partnership of Rene Henriksen and Martin Laursen. In Thomas Helveg and Jan Heintze Denmark have two of the most experienced full backs in the game. There is a no-nonsense feel about the midfield with Thomas Gravesen and Stig Tofting providing a presence that would make any international midfielder wary of bothering them. In Martin Jorgensen and Dennis Rommedahl, or alternatively Jesper Gronkjaer, Denmark have wing players who can weave their way to the byline with skill and pace. Jon Dahl Tomasson is a key player for Denmark playing in a withdrawn striker's role where he quickly becomes a partner and an option for the main striker Ebbe Sand.

# PROBABLE FORMATION 4-4-1-1

SORENSON

HELVEG · HEINTZE

HENRIKSEN · LAURSEN

TOMASSON

JORGENSEN · GRAVESEN · TOFTING · ROMMEDAHL

SAND

## ★ MEN THAT MATTER!

### EBBE SAND

Age>> 29
Club>> Schalke
Ever present (10 games) and top scorer (9 goals) during Denmark's qualification. Joined Schalke from Brondby in 2000 and became 2001 Bundesliga top scorer. Will be playing in his second World Cup.

### RENE HENRIKSEN

Age>> 31
Club>> Panathinaikos
Centre-back who is more than a stopper, with excellent pace and vision allows him to instigate and negate for Denmark. Overlooked for France 98 but played at Euro 2000.

### THOMAS SORENSON

Age>> 25
Club>> Sunderland
Emerged as Denmark's number one following retirement of Peter Schmeichel with some outstanding performances. He was third choice keeper at Euro 2000 and served plenty of bench time before getting his deserved chance.

## ★ PROBABLE SQUAD     ★ QUALIFICATION RECORD

| NAME | POSITION | CLUB | APS/GOALS | GAMES | MINS | Y/C | R/C | GOALS |
|------|----------|------|-----------|-------|------|-----|-----|-------|
| Jan Hoffmann | Goalkeeper | AB, Denmark | 0/0 | 0 | 0 | 0 | 0 | 0 |
| Peter Kjaer | Goalkeeper | Aberdeen, Scotland | 3/0 | 2 | 169 | 0 | 0 | 0 |
| Thomas Sorensen | Goalkeeper | Sunderland, England | 10/0 | 6 | 461 | 0 | 0 | 0 |
| Jan Heintze | Defender | PSV Eindhoven, Holland | 79/3 | 10 | 900 | 1 | 0 | 1 |
| Thomas Helveg | Defender | Milan, Italy | 65/2 | 10 | 880 | 1 | 0 | 0 |
| Rene Henriksen | Defender | Panathinaikos, Greece | 35/0 | 10 | 900 | 0 | 0 | 0 |
| Niclas Jensen | Defender | Copenhagen, Denmark | 4/0 | 0 | 0 | 0 | 0 | 0 |
| Martin Laursen | Defender | Milan, Italy | 12/0 | 6 | 540 | 1 | 0 | 0 |
| Steven Lustu | Defender | AB, Denmark | 3/0 | 0 | 0 | 0 | 0 | 0 |
| Jan Michaelsen | Defender | Panathinaikos, Greece | 8/1 | 4 | 91 | 0 | 0 | 1 |
| Per Frandsen | Midfielder | Bolton, England | 21/0 | 1 | 21 | 0 | 0 | 0 |
| Thomas Gravesen | Midfielder | Everton, England | 19/2 | 7 | 605 | 2 | 0 | 2 |
| Claus Jensen | Midfielder | Charlton, England | 12/1 | 7 | 222 | 1 | 0 | 1 |
| Mads Jorgensen | Midfielder | Brondby, Denmark | 1/0 | 1 | 10 | 0 | 0 | 0 |
| Christian Poulsen | Midfielder | Schalke, Germany | 2/0 | 0 | 0 | 0 | 0 | 0 |
| Brian Steen Nielsen | Midfielder | Malmo, Sweden | 61/3 | 6 | 320 | 1 | 0 | 0 |
| Peter Nielsen | Midfielder | B Munnchengladbach, Germany | 9/0 | 2 | 115 | 0 | 0 | 0 |
| Stig Tofting | Midfielder | Bolton Wanderers, England | 34/2 | 9 | 795 | 1 | 0 | 0 |
| Jesper Gronkjaer | Forward | Chelsea, England | 22/1 | 8 | 471 | 1 | 0 | 0 |
| Ebbe Sand | Forward | Schalke, Germany | 41/17 | 0 | 0 | 0 | 0 | 0 |
| Peter Madsen | Forward | Brondby, Denmark | 2/0 | 1 | 21 | 0 | 0 | 0 |
| Dennis Rommedahl | Forward | PSV Eindhoven, Holland | 15/5 | 10 | 796 | 1 | 0 | 3 |
| Jon Dahl Tomasson | Forward | Feyenoord, Holland | 35/13 | 9 | 766 | 2 | 0 | 4 |

KEY: APPS/GOALS = International Appearances/Goals; GAMES=Qualification Games played; MINS=Minutes played; Y/C= Yellow cards R/C=Red cards

# HISTORY AT THE WORLD CUP

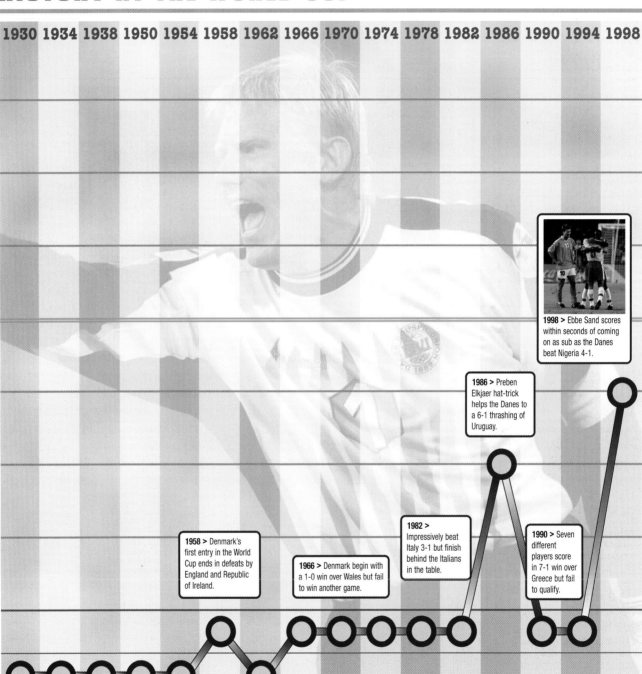

| 1930 | 1934 | 1938 | 1950 | 1954 | 1958 | 1962 | 1966 | 1970 | 1974 | 1978 | 1982 | 1986 | 1990 | 1994 | 1998 |

**1998 >** Ebbe Sand scores within seconds of coming on as sub as the Danes beat Nigeria 4-1.

**1986 >** Preben Elkjaer hat-trick helps the Danes to a 6-1 thrashing of Uruguay.

**1958 >** Denmark's first entry in the World Cup ends in defeats by England and Republic of Ireland.

**1966 >** Denmark begin with a 1-0 win over Wales but fail to win another game.

**1982 >** Impressively beat Italy 3-1 but finish behind the Italians in the table.

**1990 >** Seven different players score in 7-1 win over Greece but fail to qualify.

## ★ WORLD CUP HISTORY

| | | | |
|---|---|---|---|
| **1930** >> Did Not Enter | | **1970** >> Did Not Qualify | |
| **1934** >> Did Not Enter | | **1974** >> Did Not Qualify | |
| **1938** >> Did Not Enter | | **1978** >> Did Not Qualify | |
| **1950** >> Did Not Enter | | **1982** >> Did Not Qualify | |
| **1954** >> Did Not Enter | | **1986** >> Second Round | |
| **1958** >> Did Not Qualify | | **1990** >> Did Not Qualify | |
| **1962** >> Did Not Enter | | **1994** >> Did Not Qualify | |
| **1966** >> Did Not Qualify | | **1998** >> Quarter-Finals | |

## ★ WORLD CUP RECORDS, STORIES AND WEIRDNESS

**SUBSTITUTION** >> Ebbe Sand scored the fastest ever goal by a substitute – only 16 seconds after getting on the pitch. It was against Nigeria in 1998. Denmark won 4-1.

## GROUP G

| OPPONENT | DATE | UK TIME | VENUE |
|----------|------|---------|-------|
| Italy | **3 June** | 12.30 | **Sapporo, Japan** |
| Mexico | **9 June** | 07.30 | **Miyagi, Japan** |
| Croatia | **13 June** | 12.30 | **Yokohama, Japan** |

## *"at least they'll be acclimatised"*

# ECUADOR

Ecuador is a republic on the Equator, hence its name, on the Pacific coast of South America, big on bananas, cocoa and coffee, but not much cop at football – until now. Ecuador has finally qualified for the World Cup Finals at the 11th time of asking. The Galapagos Islands, now a national park, belong to Ecuador and that's where Charles Darwin found much evidence for his theory of evolution. Colombian coach Hernan Dario Gomez has had to introduce an evolutionary managerial policy of his own, inculcating much-needed discipline into the side.

At the halfway stage of qualifying Ecuador were in sixth place – an average side that had won four and lost four of their first nine games.

Then came the first sensation: a shock 1-0 win over Brazil at the Atalhualpa Stadium in Quito. It was Ecuador's first ever win over the Brazilians in 22 attempts. So well did Ecuador control the game that during long sequences of possession, every Ecuadorian pass was greeted with cries of 'Ole!' by the crowd. The magical party was almost spoiled by Brazil's Romario who goaded keeper Jose Francisco Cevallos into a magnificent double-save in the last minute, blocking Romario's header and the subsequent follow up.

Delgado was the goalscoring hero in a sensational comeback against an in form Paraguay. Ecuador had come from a man down – defender Augusto Poroso was sent off after 19 minutes – and a goal behind – Jose Cardozo put Paraguay ahead in the 27th minute. Delgado equalised on the

stroke of half time and scored the winner in the 53rd minute. Even more amazing was that Ecuador finished the game with nine men after midfielder Wellington Sanchez was also shown a red card in the last minute.

There followed another startling last minute victory as Ecuador won their fifth successive qualifier in Lima against Peru. Ecuador had gone behind in the second minute, but Edison Mendez, who did an excellent man-marking job on Brazil's Rivaldo, equalised ten minutes later. Ecuador weathered Peru's storm but seemed to have blown it with less than ten minutes to play when Mendez was sent off. However, in injury time Delgado broke free scoring a dramatic late winner. The result put Ecuador in third place, six points clear of fifth-placed Colombia.

Inevitably beaten by Argentina, the loss was aggravated by the dismissal of Chala, who became the sixth Ecuadorian player to be sent off in the qualifiers. Without Chala, Ecuador secured a 0-0 draw in Colombia and followed it with a sensational 5-1 win against Bolivia at La Paz – Bolivia's first home defeat in 16 years. It left Ecuador needing just a point from their last two games. Qualification, as runners up to Argentina was clinched with a 1-1 draw at home to Uruguay – Ivan Kaviedes scoring the vital goal.

During an 18-match qualifying campaign Ecuador have shown they have more than enough ability to cause an upset at the World Cup, but they remain susceptible to ill discipline.

---

### ★ THE LOWDOWN

**Population:** 13.1 million

**Capital:** Quito

**Leader:** Gustavo Nobola

**Life Expectancy:** Male: 68 yrs Female: 74 yrs

>> In the Ecuadorian Amazon live one third of all the bird species in the entire Amazon region, and 10% of all the tree species on earth.

>> Traditional Ecuadorian cuisine is not for the faint-hearted. Popular dishes include roasted guinea pig and bull penis soup! The less adventurous will be pleased to note that Macdonald's arrived in the country two years ago.

>> 11 different peoples make up the indigenous Ecuadorian population, 50% of whom now live in urban areas.

★ **ASSOCIATION:** Asociacion Ecuatoriana de Futbol

★ **JOINED FIFA:** 1926

★ **JOINED CONEMBOL:** 1930

★ **PLAYERS:** 15,700

★ **CLUBS:** 170

★ **WEBSITE:** www.ecuafutbolonline.org

★ **HONOURS:** None

*Francisco 'Pancho' Cevallos makes it clear he wants only one sugar in his half-time cuppa.*

## ★ ROAD TO QUALIFICATION

Mar 00 **Venezuela** (h) > (w) **2**-0
Delgado 17, Aguinaga Garzon 50

Apr 00 **Brazil** (a) > (l) 3-**2**
Aguinaga Garzon 12, De La Cruz, U 76

Jun 00 **Paraguay** (a) > (l) 3-**1**
Graziani Lentini 87

Jun 00 **Peru** (h) > (w) **2**-1
Chala 16, Hurtado Roa, E 51

Jul 00 **Argentina** (a) > (l) 2-**0**

Jul 00 **Colombia** (h) > (d) **0**-0

Aug 00 **Bolivia** (h) > (w) **2**-0
Delgado 18, 60

Sep 00 **Uruguay** (a) > (l) 4-**0**

Oct 00 **Chile** (h) > (w) **1**-0 Delgado 76

Nov 00 **Venezuela** (a) > (w) 1-**2**
Kaviedes 4, Sanchez 21

Mar 01 **Brazil** (h) > (w) **1**-0 Delgado 49

Apr 01 **Paraguay** (h) > (w) **2**-1
Delgado 44, 52

Jun 01 **Peru** (a) > (w) 1-**2**
Mendez, E 11, Delgado 90

Aug 01 **Argentina** (h) > (l) **0**-2

Sep 01 **Colombia** (a) > (d) 0-**0**

Oct 01 **Bolivia** (a) > (w) 1-**5**
De La Cruz, U 13, Delgado 23, Kaviedes
56, Fernandez 89, Caceres 90

Nov 01 **Uruguay** (a) > (d) 1-**1** Kaviedes 72

## ★ FINAL GROUP TABLE

| Team | P | W | D | L | F | A | Pts |
|---|---|---|---|---|---|---|---|
| Argentina | 18 | 13 | 4 | 1 | 42 | 15 | 43 |
| Ecuador | 18 | 9 | 4 | 5 | 23 | 20 | 31 |
| Brazil | 18 | 9 | 3 | 6 | 31 | 17 | 30 |
| Paraguay | 18 | 9 | 3 | 6 | 29 | 23 | 30 |
| Uruguay | 18 | 7 | 6 | 5 | 19 | 13 | 27 |
| Colombia | 18 | 7 | 6 | 5 | 20 | 15 | 27 |
| Bolivia | 18 | 4 | 6 | 8 | 21 | 33 | 18 |
| Peru | 18 | 4 | 4 | 10 | 14 | 25 | 16 |
| Venezuela | 18 | 5 | 1 | 12 | 18 | 44 | 16 |
| Chile | 18 | 3 | 3 | 12 | 15 | 27 | 12 |

## ★ RECENT RESULTS

Feb 02 **Turkey** (a) > (w) 0-**1** Tenorio 64

Mar 02 **United States** (a) > (l) 1-**0**

Mar 02 **Bulgaria** (h) > (w) **3**-0
Kaviedes 24, 82, Tenorio 51

# GROUP G

## DID YOU KNOW?

Between July 1965 (v Colombia) and November 2000 (v Venezuela) Ecuador failed to win a single away fixture in World Cup qualifying.

In Agustin Delgado and Ivan Kaviedes Ecuador have a useful striking partnership that managed 12 of Ecuador's 23 goals in qualifying. The four-man midfield provides the impetus, driven by Alex Aguinaga, the captain, and supported on the flanks by Cleber Chala and the highly rated Edison Mendez. Both players can swap positions unnerving opponents and breaking through to create chances for Delgado and Kaviedes. Alfonso Obregon provides defensive cover in midfield – largely because of his height, something the back line lacks despite the inclusion of Monterrey's tall central defender Giovani Espinoza. Defensively Ecuador are weak and are especially vulnerable in the air. Remaining defenders Ivan Hurtado. Ulises De La Cruz and Raul Guerron and keeper 'Pancho' Cevallos will be under severe pressure throughout Ecuador's tournament run – after all this is the side that conceded 20 goals in qualifying.

## PROBABLE FORMATION  4-4-2

CEVALLOS

DE LA CRUZ  GUERRON

HURTADO  ESPINOZA

CHALA  OBREGON  A AGUINAGA  MENDEZ

DELGADO  KAVIEDES

## ★ MEN THAT MATTER!

### AGUSTIN DELGADO

Age>> 27

Club>> Soton

'El Tin' scored nine goals in qualifying including the historic winner against Brazil. He is dangerous with both head and feet and the main reason for Ecuador's success.

### ULISES DE LA CRUZ

Age>> 28

Club>> Hibernian

Attacking right back, De La Cruz was ever present throughout qualifying. His pace and close control causes problems for opposing defences while few forwards can outrun him down the flank.

### IVAN KAVIEDES

Age>> 24

Club>> Celta Vigo/Porto (loan)

Kaviedes has formed an excellent attacking partnership with Delgado. He is the foil, creator and occasional scorer of many of Ecuador's goals. He is first choice with Ecuador but not his Spanish club.

## ★ PROBABLE SQUAD  ★ QUALIFICATION RECORD

| NAME | POSITION | CLUB | APS/GOALS | GAMES | MINS | Y/C | R/C | GOALS |
|------|----------|------|-----------|-------|------|-----|-----|-------|
| Jose Cevallos | Goalkeeper | Barcelona, Ecuador | 58/0 | 16 | 1440 | 5 | 0 | 0 |
| Geovani Ibarra | Goalkeeper | El Nacional, Ecuador | 20/0 | 2 | 180 | 0 | 0 | 0 |
| Jacinto Espinoza | Goalkeeper | LDU Quito, Ecuador | 1/0 | 1 | 90 | 0 | 0 | 0 |
| Marlon Ayovi | Defender | Deportivo Quito, Ecuador | 26/0 | 7 | 495 | 1 | 0 | 0 |
| Ulises De La Cruz | Defender | Hibernian, Scotland | 48/3 | 18 | 1620 | 1 | 0 | 2 |
| Giovany Espinoza | Defender | Monterrey, Mexico | 18/0 | 8 | 585 | 0 | 0 | 0 |
| Jorge Guagua | Defender | El Nacional, Ecuador | 2/0 | 2 | 70 | 0 | 0 | 0 |
| Raul Guerron | Defender | Deportivo Quito, Ecuador | 16/0 | 9 | 787 | 2 | 0 | 0 |
| Ivan Hurtado | Defender | La Piedad, Mexico | 86/4 | 17 | 1530 | 0 | 0 | 0 |
| Augusto Poroso | Defender | Emelec, Ecuador | 21/0 | 11 | 927 | 1 | 2 | 0 |
| Carlos Tenorio | Midfielder | LDU Quito, Ecuador | 4/1 | 1 | 20 | 0 | 0 | 0 |
| Juan Aguinaga | Midfielder | Espoli, Ecuador | 6/0 | 3 | 74 | 1 | 0 | 0 |
| Juan D Lara Burbano | Midfielder | El Nacional, Ecuador | 17/0 | 8 | 416 | 2 | 0 | 0 |
| Cleber Chala | Midfielder | Southampton, England | 59/6 | 14 | 896 | 0 | 1 | 1 |
| Luis Gomez | Midfielder | Barcelona, Ecuador | 7/1 | 1 | 90 | 1 | 0 | 0 |
| Edison Mendez | Midfielder | Deportivo Quito, Ecuador | 20/2 | 8 | 658 | 1 | 1 | 1 |
| Alfonso Obregon | Midfielder | Delfin, Ecuador | 35/0 | 14 | 1154 | 6 | 0 | 0 |
| Edwin Tenorio | Midfielder | Aucas, Ecuador | 30/0 | 14 | 1114 | 8 | 0 | 0 |
| Alex Aguinaga | Forward | Necaxa, Mexico | 88/20 | 13 | 950 | 4 | 0 | 2 |
| Nicolas Asencio | Forward | Barcelona, Ecuador | 13/0 | 0 | 0 | 0 | 0 | 0 |
| Agustin Delgado | Forward | Southampton, England | 44/20 | 16 | 1305 | 1 | 0 | 9 |
| Angel Fernandez | Forward | El Nacional, Ecuador | 66/12 | 5 | 198 | 0 | 0 | 1 |
| Ivan Kaviedes | Forward | Celta Vigo, Spain | 24/8 | 13 | 817 | 0 | 0 | 3 |

KEY: APPS/GOALS = International Appearances/Goals; GAMES=Qualification Games played; MINS=Minutes played; Y/C= Yellow cards R/C=Red cards

# HISTORY AT THE WORLD CUP

1930 1934 1938 1950 1954 1958 1962 1966 1970 1974 1978 1982 1986 1990 1994 1998

**1974 >** Ecuador's qualification hopes ended by two draws with Colombia and two defeats by Uruguay.

**1978 >** Ecuador again fail to win against Chile and Peru in their qualification group.

**1970 >** Ecuador fail to win any of the World Cup qualifiers.

**1986 >** Ecuador suffer 6-2 defeat by Chile in qualifying.

**1962 >** Ecuador's first World Cup qualifier ends in a 6-3 defeat at home to Argentina.

**1982 >** Ecuador beat Paraguay 1-0 in qualifying but again fail to progress.

**1966 >** Ecuador lose 2-1 to Chile in a qualification play-off in Peru.

**1990 >** Ecuador record only a single win over Paraguay in their qualification campaign.

## ★ WORLD CUP HISTORY

| | | | |
|---|---|---|---|
| 1930 >> Did Not Enter | 1970 >> Did Not Qualify |
| 1934 >> Did Not Enter | 1974 >> Did Not Qualify |
| 1938 >> Did Not Enter | 1978 >> Did Not Qualify |
| 1950 >> Did Not Enter | 1982 >> Did Not Qualify |
| 1954 >> Did Not Enter | 1986 >> Did not Qualify |
| 1958 >> Did Not Enter | 1990 >> Did Not Qualify |
| 1962 >> Did Not Qualify | 1994 >> Did Not Qualify |
| 1966 >> Did Not Qualify | 1998 >> Did Not Qualify |

## ★ WORLD CUP RECORDS, STORIES AND WEIRDNESS

**QUALIFYING GOALS** >> Ecuador scored a total of 23 goals in qualifying, making them 29th equal top scorer with Iran, Iraq, Syria, Uzbekistan and Australia (on 73) ahead of them!

# GROUP F

| OPPONENT | DATE | UK TIME | VENUE |
|----------|------|---------|-------|
| Sweden | **2 June** | 10.30 | **Saitama, Japan** |
| Argentina | **7 June** | 12.30 | **Sapporo, Japan** |
| Nigeria | **12 June** | 07.30 | **Osaka, Japan** |

## "if Becks plays, serious semi-final contenders"

# ENGLAND

England are reeling from the news that their captain, midfield supremo and free kick genius is seriously in doubt for the Finals.

A dastardly late lunge by Argentinian Pedro Duscher during Manchester United's quarter-final Champions League clash broke a bone in Beckham's foot and may have ruled him out of the tournament.

It all began in Munich, Germany on September 1st 2001 as England thrash Germany 5-1 in a World Cup qualifier. A hat-trick from Michael Owen, a first goal for Steven Gerrard and an amazing fifth goal from Emile Heskey complete a magical night for England, a night that proves to be a turning point in the group after England had started its qualifying run so disastrously.

Towards the end of 2000 England had hit rock bottom. Marking the closing of Wembley Stadium with a 1-0 home defeat by Germany in their opening World Cup qualifier had followed a disastrous Euro 2000 tournament. Boss Kevin Keegan resigned admitting he was not up to the job leaving the FA's Director of Football Howard Wilkinson to retrieve something from a trip to Finland. A goalless draw, which England fans had to pay to see on television for the first time, led to country-wide pessimism about the state of English football.

The FA took the radical, and controversial, step of appointing foreign coach Swede Sven Goran Eriksson to re-vitalise England's qualification campaign. Eriksson brought to the role a calming and confidence-building influence. Deciding on his favoured 4-4-2 system, he took the common sense step of playing players in their familiar positions and, after watching more English league matches with his assistant Tord Grip than any of his predecessors, unearthed surprising new international talent in left-backs 31-year-old Chris Powell and 19-year-old Ashley Cole.

The return match against Finland at Anfield saw England come back from a goal behind to win 2-1 with goals from Owen and new captain David Beckham. A trip to Tirana saw a resilient Albanian outfit hold out until the 74th minute when Owen, Paul Scholes and Andy Cole scored for a 3-1 win. A successful trip to Athens earned a 2-0 win over Greece with Scholes and Beckham on target.

Then came that magnificent win in Munich followed by a 2-0 win over Albania which put England in the driving seat for the first time. But in their final game against Greece at Old Trafford, England, without Owen, made hard work of it. They went a goal down and had goalkeeper Nigel Martyn to thank for not going further behind after he made two superb saves. A vital English substitution brought on Teddy Sheringham, who equalised with his very first touch of the ball, before Greece took the lead again.

At the same time Germany were being held to a goalless draw by Finland and England looked destined for the lottery of the play-offs but, in injury time, Sheringham was fouled and Beckham was left with one of the most important free kicks of his career. The England captain did not disappoint – curling a superb kick from 30 yards out and into the back of the net to earn the single point that took England to the World Cup Finals. And now England can only hope…

★ **ASSOCIATION:** The Football Association

★ **JOINED FIFA:** 1946

★ **JOINED UEFA:** 1954

★ **PLAYERS:** 2,250,000

★ **CLUBS:** 42,000

★ **WEBSITE:** www.the-fa.org

★ **HONOURS:** World Cup – 1966; Olympics – 1908, 1912

*Beckham, free kick maestro – but will he be fit enough to play?*

## ★ ROAD TO QUALIFICATION

Oct 00 **Germany** (h) > (l) **0**-1

Oct 00 **Finland** (a) > (d) 0-**0**

Mar 01 **Finland** (h) > (w) **2**-1
Owen 43, Beckham 49

Mar 01 **Albania** (a) > (w) 1-**3**
Owen 73, Scholes 85, Cole, Andy 90

Jun 01 **Greece** (a) > (w) 0-**2**
Scholes 63, Beckham 86

Sep 01 **Germany** (a) > (w) 1-**5**
Owen 13, 48, 66 Gerrard 45, Heskey 74

Sep 01 **Albania** (h) > (w) **2**-0
Owen 44, Fowler 88

Oct 01 **Greece** (h) > (d) **2**-2
Sheringham 67, Beckham 90

## ★ FINAL GROUP TABLE

| Team | P | W | D | L | F | A | Pts |
|---|---|---|---|---|---|---|---|
| England | 8 | 5 | 2 | 1 | 16 | 6 | 17 |
| Germany | 8 | 5 | 2 | 1 | 14 | 10 | 17 |
| Finland | 8 | 3 | 3 | 2 | 12 | 7 | 12 |
| Greece | 8 | 2 | 1 | 5 | 7 | 17 | 7 |
| Albania | 8 | 1 | 0 | 7 | 5 | 14 | 3 |

## ★ RECENT RESULTS

Feb 02 **Holland** (a) > (d) 1-1 Vassell 61

Mar 02 **Italy** (h) > (l) **1**-2 Fowler 62

53

## DID YOU KNOW?

Bryan Robson scored England's quickest World Cup goal after 27 seconds against Czechoslovakia at Bilbao in Spain on June 16, 1982.

Under Sven Goran Eriksson, revitalised England have evolved a settled way of playing in the 4-4-2 formation familiar to Premiership players, and have selected a younger and better balanced squad. David Seaman is England's first choice goalkeeper when fit with Nigel Martyn (probably) as alternative if he's not. Sol Campbell and Rio Ferdinand have established themselves as England's centre backs with Gary Neville and Ashley Cole at full back. In midfield the supremely talented and talismanic Steven Gerrard will be the defensive anchor – if only he can stay fit – while Paul Scholes will play in the hole behind the front two, given free rein to attack from midfield. Owen Hargreaves takes the right of the midfield position if Beckham is ruled out and on England's problematic left side Steve McManaman should get the nod although Emile Heskey could be asked to play the role. Heskey, however, will probably be first choice, among an abundance of other striking talent including Robbie Fowler and Darius Vassell, to play alongside the prolific Michael Owen in attack. Teddy Sheringham's reputation as England's supersub goes before him and he'll be ready to come on to make his mark if Owen or Heskey haven't already made theirs.

## PROBABLE FORMATION 4-4-2

SEAMAN

G NEVILLE

Ashley COLE

FERDINAND    CAMPBELL

HARGREAVES    GERRARD    SCHOLES    McMANAMAN

HESKEY    OWEN

## ★ MEN THAT MATTER!

### DAVID BECKHAM

Age>> 27

Club>> Man. United

Indispensable Captain, free kick specialist and one of England's most successful players, but fighting to recover from injury in time for the Finals.

### MICHAEL OWEN

Age>> 22

Club>> Liverpool

Stormed on to the scene at France 98 scoring a stunning goal against Argentina. Scored a hat-trick against Germany in the qualifiers. Lightening pace and prolific scoring makes him England's main marksman.

### STEVEN GERRARD

Age>> 22

Club>> Liverpool

Pivotal player for England in the midfield anchor role that allows Beckham plenty of freedom. This determined and tenacious player has always been excellent for England when free from injury.

## ★ PROBABLE SQUAD                    ★ QUALIFICATION RECORD

| NAME | POSITION | CLUB | APS/GOALS | GAMES | MINS | Y/C | R/C | GOALS |
|---|---|---|---|---|---|---|---|---|
| David James | Goalkeeper | West Ham, England | 7/0 | 0 | 0 | 0 | 0 | 0 |
| Nigel Martyn | Goalkeeper | Leeds, England | 21/0 | 1 | 90 | 0 | 0 | 0 |
| David Seaman | Goalkeeper | Arsenal, England | 67/0 | 7 | 630 | 0 | 0 | 0 |
| Wayne Bridge | Defender | Southampton, England | 2/0 | 0 | 0 | 0 | 0 | 0 |
| Sol Campbell | Defender | Arsenal, England | 44/0 | 4 | 299 | 0 | 0 | 0 |
| Jamie Carragher | Defender | Liverpool, England | 7/0 | 2 | 14 | 0 | 0 | 0 |
| Ashley Cole | Defender | Arsenal, England | 7/0 | 5 | 438 | 1 | 0 | 0 |
| Rio Ferdinand | Defender | Leeds, England | 20/0 | 6 | 540 | 0 | 0 | 0 |
| Martin Keown | Defender | Arsenal, England | 40/2 | 4 | 360 | 0 | 0 | 0 |
| Gary Neville | Defender | Manchester United, England | 51/0 | 6 | 496 | 1 | 0 | 0 |
| Philip Neville | Defender | Manchester United, England | 36/0 | 2 | 180 | 0 | 0 | 0 |
| David Beckham | Midfielder | Manchester United, England | 49/6 | 7 | 623 | 0 | 0 | 3 |
| Nicky Butt | Midfielder | Manchester United, England | 17/0 | 3 | 93 | 0 | 0 | 0 |
| Kieron Dyer | Midfielder | Newcastle, England | 8/0 | 1 | 44 | 0 | 0 | 0 |
| Steven Gerrard | Midfielder | Liverpool, England | 9/1 | 5 | 431 | 1 | 0 | 1 |
| Owen Hargreaves | Midfielder | Bayern Munich, Germany | 3/0 | 1 | 12 | 0 | 0 | 0 |
| Steve McManaman | Midfielder | Real Madrid, Spain | 37/3 | 7 | 216 | 1 | 0 | 0 |
| Paul Scholes | Midfielder | Manchester United, England | 41/13 | 8 | 711 | 2 | 0 | 2 |
| Robbie Fowler | Forward | Leeds, England | 23/6 | 4 | 190 | 0 | 0 | 1 |
| Emile Heskey | Forward | Liverpool, England | 22/3 | 7 | 462 | 1 | 0 | 1 |
| Michael Owen | Forward | Liverpool, England | 33/14 | 6 | 532 | 0 | 0 | 6 |
| Teddy Sheringham | Forward | Tottenham, England | 44/11 | 1 | 23 | 0 | 0 | 1 |
| Darius Vassell | Forward | Aston Villa, England | 2/1 | 0 | 0 | 0 | 0 | 0 |

KEY: APPS/GOALS = International Appearances/Goals; GAMES=Qualification Games played; MINS=Minutes played; Y/C= Yellow cards R/C=Red cards

# HISTORY AT THE WORLD CUP

1930 1934 1938 1950 1954 1958 1962 1966 1970 1974 1978 1982 1986 1990 1994 1998

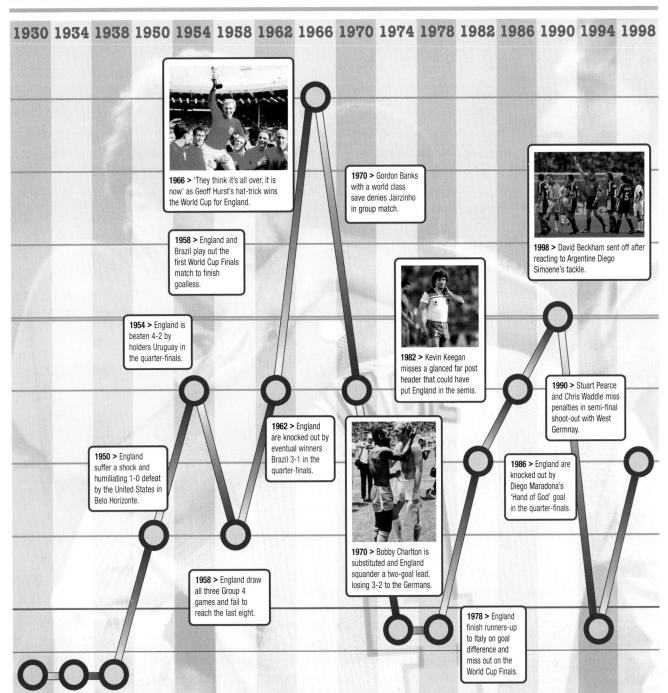

**1966 >** 'They think it's all over, it is now' as Geoff Hurst's hat-trick wins the World Cup for England.

**1970 >** Gordon Banks with a world class save denies Jairzinho in group match.

**1998 >** David Beckham sent off after reacting to Argentine Diego Simoene's tackle.

**1958 >** England and Brazil play out the first World Cup Finals match to finish goalless.

**1954 >** England is beaten 4-2 by holders Uruguay in the quarter-finals.

**1982 >** Kevin Keegan misses a glanced far post header that could have put England in the semis.

**1990 >** Stuart Pearce and Chris Waddle miss penalties in semi-final shoot-out with West Germnay.

**1962 >** England are knocked out by eventual winners Brazil 3-1 in the quarter-finals.

**1950 >** England suffer a shock and humiliating 1-0 defeat by the United States in Belo Horizonte.

**1986 >** England are knocked out by Diego Maradona's 'Hand of God' goal in the quarter-finals.

**1970 >** Bobby Charlton is substituted and England squander a two-goal lead, losing 3-2 to the Germans.

**1958 >** England draw all three Group 4 games and fail to reach the last eight.

**1978 >** England finish runners-up to Italy on goal difference and miss out on the World Cup Finals.

## ★ WORLD CUP HISTORY

| | | | |
|---|---|---|---|
| **1930** >> Did Not Enter | | **1970** >> Quarter-Final | |
| **1934** >> Did Not Enter | | **1974** >> Did Not Qualify | |
| **1938** >> Did Not Enter | | **1978** >> Did Not Qualify | |
| **1950** >> First Round | | **1982** >> Second Round | |
| **1954** >> Quarter-Final | | **1986** >> Quarter-Final | |
| **1958** >> First Round | | **1990** >> Fourth Place | |
| **1962** >> Quarter-Final | | **1994** >> Did Not Qualify | |
| **1966** >> Winners | | **1998** >> Second Round | |

## ★ WORLD CUP RECORDS, STORIES AND WEIRDNESS

**MOST GOALS** >> In 1990 England reached the semi-final of the World Cup, Gary Lineker scoring four goals on the way there. Making him only the 8th player in World Cup history to score 10 goals or more.

**CONTROVERSEY** >> 1966 and Geoff Hurst's was it over the line goal? Few, if any goals have been as repeatedly discussed. It's 2-2 in extra time in the 1966 Final against West Germany; Hurst receives the ball in the penalty area, turns and shoots – the ball hits the bar and bounces down on or over the line. The referee ultimately awards the goal after conferring with the Russian linesman.

| OPPONENT | DATE | UK TIME | VENUE |
|----------|------|---------|-------|
| Senegal | **31 May** | **12.30** | **Seoul, Korea** |
| Uruguay | **6 June** | **12.30** | **Busan, Korea** |
| Denmark | **11 June** | **07.30** | **Incheon, Korea** |

## "defending champions and still the best"

# FRANCE

### ★ THE LOWDOWN

**Population:** 59.5 million

**Capital:** Paris

**Leader:** Lionel Jospin

**Life Expectancy:** Male: 75 yrs
Female: 83 yrs

>> France is the largest Western European nation and is approximately 7 times bigger than England.

>> Most frogs' legs served up in French restaurants come from Asian bullfrogs; mainly from Bangladesh, Malaysia and India.

>> A diet of garlic, frogs' legs and snails, washed down with plenty of vin de table must be good for you; the French football team are the current holders of both the European and the World Cups. Zut alors!!

Devastating fluidity in attack, and possessed of an almost impenetrable defence, France are probably the best international side in the world. Frankly, since winning the World Cup on home soil in 1998 and the 2000 European Championship in Rotterdam, no side has come close to matching their flawless organisation, rock-like defence, highly skilled and ferocious midfield and swooping, clinical-finishing attack.

Eighteen players featured in both the 1998 World Cup and Euro 2000 squads with nine players – Lizarazu, Vieira, Djorkaeff, Deschamps, Desailly, Zidane, Thuram, Barthez and Dugarry – playing in both Finals. Laurent Blanc and Didier Deschamps have since retired from the international scene (Blanc's departure has led to some questions about the effectiveness of the new central defence pairing of Manchester United's Mikaël Silvestre and captain Marcel Desailly), but the core of this almost invincible French side remains.

And while coach Roger Lemerre faces certain selection headaches, the seamless blending of new talent has been achieved without any signs of disruption.

An experimental squad of experienced and new players beat Japan 1-0 in the Final of 2001 Confederations Cup held in Japan/Korea with a Vieira goal. What better preparation for the 2002 World Cup Finals? Particularly when you remember that from that point on France would only be playing friendlies (no need to qualify as reigning champions).

Lemerre's side have played teams from the five football-playing continents of varying ability and different styles and, almost invariably, beaten them. They've travelled to Africa, Australia, South America and, most importantly, to Asia. Consequently France are the best prepared of any of the finalists. There is a realistic chance that France could become the first team since Brazil in 1958 and 1962 to win successive World Cup Finals.

And France look set to continue to be a major football power for years to come. The production line that led to the current crop of world class players continues to turn out talented youngsters as demonstrated by France lifting the 2000 European Under-18 Championship and 2001 World Under-17 Championship.

★ **ASSOCIATION:** Federation Francaise de Football

★ **JOINED FIFA:** 1904

★ **JOINED UEFA:** 1954

★ **PLAYERS:** 1,692,300

★ **CLUBS:** 21,629

★ **WEBSITE:** www.fff.fr

★ **HONOURS:** World Cup – 1998; European Championship – 1984, 2000.

*Fabian Barthez launches another French onslaught.*

The world knows how defending Champions France will play at the 2002 World Cup – Roger Lemerre's team will play how they have always played because, quite frankly, they are so good at it and there is very little the opposition can do to stop them. France is blessed with a depth and quality in their squad that can deal with injuries and suspensions far better than most. And play incisive, tireless attack-minded football. Goalkeeper Fabian Barthez will be protected by a four-man defence of Lilian Thuram and Bixente Lizarazu at full back, with Marcel Desailly and Franck Leboeuf as centre backs. Manchester United's Mikael Silvestre, Roma's Vincent Candela and Bayern Munich's Willy Sagnol provide cover. Robert Pires is still struggling with injury, but Emmanuel Petit and Patrick Vieira can provide both defensive and attacking midfield strategies leaving one of the world's greatest footballers Zinedine Zidane free reign to cause as much damage as possible behind the front men David Trezeguet and Sylvain Wiltord.

## PROBABLE FORMATION  4-3-1-2

## ★ MEN THAT MATTER!

### ZINEDINE ZIDANE

Age>> 29
Club>> R. Madrid
Zidane, a former World Player of the Year and Euro 2000 winner, is the world's most expensive player at £47.2 million. He scored twice in the 1998 World Cup Final against Brazil.

### DAVID TREZEGUET

Age>> 24
Club>> Juventus
Scored the golden goal against Italy that won France the 2000 European Championship. Played in every match of France 98 except the Final. He is currently France's first choice striker.

### PATRICK VIEIRA

Age>> 25
Club>> Arsenal
Widely regarded as one of the best midfielders in the world both in defence and attack. A World Cup Final substitute at France 98 and also a Euro 2000 winner.

## ★ PROBABLE SQUAD  ★ QUALIFICATION RECORD

| NAME | POSITION | CLUB | APS/GOALS | GAMES | MINS | Y/C | R/C | GOALS |
|---|---|---|---|---|---|---|---|---|
| Fabien Barthez | Goalkeeper | Manchester United, England | 44/0 | - | - | - | - | - |
| Gregory Coupet | Goalkeeper | Lyon, France | 1/0 | - | - | - | - | - |
| Ulrich Rame | Goalkeeper | Bordeaux, France | 8/0 | - | - | - | - | - |
| Vincent Candela | Defender | Roma, Italy | 31/2 | - | - | - | - | - |
| Marcel Desailly | Defender | Chelsea, England | 88/3 | - | - | - | - | - |
| William Gallas | Defender | Chelsea, England | 43/3 | - | - | - | - | - |
| Bixente Lizarazu | Defender | Bayern Munich, Germany | 70/2 | - | - | - | - | - |
| Willy Sagnol | Defender | Bayern Munich, Germany | 8/0 | - | - | - | - | - |
| Mickael Silvestre | Defender | Manchester United, England | 9/1 | - | - | - | - | - |
| Lilian Thuram | Defender | Juventus, Italy | 70/2 | - | - | - | - | - |
| Alain Boghossain | Midfielder | Parma, Italy | 23/2 | - | - | - | - | - |
| Eric Carriere | Midfielder | Lyon, France | 5/2 | - | - | - | - | - |
| Youri Djorkaeff | Midfielder | Bolton Wanderers, England | 75/28 | - | - | - | - | - |
| Christian Karembeu | Midfielder | Olympiakos, Greece | 51/1 | - | - | - | - | - |
| Claude Makelele | Midfielder | Real Madrid, Spain | 12/0 | - | - | - | - | - |
| Emmanuel Petit | Midfielder | Chelsea, England | 52/5 | - | - | - | - | - |
| Patrick Vieira | Midfielder | Arsenal, England | 47/2 | - | - | - | - | - |
| Zinedine Zidane | Midfielder | Real Madrid, Spain | 69/18 | - | - | - | - | - |
| Nicolas Anelka | Forward | Liverpool, England | 26/6 | - | - | - | - | - |
| Thierry Henry | Forward | Arsenal, England | 31/11 | - | - | - | - | - |
| Laurent Robert | Forward | Newcastle, England | 9/1 | - | - | - | - | - |
| David Trezeguet | Forward | Juventus, Italy | 32/14 | - | - | - | - | - |
| Sylvain Wiltord | Forward | Arsenal, England | 34/12 | - | - | - | - | - |

**KEY:** APPS/GOALS = International Appearances/Goals; GAMES=Qualification Games played; MINS=Minutes played; Y/C= Yellow cards R/C=Red cards

# HISTORY OF THE WORLD CUP

1930 1934 1938 1950 1954 1958 1962 1966 1970 1974 1978 1982 1986 1990 1994 1998

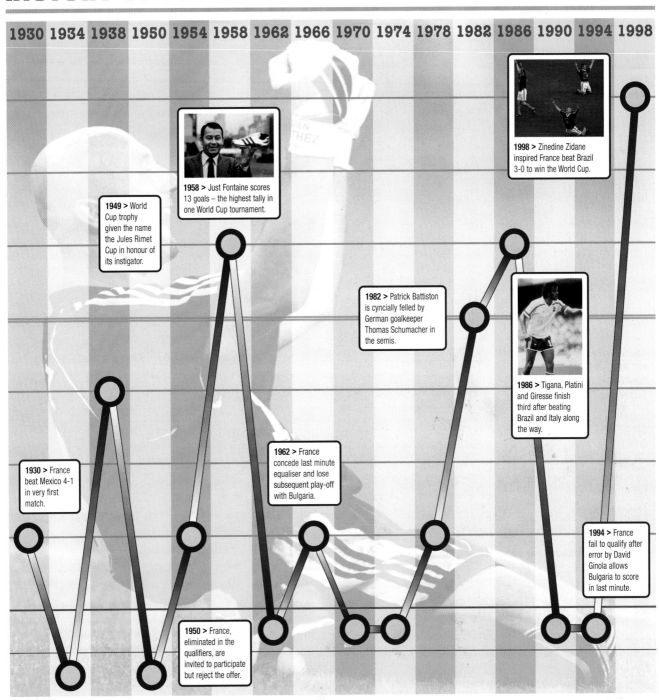

**1958 >** Just Fontaine scores 13 goals – the highest tally in one World Cup tournament.

**1949 >** World Cup trophy given the name the Jules Rimet Cup in honour of its instigator.

**1998 >** Zinedine Zidane inspired France beat Brazil 3-0 to win the World Cup.

**1982 >** Patrick Battiston is cyncially felled by German goalkeeper Thomas Schumacher in the semis.

**1962 >** France concede last minute equaliser and lose subsequent play-off with Bulgaria.

**1930 >** France beat Mexico 4-1 in very first match.

**1986 >** Tigana, Platini and Giresse finish third after beating Brazil and Italy along the way.

**1994 >** France fail to qualify after error by David Ginola allows Bulgaria to score in last minute.

**1950 >** France, eliminated in the qualifiers, are invited to participate but reject the offer.

## ★ WORLD CUP HISTORY

| | | | |
|---|---|---|---|
| 1930 >> First Round | | 1970 >> Did Not Qualify | |
| 1934 >> Did Not Enter | | 1974 >> Did Not Qualify | |
| 1938 >> Quarter-Final | | 1978 >> First Round | |
| 1950 >> Did Not Qualify | | 1982 >> Fourth Place | |
| 1954 >> First Round | | 1986 >> Third Place | |
| 1958 >> Third Place | | 1990 >> Did Not Qualify | |
| 1962 >> Did Not Qualify | | 1994 >> Did Not Qualify | |
| 1966 >> First Round | | 1998 >> Winners | |

## ★ WORLD CUP RECORDS, STORIES AND WEIRDNESS

**MOST GOALS IN A TOURNAMENT** >> Just Fontaine's record 13 World Cup goals in 1958 included four in the third place play-off against West Germany.

**FIRST EVER GOLDEN GOAL** >> When France beat Paraguay 1-0 in the second round in 1988, Laurent Blanc scored the first ever Golden Goal in a World Cup match. It is, so far, the only one.

# GROUP E

| OPPONENT | DATE | UK TIME | VENUE |
|----------|------|---------|-------|
| Saudi Arabia | **1 June** | **12.30** | **Sapporo, Korea** |
| Ireland | **5 June** | **12.30** | **Ibaraki, Japan** |
| Cameroon | **11 June** | **12.30** | **Shizuoka, Japan** |

## "not what they were?"

# GERMANY

**G**ermany are no longer the reliable quality side who always do well. After failing to win a single game during Euro 2000, Germany launched a search for a new managerial messiah to deliver them from the decline associated with what was becoming an ageing side. That man was to be Christoph Daum but, dogged by scandal, he was quickly forced to leave the job.

Former German international striker Rudi Voller, appointed caretaker boss, was soon persuaded to take over permanently. Voller started brightly winning his first three games in charge – including World Cup qualifying victories over Greece and, more importantly, over England at Wembley.

After a honeymoon period nothing could disguise the fact that, by previous standards, this was a very ordinary German side. They struggled against Albania in Leverkusen and only secured victory with two minutes to spare through substitute Miroslav Klose. They also surrendered a two-goal lead in Athens against Greece, had Sebastian Deisler sent off on the hour, and had to rely on substitutes Klose and Marco Bode to get the points with two goals in the last nine minutes.

It was a similar story in Helinski where the Germans gave an awful first half performance that saw them trail 2-0. A Michael Ballack penalty and a Carsten Jancker goal salvaged a point. In Tirana, Marko Rehmer gave Germany the lead but it immediately came under threat when Carsten Ramelow was dismissed. The Germans struggled until Ballack found the net midway through the second half.

But despite the poor quality of these performances, Germany remained unbeaten and the value of the win in England could not be underestimated. Five points clear and with a superior goal difference, Germany looked certain to qualify for the World Cup Finals.

Then, on September 1st in Munich, Germany suffered their worst home defeat since 1930, as England thrashed Voller's team 5-1. The *Die Welt* newspaper described it as "the greatest-ever slap in the face for German football". It was a disastrous night for Voller both professionally and personally as his father, Kurt, was rushed to hospital after suffering a heart attack.

A month later Germany faced Finland at home while England entertained Greece. Germany knew they had to better the result of the English and Voller made a point of banning news of events in England from reaching his players. Against the Finns both Oliver Bierhoff and Olivier Neuville missed chances as the Germans failed to score, the game ending 0-0. But automatic qualification still seemed likely with the news that Greece led England 2-1 and just seconds remaining. German midfielder Sebastian Deisler managed to get to a TV set only to witness David Beckham's spectacular equalising free kick.

Paired with a lacklustre Ukraine in the play-offs, Germany put in two of their best performances with a 1-1 draw in Kiev that would make for a tense second leg at home. In the event the tie in Dortmund was over by the 14th minute as Ballack, Neuville and Rehmer found the net on the way to an overall 5-2 aggregate victory.

## ★ THE LOWDOWN

**Population:** 83 million

**Capital:** Berlin

**Leader:** Gerhard Schroeder

**Life Expectancy:** Male: 74 yrs Female: 81 yrs

>> The Germans are a polite bunch. It is still customary to shake hands when meeting or saying good-bye; to be particularly polite a small bow should also be performed at the same time.

>> East and West Germany were formally re-unified on 3rd October 1990; the Germans celebrate "Unity Day" every year.

>> It is popular to drink black tea in Germany and eat black bread, especially by those Germans living in the Black Forest. Strange lot!

★ **ASSOCIATION:** Deutsche Fussbull-Bund

★ **JOINED FIFA:** 1950

★ **JOINED UEFA:** 1954

★ **PLAYERS:** 5,260,320

★ **CLUBS:** 26,800

★ **WEBSITE:** www.dfb.de

★ **HONOURS:** World Cup - *1954/*74/*90; European Championships: *1972/*80/96; Olympics - **1976.
(*as West Germany; **as East Germany)

*Sebastien Deisler – a young talented midfielder.*

## ★ ROAD TO QUALIFICATION

Sep 00 **Greece** (h) > (w) **2**-0
Deisler 17, Ouzounidis 75 og

Oct 00 **England** (a) > (w) 0-**1** Hamann 13

Mar 01 **Albania** (h) > (w) **2**-1
Deisler 50, Klose 87

Mar 01 **Greece** (a) > (w) 2-**4**
Rehmer 6, Ballack 25 pen, Klose 82, Bode 90

Jun 01 **Finland** (a) > (d) 2-2
Ballack 68 pen, Jancker 72

Jun 01 **Albania** (a) > (w) 0-**2**
Rehmer 28, Ballack 68

Sep 01 **England** (h) > (l) **1**-5 Jancker 6

Oct 01 **Finland** (h) > (d) 0-0

Nov 01 **Ukraine** (a) > (d) 1-1 Ballack 31

Nov 01 **Ukraine** (h) > (w) **4**-1 (agg **5**-2)
Ballack 5, 51, Neuville 11, Rehmer 16

## ★ FINAL GROUP TABLE

| Team | P | W | D | L | F | A | Pts |
|------|---|---|---|---|---|---|-----|
| England | 8 | 5 | 2 | 1 | 16 | 6 | 17 |
| Germany | 8 | 5 | 2 | 1 | 14 | 10 | 17 |
| Finland | 8 | 3 | 3 | 2 | 12 | 7 | 12 |
| Greece | 8 | 2 | 1 | 5 | 7 | 17 | 7 |
| Albania | 8 | 1 | 0 | 7 | 5 | 14 | 3 |

## ★ RECENT RESULTS

Feb 02 **Israel** (h) > (w) **7**-1
Klose 49, 51, 65, Hamann 62, Bierhoff 69, Asamoah 75, Ricken 77

Mar 02 **United States** (h) > (w) **4**-2
Ziege 44, Neuville 61, Bierhoff 65, Frings 68

Germany have always played 3-5-2 but Rudi Voller's side had to revise this system to achieve adequate results during qualifying. Like France, teams know how Germany will play, but unlike France, Germany currently lacks the quality to be good at it. As something of a last resort, goalkeeper Oliver Kahn has become an increasingly valuable member of the team. Marco Rehmer and Jens Nowotny have been ever present in a shaky back line. No nonsense Thomas Linke completes the defence. In the midfield engine room Michael Ballack, Carsten Ramelow and Sebastian Deisler are regarded as the best, if not the most consistent, combination. Jens Jeremies, if back to form, can play the anchor role and Bernd Schneider on the right and Christian Ziege on the left will play down the flanks. The goals are expected to come from the nippy Oliver Neuville and his towering partner Carsten Jancker.

## PROBABLE FORMATION 3-5-2

KAHN

REHMER LINKE

NOWOTNY

SCHNEIDER BALLACK DEISLER ZIEGE

RAMELOW

NEUVILLE JANCKER

---

## ★ MEN THAT MATTER!

### OLIVER KAHN

Age>> 32

Club>> Bayern Munich

Captain of Germany and one of the best goalkeepers in the world. This is his third World Cup but he spent all of USA 94 (third choice) and France 98 (second choice) on the bench.

### MICHAEL BALLACK

Age>> 25

Club>> Bayer Leverkusen

Goalscoring midfielder who was Germany's leading marksman in qualifying. He was superb in the play-offs against Ukraine scoring three goals – two far post headers and a tap in.

### SEBASTIEN DEISLER

Age>> 22

Club>> Hertha Berlin

Deisler is one of the few creative players in the German side. This will be the first World Cup for this young talented midfielder although he did feature at Euro 2000.

## ★ PROBABLE SQUAD        ★ QUALIFICATION RECORD

| NAME | POSITION | CLUB | APS/GOALS | GAMES | MINS | Y/C | R/C | GOALS |
|---|---|---|---|---|---|---|---|---|
| Hans-Jorg Butt | Goalkeeper | Bayer Leverkusen, Germany | 1/0 | 0 | 0 | 0 | 0 | 0 |
| Oliver Kahn | Goalkeeper | Bayern Munich, Germany | 42/0 | 10 | 900 | 0 | 0 | 0 |
| Jens Lehmann | Goalkeeper | Borussia Dortmund, Germany | 13/0 | 0 | 0 | 0 | 0 | 0 |
| Frank Baumann | Defender | Werder Bremen, Germany | 7/2 | 2 | 9 | 0 | 0 | 0 |
| Jorg Heinrich | Defender | Borussia Dortmund, Germany | 34/2 | 2 | 136 | 1 | 0 | 0 |
| Thomas Linke | Defender | Bayern Munich, Germany | 28/0 | 6 | 494 | 1 | 0 | 0 |
| Jens Nowotny | Defender | Bayer Leverkusen, Germany | 35/0 | 10 | 900 | 1 | 0 | 0 |
| Marko Rehmer | Defender | Hertha Berlin, Germany | 27/4 | 10 | 852 | 0 | 0 | 3 |
| Christian Worns | Defender | Borussia Dortmund, Germany | 38/0 | 4 | 316 | 1 | 0 | 0 |
| Michael Ballack | Midfielder | Bayer Leverkusen, Germany | 21/6 | 9 | 787 | 3 | 0 | 6 |
| Marco Bode | Midfielder | Werder Bremen, Germany | 32/6 | 5 | 347 | 1 | 0 | 1 |
| Sebastian Deisler | Midfielder | Hertha Berlin, Germany | 16/2 | 7 | 623 | 0 | 1 | 2 |
| Dietmar Hamann | Midfielder | Liverpool, England | 37/3 | 5 | 406 | 3 | 0 | 1 |
| Jens Jeremies | Midfielder | Bayern Munich, Germany | 28/1 | 2 | 182 | 0 | 0 | 0 |
| Carsten Ramelow | Midfielder | Bayer Leverkusen, Germany | 22/0 | 9 | 718 | 1 | 1 | 0 |
| Lars Ricken | Midfielder | Borussia Dortmund, Germany | 14/0 | 4 | 141 | 1 | 0 | 0 |
| Mehmet Scholl | Midfielder | Bayern Munich, Germany | 35/8 | 3 | 270 | 2 | 0 | 0 |
| Christian Ziege | Midfielder | Tottenham, England | 63/8 | 7 | 475 | 1 | 0 | 0 |
| Gerald Asamoah | Forward | Schalke, Germany | 7/1 | 5 | 337 | 0 | 0 | 0 |
| Oliver Bierhoff | Forward | Monaco, France | 60/32 | 5 | 265 | 0 | 0 | 0 |
| Carsten Jancker | Forward | Bayern Munich, Germany | 21/6 | 8 | 555 | 0 | 0 | 2 |
| Oliver Neuville | Forward | Bayer Leverkusen, Germany | 29/2 | 7 | 484 | 2 | 0 | 1 |
| Alexander Zickler | Forward | Bayern Munich, Germany | 8/2 | 3 | 183 | 0 | 0 | 0 |

**KEY:** APPS/GOALS = International Appearances/Goals; GAMES=Qualification Games played; MINS=Minutes played; Y/C= Yellow cards R/C=Red cards

# HISTORY AT THE WORLD CUP

**1930 1934 1938 1950 1954 1958 1962 1966 1970 1974 1978 1982 1986 1990 1994 1998**

**1954 >** West Germany come from 2-0 down in the Final to beat favourites Hungary 3-2.

**1966 >** West Germany lose Final to hosts England after controversial Hurst goal adjudged over the line.

**1970 >** Gerd Müller scores ten goals including hat-tricks against Bulgaria and Peru.

**1974 >** Franz Beckenbauer captains host West Germany to World Cup victory in Munich.

**1986 >** Coach Franz Beckenbauer guides West Germany to the World Cup runners-up spot.

**1990 >** Andreas Brehme penalty wins Beckenabuer's West Germany the World Cup in Rome.

**1994 >** Against South Korea, German Stefan Effenberg is sent off for a gesture towards the fans.

**1998 >** Lothar Matthaus in his fifth tournament makes a World Cup record 25th appearance against Croatia.

## ★ WORLD CUP HISTORY

| | |
|---|---|
| **1930** >> Did Not Enter | **1970** >> Third Place |
| **1934** >> Third Place | **1974** >> Winners |
| **1938** >> First Round | **1978** >> Second Round |
| **1950** >> Did Not Enter | **1982** >> Runners-Up |
| **1954** >> Winners | **1986** >> Runners-Up |
| **1958** >> Fourth Place | **1990** >> Winners |
| **1962** >> Quarter-Finals | **1994** >> Quarter-Final |
| **1966** >> Runners-Up | **1998** >> Quarter-Final |

## ★ WORLD CUP RECORDS, STORIES AND WEIRDNESS

**MOST GOALS** >> Gerd Müller, "Der Bomber", is the most prolific striker in World Cup history with a record of 14 goals in two tournaments.

**SUCCES AS PLAYER AND MANAGER** >> Franz Beckenbauer was appointed national coach in 1984 and steered West Germany to the final in both 1986 and 1990. At the latter he became only the second man in World Cup history, Zagalo of Brazil was the other, to achieve success as both a player and manager.

| OPPONENT | DATE | UK TIME | VENUE |
|---|---|---|---|
| Cameroon | **1 June** | 07.30 | **Niigata, Japan** |
| Germany | **5 June** | 12.30 | **Ibaraki, Japan** |
| Saudi Arabia | **11 June** | 12.30 | **Yokohama, Japan** |

## "second round candidates, with luck"

# IRELAND

The Republic of Ireland must have dreaded the prospect of a play-off after finishing unbeaten but second to Portugal (on goal difference) in European Qualifying Group Two. Three previous competitions – Euro 96, World Cup 98 and Euro 2000 – had seen the Irish denied a place in the Finals after falling at the play-off stage. The draw for the 2002 World Cup play-offs paired them with Iran.

As it happens this time the Irish had nothing to fear. The first leg in Dublin saw the Irish defeat the Iranians 2-0 thanks to a penalty from Ian Harte on the stroke of half time and a 51st minute goal from Robbie Keane. Despite losing to a last minute goal in Tehran, Ireland's qualification was never really threatened.

Mick McCarthy's team deserved to reach Japan/Korea after some stunning performances, which ultimately led to the elimination of Holland. A particularly satisfying outcome, since the Dutch had denied the Irish a place at the last World Cup and Euro 96.

The Irish began their campaign with their two toughest away fixtures against Holland and Portugal – securing a point from each game – but it could have easily been much more. Robbie Keane and Jason McAteer established a two-goal lead against the Dutch with 25 minutes left. Holland fought back to claim a point. In Lisbon, McCarthy's team were under enormous pressure throughout, but Matt Holland managed to find the target cancelling out Sergio Conceicao's effort.

Maximum points were achieved against Estonia, Cyprus and Andorra before Portugal arrived in Dublin. It was an eventful game for captain Roy Keane as the Manchester United midfielder put the Irish in the lead with a deflected shot and was later sent off. Luis Figo's goal secured the draw. Both Keanes, Roy (suspension) and Robbie (injury), missed the trip to Estonia four days later, but the Irish strolled to a comfortable 2-0 win.

Then came the night when all Ireland supped from the cold dish of revenge. A single goal from Jason McAteer proved enough to beat Holland and knock the Dutch out of the World Cup.

The 4-0 win over Cyprus was marked by Niall Quinn's long awaited 21st goal for his country making him the Republic of Ireland's all-time top goalscorer.

This will be Ireland's third time at the World Cup Finals after the glory days of Italia 90 and USA 94. England 1966 World Cup winner Jack Charlton was in charge with a squad in 1990 that reached the last eight and featured Mick McCarthy, Leeds boss David O'Leary and Niall Quinn. Four years later Quinn was joined by current squad members Gary Kelly, Jason McAteer and Steve Staunton, as the Irish reached the second round (beaten by Holland).

Ireland can be expected to do well again. Mick McCarthy's team has shown they can, on their day, match any side in the world and it will require a very good team to stop the boys in green progressing.

### ★ THE LOWDOWN

**Population:** 3.8 million

**Capital:** Dublin

**Leader:** Bertie Ahern

**Life Expectancy:** Male: 74 yrs
Female: 80 yrs

>> Southern Ireland is divided into 27 counties and 5 county boroughs. Irish-speaking areas are known as "Gaeltacht".

>> The harp is a national Irish symbol. Arthur Guinness deliberately chose it as his logo for this reason. However, the Guinness harp faces left, whilst the official government version faces right. After 7 or 8 pints of the black stuff who cares?!

>> St Patrick's Day is celebrated the world over on March 17th.

* **ASSOCIATION:** Football Association of Ireland
* **JOINED FIFA:** 1923
* **JOINED UEFA:** 1954
* **PLAYERS:** 124,700
* **CLUBS:** 3,190
* **WEBSITE:** www.fai.ie
* **HONOURS:** None

*Roy Keane shows balletic poise under pressure.*

## ★ ROAD TO QUALIFICATION

Sep 00 **Holland** (a) > (d) **2**-**2**
Keane, Robbie 21, McAteer 65

Oct 00 **Portugal** (a) > (d) 1-**1** Holland 73

Oct 00 **Estonia** (h) > (w) **2**-0
Kinsella 24, Dunne 50

Mar 01 **Cyprus** (a) > (w) 0-**4**
Keane, Roy 32, 88, Harte 42 pen,
Kelly, G 80

Mar 01 **Andorra** (a) > (w) 0-**3**
Harte 32 pen, Kilbane 75, Holland 80

Apr 01 **Andorra** (h) > (w) **3**-1
Kilbane 33, Kinsella 36, Breen 73

Jun 01 **Portugal** (h) > (d) **1**-1
Keane, Roy 67

Jun 01 **Estonia** (a) > (w) 0-**2**
Dunne 9, Holland 39

Sep 01 **Holland** (h) > (w) **1**-0 McAteer 67

Oct 01 **Cyprus** (h) > (w) **4**-0
Harte 3, Quinn, N 11, Connolly 63,
Keane, Roy 66

Nov 01 **Iran** (h) > (w) **2**-0
Harte 44 pen, Keane, Robbie 50

Nov 01 **Iran** (a) > (l) 1-**0** (agg **2**-1)

## ★ FINAL GROUP TABLE

| Team | P | W | D | L | F | A | Pts |
|---|---|---|---|---|---|---|---|
| Portugal | 10 | 7 | 3 | 0 | 33 | 7 | 24 |
| Rep of Ireland | 10 | 7 | 3 | 0 | 23 | 5 | 24 |
| Netherlands | 10 | 6 | 2 | 2 | 30 | 9 | 20 |
| Estonia | 10 | 2 | 2 | 6 | 10 | 26 | 8 |
| Cyprus | 10 | 2 | 2 | 6 | 13 | 31 | 8 |
| Andorra | 10 | 0 | 0 | 10 | 5 | 36 | 0 |

## ★ RECENT RESULTS

Feb 02 **Russia** (h) > (w) **2**-0
Reid 3, Keane, Robbie 20

Mar 02 **Denmark** (h) > (w) **3**-0
Harte 19, Keane, Robbie 54, Morrison 90

## DID YOU KNOW?

**On their World Cup debut in 1990 the Republic of Ireland reached the quarter-finals by virtue of just scoring two goals against England and Holland, and without winning a game.**

Nobody really expected Mick McCarthy's Republic of Ireland side to qualify for the Finals out of "the group of death" that included Portugal and Holland, but here they are again, finalists for the third time. Lining up in a strict 4-4-2 formation, we can expect the Irish to be tough act to deal with, especially now that their captain and midfield powerhouse, Roy Keane, is delivering at international level as has for his club for the last few years. Keane's influence over his Irish teamates can't be underestimated as he lifts their performances to levels they'd rarely achieve on their own. Keane will be keeping good company in Japan/Korea with a young and fast-developing side. The midfield is full of skill and invention featuring Matt Holland, who can also deputise for Keane if necessary, Kevin Kilbane – excellent on the left flank and Jason McAteer, who's back in favour on the right. Ireland's main striker Robbie Keane would hold a place in any European club and will be partnered with the height of either Niall Quinn, if fit, or David Connolly. Shay Given is first choice keeper and at right back either Gary Kelly or Steve Finnan should get the nod. Otherwise the back line, which is always difficult to break down, picks itself.

## PROBABLE FORMATION 4-4-2

GIVEN

Gary KELLY — HARTE

BREEN — STAUNTON

McATEER — Roy KEANE — HOLLAND — KILBANE

Robbie KEANE — QUINN

## ★ MEN THAT MATTER!

### ROY KEANE

Age>> 30

Club>> Man. United

Inspirational captain of the Irish side, who played at USA 94, leads by example scoring four goals in qualifying. He is a no-nonsense midfielder who has won a host of honours with his club.

### ROBBIE KEANE

Age>> 21

Club>> Leeds United

Ireland's most expensive player after two moves totalling £20 million in transfer fees. A young striker who is always a handful for defences. Scored the first and last goals in Ireland's qualifying campaign.

### IAN HARTE

Age>> 24

Club>> Leeds United

Ever present at left back and Ireland's first choice penalty-taker. He converted three penalties — against Cyprus, Andorra and Iran — and is also a real danger at set pieces.

## ★ PROBABLE SQUAD / ★ QUALIFICATION RECORD

| NAME | POSITION | CLUB | APS/GOALS | GAMES | MINS | Y/C | R/C | GOALS |
|---|---|---|---|---|---|---|---|---|
| **Shay Given** | Goalkeeper | Newcastle, England | 36/0 | 9 | 840 | 0 | 0 | 0 |
| **Alan Kelly** | Goalkeeper | Blackburn, England | 34/0 | 3 | 270 | 0 | 0 | 0 |
| **Dean Kiely** | Goalkeeper | Charlton, England | 4/0 | 0 | 0 | 0 | 0 | 0 |
| **Gary Breen** | Defender | Coventry, England | 42/5 | 9 | 832 | 0 | 0 | 1 |
| **Gary Doherty** | Defender | Tottenham, England | 8/0 | 5 | 249 | 0 | 0 | 0 |
| **Richard Dunne** | Defender | Manchester City, England | 12/3 | 7 | 630 | 0 | 0 | 2 |
| **Steve Finnan** | Defender | Fulham, England | 12/1 | 8 | 359 | 0 | 0 | 0 |
| **Ian Harte** | Defender | Leeds, England | 36/7 | 12 | 1110 | 0 | 0 | 4 |
| **Gary Kelly** | Defender | Leeds, England | 43/2 | 9 | 599 | 1 | 1 | 1 |
| **Steve Staunton** | Defender | Aston Villa, England | 95/7 | 8 | 543 | 0 | 0 | 0 |
| **Lee Carsley** | Midfielder | Everton, England | 19/0 | 1 | 26 | 0 | 0 | 0 |
| **Matt Holland** | Midfielder | Ipswich, England | 15/3 | 10 | 732 | 0 | 0 | 3 |
| **Roy Keane** | Midfielder | Manchester United, England | 57/9 | 9 | 840 | 2 | 0 | 4 |
| **Mark Kennedy** | Midfielder | Wolves, England | 33/3 | 2 | 154 | 0 | 0 | 0 |
| **Kevin Kilbane** | Midfielder | Sunderland, England | 30/3 | 12 | 1040 | 0 | 0 | 2 |
| **Mark Kinsella** | Midfielder | Charlton, England | 25/2 | 8 | 697 | 1 | 0 | 2 |
| **Jason McAteer** | Midfielder | Sunderland, England | 45/3 | 7 | 531 | 2 | 0 | 2 |
| **David Connolly** | Forward | Wimbledon, England | 30/8 | 6 | 404 | 0 | 0 | 1 |
| **Damien Duff** | Forward | Blackburn, England | 22/1 | 7 | 399 | 0 | 0 | 0 |
| **Dominic Foley** | Forward | QPR, England | 6/2 | 1 | 3 | 0 | 0 | 0 |
| **Robbie Keane** | Forward | Leeds, England | 29/8 | 9 | 754 | 2 | 0 | 2 |
| **Clinton Morrison** | Forward | Crystal Palace, England | 3/1 | 2 | 36 | 0 | 0 | 0 |
| **Niall Quinn** | Forward | Sunderland, England | 87/21 | 8 | 480 | 1 | 0 | 1 |

**KEY:** APPS/GOALS = International Appearances/Goals; GAMES=Qualification Games played; MINS=Minutes played; Y/C= Yellow cards R/C=Red cards

# HISTORY AT THE WORLD CUP

1930 1934 1938 1950 1954 1958 1962 1966 1970 1974 1978 1982 1986 1990 1994 1998

**1990 >** David O'Leary converts penalty against Romania to put the Irish into the last eight.

**1994 >** An appalling goalkeeping error by Pat Bonner leads the Irish to defeat against Holland.

**1982 >** Republic of Ireland fail to qualify on goal difference losing out to France.

**1958 >** Republic of Ireland finish as runners-up to England but fail to qualify.

**1966 >** Republic of Ireland lose out after three qualifying matches with Spain in Dublin, Madrid and Paris.

## ★ WORLD CUP HISTORY

| | |
|---|---|
| **1930** >> Did Not Enter | **1970** >> Did Not Qualify |
| **1934** >> Did Not Qualify | **1974** >> Did Not Qualify |
| **1938** >> Did Not Qualify | **1978** >> Did Not Qualify |
| **1950** >> Did Not Qualify | **1982** >> Did Not Qualify |
| **1954** >> Did Not Qualify | **1986** >> Did not Qualify |
| **1958** >> Did Not Qualify | **1990** >> Quarter-Finals |
| **1962** >> Did Not Qualify | **1994** >> Second Round |
| **1966** >> Did Not Qualify | **1998** >> Did Not Qualify |

## ★ WORLD CUP RECORDS, STORIES AND WEIRDNESS

**MOST DRAWS** >> Ireland hold the unlikely record of having secured more (4 in 1990) successive draws than any other team.

| OPPONENT | DATE | UK TIME | VENUE |
|---|---|---|---|
| Ecuador | **3 June** | 12.30 | **Sapporo, Japan** |
| Croatia | **8 June** | 10.00 | **Ibaraki, Japan** |
| Mexico | **13 June** | 12.30 | **Oita, Japan** |

## *"a last-four certainty"*

# ITALY

Coach Giovanni Trapattoni expects Italy to at least reach the semi-finals at the 2002 World Cup. A not unreasonable expectation considering Italy were runners up at Euro 2000 and quarter-finalists at France 98. In both tournaments Italy were knocked out by eventual tournament winners France – in 1998 on a penalty shoot-out and by a golden goal in 2000.

Trapattoni took over Italy after Euro 2000, inheriting a comparatively young side that he has nurtured through qualification. Italy still lack a couple of players that would make them the equal of Italy's 1982 World Cup-winning side, but it should be noted that since Euro 2000 only World Cup favourites Argentina have beaten them.

Alessandro Del Piero netted from one of his trademark free kicks for the winning goal against Hungary in their last group game to confirm qualification, but Italy's place in the Finals would have been booked a game earlier but for a disappointing below par performance in Lithuania, where the hosts earned a well-deserved 0-0 draw.

Throughout qualification, the real goalscoring hero has been Milan's Filippo Inzaghi who scored seven goals in just six appearances. He scored both first half goals in the 2-2 draw with Hungary in Budapest; opened the scoring for the 3-0 home drubbing of Romania and netted both goals in the 2-0 win in Bucharest. Inzaghi also scored two goals, as did Del Piero, in the 4-0 home thrashing of Lithuania.

The national side has been a boon to Italian soccer, where the league game has been rocked by a series of scandals involving drugs, faked passports and match fixing. On top of that Italian clubs – which have been a dominant force in European competition for the past 20 years – have not been performing at anything like the same level. The last Italian club to lift a major European trophy was Lazio which won the European Cup Winners' Cup in 1999.

The national side currently has a plethora of playmakers and lethal attackers. In the former category are Demetrio Albertini, Luigi Di Biagio, Alessio Tacchinardi, Damiano Tommasi and Gianluca Zambrotta. In attack, where often three players are selected, Del Piero and Inzaghi are joined or replaced by Marco Delvecchio and Francesco Totti.

Such an abundance of midfield and attacking talent, when combined with Italy's traditional ability to defend, and defend well, makes a serious challenge for the trophy a real possibility. Italy has always done well at the World Cup; they have won the competition three times in 1934, 1938 and 1982 and have been runners-up twice (both times to Brazil) in 1970 and 1994. Such a history and impressive recent form at major tournaments breeds a high level of expectation from both fans and the Italian media. Anything less than a place in the last four will be considered a disaster for the Italians!

### ★ THE LOWDOWN

**Population:** 57.6 million

**Capital:** Rome

**Leader:** Silvio Berlusconi

**Life Expectancy:** Male: 76 yrs Female: 82 yrs

>> Bocce is the name given to a popular Italian sport. It is similar to bowls; each player tries to throw his or her four bowls nearest to a target bowl which is about 25 feet away.

>> Eating is an important part of Italian culture. Some shops close for many hours during meal times and about half the primary school children return home for lunch.

>> Ferrari cars are made in Italy, although they are now 51% owned by Fiat. Just think, the Testerossa is owned by the same people that came up with the Fiat Cinquencento - aahh bless!

★ **ASSOCIATION:** Federazione Italiana Giuoco Calcio
★ **JOINED FIFA:** 1905
★ **JOINED UEFA:** 1954
★ **PLAYERS:** 1,421,000

★ **CLUBS:** 20,961
★ **WEBSITE:** www.figc.it
★ **HONOURS:** World Cup – 1934, 1938, 1982;
European Championship – 1968; Olympic Games – 1936.

*Alessandro Del Piero models the best shirts in football.*

## ★ ROAD TO QUALIFICATION

Sep 00 **Hungary** (a) > (d) 2-**2**
Inzaghi, F 26, 35

Oct 00 **Romania** (h) > (w) 3-0
Inzaghi, F 12, Delvecchio 16, Totti 41

Oct 00 **Georgia** (h) > (w) **2**-0
Del Piero 46 pen, 88 pen

Mar 01 **Romania** (a) > (w) 0-**2**
Inzaghi, F 28, 32

Mar 01 **Lithuania** (h) > (w) 4-0
Inzaghi, F 17, 64, Del Piero 49, 79

Jun 01 **Georgia** (a) > (w) 1-**2**
Delvecchio 45, Totti 66

Sep 01 **Lithuania** (a) > (d) 0-**0**

Oct 01 **Hungary** (h) > (w) **1**-0 Del Piero 44

## ★ FINAL GROUP TABLE

| Team | P | W | D | L | F | A | Pts |
|---|---|---|---|---|---|---|---|
| Italy | 8 | 6 | 2 | 0 | 16 | 3 | 20 |
| Romania | 8 | 5 | 1 | 2 | 10 | 7 | 16 |
| Georgia | 8 | 3 | 1 | 4 | 12 | 12 | 10 |
| Hungary | 8 | 2 | 2 | 4 | 14 | 13 | 8 |
| Lithuania | 8 | 0 | 2 | 6 | 3 | 20 | 2 |

## ★ RECENT RESULTS

Feb 02 **United States** (h) > (w) **1**-0
Del Piero 61

Mar 02 **England** (a) > (w) 1-**2**
Montella 67, 90

## DID YOU KNOW?

**Christian Vieiri received 264 bottles of wine from Italy's National Wine Cities Association for scoring Italy's first goal at France 98.**

Italy's 3-5-2 line-up was introduced at France 98 – a change from their traditional 4-4-2 – but the emphasis remains on strong defence, quality midfield and lethal strikers. A truly world class back three in Fabio Cannavaro, Alessandro Nesta and captain Paolo Maldini can be bolstered, if needed, by right wing-back Gianluca Zambrotta. The right side is perhaps not Italy's strongest but Zambrotta is effective and Francesco Coco offers the same service on the left. Demetrio Albertini is the conductor of the Italian side, dictating pace and strategy – aided by the improving Damiano Tommasi. Francesco Totti plays just behind the front two of Filippo Inzaghi and Alessandro Del Piero. These three players will be a serious handful for any defence and if, for some reason, they don't do the job then there are always Marco Delvecchio and Christian Vieri to call upon. Quality pervades the whole squad.

## PROBABLE FORMATION   3-5-2

BUFFON

CANNAVARO    MALDINI

NESTA

ZAMBROTTA    TOMMASI    ALBERTINI    COCO

TOTTI

INZAGHI    DEL PIERO

## ★ MEN THAT MATTER!

### FILIPPO INZAGHI

Age>> 28

Club>> AC Milan

Inzaghi is £26 million worth of goal poaching excellence who, in six appearances, netted seven goals during qualifying. Substitute at France 98 managing 50 minutes play over two games.

### ALESSANDRO DEL PIERO

Age>> 27

Club>> Juventus

Hailed as Italy's golden boy since his goalscoring debut against Wales in 1995. This is his fourth major tournament appearance, including a disappointing France 98.

### ALESSANDRO NESTA

Age>> 26

Club>> Lazio

Damaged ligaments ruled him out of the France 98 knock out stage. He is regarded as one of the best central defenders in Italian soccer and on the international scene.

## ★ PROBABLE SQUAD    ★ QUALIFICATION RECORD

| NAME | POSITION | CLUB | APS/GOALS | GAMES | MINS | Y/C | R/C | GOALS |
|---|---|---|---|---|---|---|---|---|
| **Christian Abbiati** | Goalkeeper | Milan, Italy | 0/0 | 0 | 0 | 0 | 0 | 0 |
| **Gianluigi Buffon** | Goalkeeper | Juventus, Italy | 23/0 | 5 | 450 | 0 | 0 | 0 |
| **Francessco Toldo** | Goalkeeper | Internazionale, Italy | 20/0 | 3 | 270 | 0 | 0 | 0 |
| **Fabio Cannavaro** | Defender | Parma, Italy | 54/0 | 8 | 720 | 1 | 0 | 0 |
| **Mark Iuliano** | Defender | Juventus, Italy | 13/1 | 1 | 90 | 0 | 0 | 0 |
| **Paolo Maldini** | Defender | Milan, Italy | 121/7 | 7 | 630 | 0 | 0 | 0 |
| **Marco Materazzi** | Defender | Internazionale, Italy | 4/0 | 2 | 120 | 0 | 0 | 0 |
| **Alessandro Nesta** | Defender | Lazio, Italy | 40/0 | 7 | 600 | 0 | 0 | 0 |
| **Giuseppe Pancaro** | Defender | Lazio, Italy | 12/0 | 5 | 320 | 2 | 0 | 0 |
| **Demetrio Albertini** | Midfielder | Milan, Italy | 78/2 | 5 | 432 | 1 | 0 | 0 |
| **Francesco Coco** | Midfielder | Barcelona, Spain | 9/0 | 5 | 368 | 0 | 0 | 0 |
| **Luigi Di Biagio** | Midfielder | Internazionale, Italy | 23/2 | 2 | 38 | 0 | 0 | 0 |
| **Stefano Fiore** | Midfielder | Lazio, Italy | 21/2 | 6 | 289 | 0 | 0 | 0 |
| **Gennaro Gattuso** | Midfielder | Milan, Italy | 9/0 | 3 | 80 | 0 | 0 | 0 |
| **Alessio Tacchinardi** | Midfielder | Juventus, Italy | 10/0 | 4 | 298 | 2 | 0 | 0 |
| **Damiano Tommasi** | Midfielder | Roma, Italy | 10/1 | 5 | 450 | 1 | 0 | 0 |
| **Gianlucca Zambrotta** | Midfielder | Juventus, Italy | 20/0 | 6 | 522 | 1 | 0 | 0 |
| **Alessandro Del Piero** | Forward | Juventus, Italy | 47/17 | 8 | 520 | 0 | 0 | 5 |
| **Marco Delvecchio** | Forward | Roma, Italy | 14/3 | 4 | 218 | 0 | 0 | 2 |
| **Filippo Inzaghi** | Forward | Milan, Italy | 36/15 | 6 | 445 | 0 | 0 | 7 |
| **Francesco Totti** | Forward | Roma, Italy | 28/5 | 7 | 606 | 2 | 0 | 2 |
| **Christian Vieri** | Forward | Internazionale, Italy | 22/10 | 1 | 90 | 0 | 0 | 0 |
| **Vincenzo Montella** | Forward | Roma, Italy | 12/3 | 4 | 44 | 0 | 0 | 0 |

**KEY:** APPS/GOALS = International Appearances/Goals; GAMES=Qualification Games played; MINS=Minutes played; Y/C= Yellow cards R/C=Red cards

# HISTORY AT THE WORLD CUP

**1930 1934 1938 1950 1954 1958 1962 1966 1970 1974 1978 1982 1986 1990 1994 1998**

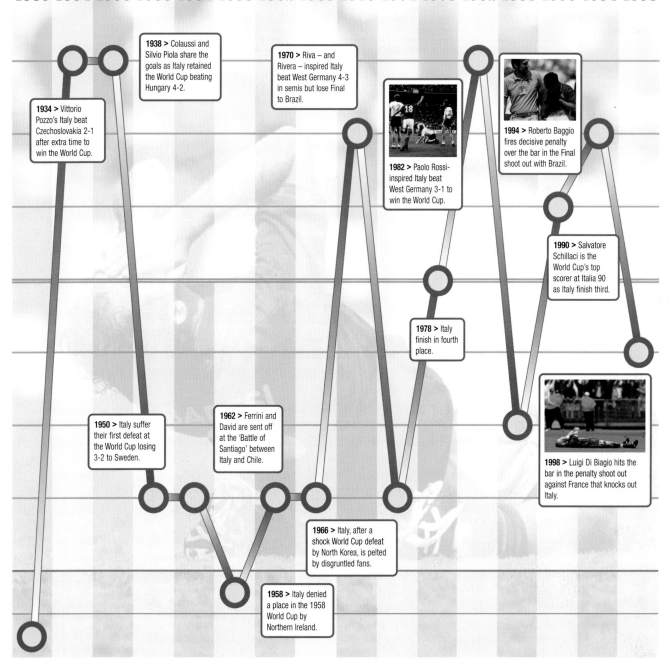

**1938 >** Colaussi and Silvio Piola share the goals as Italy retained the World Cup beating Hungary 4-2.

**1934 >** Vittorio Pozzo's Italy beat Czechoslovakia 2-1 after extra time to win the World Cup.

**1970 >** Riva – and Rivera – inspired Italy beat West Germany 4-3 in semis but lose Final to Brazil.

**1982 >** Paolo Rossi-inspired Italy beat West Germany 3-1 to win the World Cup.

**1994 >** Roberto Baggio fires decisive penalty over the bar in the Final shoot out with Brazil.

**1990 >** Salvatore Schillaci is the World Cup's top scorer at Italia 90 as Italy finish third.

**1978 >** Italy finish in fourth place.

**1950 >** Italy suffer their first defeat at the World Cup losing 3-2 to Sweden.

**1962 >** Ferrini and David are sent off at the 'Battle of Santiago' between Italy and Chile.

**1998 >** Luigi Di Biagio hits the bar in the penalty shoot out against France that knocks out Italy.

**1966 >** Italy, after a shock World Cup defeat by North Korea, is pelted by disgruntled fans.

**1958 >** Italy denied a place in the 1958 World Cup by Northern Ireland.

## ★ WORLD CUP HISTORY

| | | | |
|---|---|---|---|
| **1930** >> Did Not Enter | | **1970** >> Runners Up | |
| **1934** >> Winners | | **1974** >> First Round | |
| **1938** >> Winners | | **1978** >> Fourth Place | |
| **1950** >> First Round | | **1982** >> Winners | |
| **1954** >> First Round | | **1986** >> Second Round | |
| **1958** >> Did Not Qualify | | **1990** >> Third Place | |
| **1962** >> First Round | | **1994** >> Runners-Up | |
| **1966** >> First Round | | **1998** >> Quarter-Finals | |

## ★ WORLD CUP RECORDS, STORIES AND WEIRDNESS

**MOST GOALS IN A TOURNAMENT** >> At the 1982 Final Paolo Rossi made a poor start, but in a memorable game where Brazil only needed a draw to reach the semi-final, Rossi scored a magnificent hat-trick, Italy winning 3-2. He continued to impress in the semi-final against Poland, scoring both goals in the 2-0 win. In the final he scored the first in the 3-1 victory over West Germany and with that goal secured the topscorer title of the tournament.

| OPPONENT | DATE | UK TIME | VENUE |
|---|---|---|---|
| Belgium | **4 June** | 10.00 | **Saitama, Japan** |
| Russia | **9 June** | 12.30 | **Yokohama, Japan** |
| Tunisia | **14 June** | 07.30 | **Osaka, Japan** |

## ★ THE LOWDOWN

**Population:** 126.6 million

**Capital:** Tokyo

**Leader:** Junichiro Koizumi

**Life Expectancy:** Male: 77 yrs
Female: 84 yrs

>> Japan has one of the world's largest fishing fleets and accounts for nearly 15% of the world's global catch – eat your heart out John Wilson!

>> It is considered quite rude in Japan to blow your nose in public.

>> Of the world's 720,000 working robots, 410,000 are slaving away in Japan.

>> Japan has 18 active volcanoes and is subject to earthquakes. So you'd better take a helmet!

## "desperately seeking second round success"

# JAPAN

For World Cup co-hosts Japan, reaching the second-round would make Japanese footballing history. Even so, their fanatical supporters will be expecting much more. The Japanese side is undoubtedly the stronger of the two co-hosts and under coach Philippe Troussier there's been three years of solid preparation – resulting in huge improvement on the side that looked outclassed at France 98.

Japan's long overdue debut at the last World Cup was a big disappointment. The newcomers failed to pick up a single point losing to Argentina (1-0), Croatia (1-0) and Jamaica (2-1), although Masashi Nakayama delighted in the honour of scoring Japan's first ever World Cup goal.

Troussier inherited a relatively young squad and has developed them into a mature outfit. He has positively encouraged Japanese players to move abroad to improve their game. Goalkeeper Yoshikatsu Kawaguchi and midfielder Junichi Inamoto both play in England for Portsmouth and Arsenal respectively. A third player, defender Tsuneyasu Miyamoto, was bound for West Ham but visa problems stalled the move. Japan's most famous player Hidetoshi Nakata plays in Italy with Parma while fellow midfielder Shinji Ono plays in Holland for Feyenoord. Forward Naohiro Takahara, meanwhile, has joined Boca Juniors of Argentina.

Japan's World Cup Squad will be drawn from a pool of 28 tried and tested players all of whom possess good technique and pace, but more recently controlled aggression has been an added feature of their playing style – as was amply demonstrated during their 1-1 draw with Italy, one of the tournament favourites.

Confidence has been built up and this has been reflected in two impressive tournament performances. In 2000, Japan became Asian Champions, winning the title for the second time in eight years. Japan overcame Asia's best beating Saudi Arabia 4-1, Uzbekistan 8-1 (in which both Akinori Nishizawa and Naohiro Takahara got hat-tricks) and drew 1-1 with Qatar. Iraq were defeated 4-1 in the quarter-finals and China 3-2 in the semi-finals.

In the Final, Japan faced Saudi Arabia again for an incident-packed game. Shigeyoshi Mochizuki, playing only because Inamoto was suspended, gave away a penalty in the seventh minute but goalkeeper Kawaguchi survived the spot kick as Talal Al-Meshal put it wide. The relieved Mochizuki went on to score the winning goal in the 29th minute stabbing home Shunsuke Nakamura's free kick. Hiroshi Nanami was voted Player of the Tournament.

Nine months later, Japan co-hosted the Confederations Cup with South Korea and gave a magnificent performance. They went all the way to the Final beating Canada 2-0, Cameroon 2-0 and drawing 0-0 with Brazil before defeating Australia with a Nakata goal. In the Final, Japan suffered defeat by World Cup holders France by a single goal.

Goalkeeper Yawaguchi was once again in superb form while Shonji Ono showed why he was such a danger at free kicks with the goal of the tournament against Canada.

★ **ASSOCIATION:** The Football Association of Japan

★ **JOINED FIFA:** 1950

★ **JOINED AFC:** 1954

★ **PLAYERS:** 359,000

★ **CLUBS:** 13,100

★ **WEBSITE:** www.jfa.or.jp

★ **HONOURS:** Asian Championship – 1992, 2000

*On my rising head, son!*

## DID YOU KNOW?

**Japan reached the World Youth Cup Final in Nigeria under national team coach Philippe Troussier.**

Japan's 3-5-2 formation is built for a quick passing game that can quickly turn defence into attack. Coach Philippe Troussier has instilled much needed aggression into the side and Japan can now compete to win the ball instead of relying on interceptions and their opposition's wayward passes. However, once the pressure is on, the five-man midfield drifts back to act as a five-man defence and struggles to regain any sort of attacking impetus thereafter. Many of their attacks come from the lightening pace and crossing ability of Yasuhiro Hato and Toshiro Hattori, but if these two are pushed back to defend their attacking ability is nullified. Hidetoshi Nakata will be the main creator in midfield. The Kashima Antlers' striking pair of Takayuki Suzuki and Atsushi Yanagisawa can cause problems around the goal, if they get any sort of service, and it's noticeable that Japan have begun to score more goals of late.

## PROBABLE FORMATION 3-5-2

KAWAGUCHI

MORIOKA — K NAKATA

MIYAMOTO

HATO — INAMOTO — ONO — HATTORI

H NAKATA

YANAGISAWA — SUZUKI

## ★ MEN THAT MATTER!

### JUNICHI INAMOTO

Age>> 22
Club>> Arsenal
Defensive midfielder Inamoto is a pivotal player for Japan. He has represented Japan at every level from schoolboy (age 14) upwards. He was an influential member of Japan's 2000 Asian Cup team.

### HIDETOSHI NAKATA

Age>> 25
Club>> Parma
Japan's most famous export has made an impressive mark in Italy with Roma and Parma. He played at France 98 but chose to miss Japan's 2000 Asian Cup triumph.

### SHINJI ONO

Age>> 22
Club>> Feyenoord
Recovered from a ligament injury suffered in Olympic qualifying and went onto impress at the 2001 Confederations Cup after being restricted to substitute at France 98 and the 2000 Asian Cup.

## ★ PROBABLE SQUAD / ★ QUALIFICATION RECORD

| NAME | POSITION | CLUB | APS/GOALS | GAMES | MINS | Y/C | R/C | GOALS |
|------|----------|------|-----------|-------|------|-----|-----|-------|
| Yoshi Kawaguchi | Goalkeeper | Portsmouth, England | 51\0 | - | - | - | - | - |
| Seigo Narazaki | Goalkeeper | Nagoya Grampus Eight, Japan | 15\0 | - | - | - | - | - |
| Hitoshi Sogahata | Goalkeeper | Kashima Antlers, Japan | 1\0 | - | - | - | - | - |
| Yasuhiro Hato | Defender | Yokohama F Marinos, Japan | 10/0 | - | - | - | - | - |
| Toshihiro Hattori | Defender | Jubilo Iwata, Japan | 35/2 | - | - | - | - | - |
| Naoki Matsuda | Defender | Yokohama F Marinos, Japan | 24/0 | - | - | - | - | - |
| Tsuneyasu Miyamoto | Defender | Gamba Osaka, Japan | 5/0 | - | - | - | - | - |
| Ryuzo Morioka | Defender | Shimizu S-Pulse, Japan | 32/0 | - | - | - | - | - |
| Koji Nakata | Defender | Kashima Antlers, Japan | 20/0 | - | - | - | - | - |
| Junichi Inamoto | Midfielder | Arsenal, England | 25/1 | - | - | - | - | - |
| Teruyoshi Ito | Midfielder | Shimizu S-Pulse, Japan | 27/0 | - | - | - | - | - |
| Hiroaki Morishima | Midfielder | Cerezo Osaka, Japan | 57/11 | - | - | - | - | - |
| Tomokazu Myojin | Midfielder | Kashiwa Reysol, Japan | 16/2 | - | - | - | - | - |
| Hidetoshi Nakata | Midfielder | Parma, Italy | 40/7 | - | - | - | - | - |
| Daisuke Oku | Midfielder | Jubilo Iwata, Japan | 22/2 | - | - | - | - | - |
| Shinji Ono | Midfielder | Feyenoord, Holland | 24/2 | - | - | - | - | - |
| Kazuyuki Toda | Midfielder | Shimizu S-Pulse, Japan | 10/0 | - | - | - | - | - |
| Masashi Nakayama | Forward | Jubilo Iwata, Japan | 47/21 | - | - | - | - | - |
| Akinori Nishizawa | Forward | Cerezo Osaka, Japan | 24/9 | - | - | - | - | - |
| Takayuki Suzuki | Forward | Kashima Antlers, Japan | 10/3 | - | - | - | - | - |
| Naohiro Takahara | Forward | Boca Juniors, Argentina | 15/8 | - | - | - | - | - |
| Atsushi Yanagisawa | Forward | Kashima Antlers, Japan | 22/9 | - | - | - | - | - |
| Tatsuhiko Kubo | Forward | Sanfrecce Hiroshima, Japan | 7/0 | - | - | - | - | - |

KEY: APPS/GOALS = International Appearances/Goals; GAMES=Qualification Games played; MINS=Minutes played; Y/C= Yellow cards R/C=Red cards

# HISTORY AT THE WORLD CUP

**1930 1934 1938 1950 1954 1958 1962 1966 1970 1974 1978 1982 1986 1990 1994 1998**

**1994 >** Japan cruelly missed out on their first Finals when Iraqi score an injury time goal.

**1990 >** North Korea stops Japan's progress in the qualifiers as the Japanese finish runners-up.

**1982 >** Japan beaten 1-0 by North Korea in the Asian Qualifying semi-finals.

**1978 >** Japan finish behind South Korea, again, and Israel.

**1998 >** Masashi Nakayama scores Japan's first World Cup Finals goal, but they suffer a third successive defeat.

**1974 >** Japan are beaten 1-0 by Israel in the Asia Qualifying semi-finals.

**1954 >** Japan, despite playing in Tokyo twice, lose 7-3 on aggregate to South Korea in the qualifiers.

**1962 >** Japan beaten twice by South Korea 2-1 and 2-0 in Group 10.

**1970 >** Japan finish bottom of the Asia-Oceania group behind Australia and South Korea.

**1986 >** Once again Japan lose out to South Korea 3-1 on aggregate.

---

## ★ WORLD CUP HISTORY

| | |
|---|---|
| 1930 >> Did Not Enter | 1970 >> Did Not Qualify |
| 1934 >> Did Not Enter | 1974 >> Did Not Qualify |
| 1938 >> Did Not Enter | 1978 >> Did Not Qualify |
| 1950 >> Did Not Enter | 1982 >> Did Not Qualify |
| 1954 >> Did Not Qualify | 1986 >> Did Not Qualify |
| 1958 >> Did Not Enter | 1990 >> Did Not Qualify |
| 1962 >> Did Not Qualify | 1994 >> Did Not Qualify |
| 1966 >> Did Not Enter | 1998 >> First Round |

## ★ WORLD CUP RECORDS, STORIES AND WEIRDNESS

**QUALIFYING PAIN** >> Captain Tetsuji Hashiratani was taken from the field weeping after Japan had come within 17 seconds of qualifying for 1994 World Cup Finals. They'd conceded an injury time goal to Iraq, and that was that.

**CO-HOSTS** >> Japan beat South Korea for the first time ever in a World Cup competition during the 1994 qualification tournament.

**PRECOCIOUS DEBUTANTE** >> On the 1st of March 1994 Shinji Ono left school, he then averaged a goal a game in the J. League and made his debut for the national side in July, aged 18. From schoolboy to international in just 4 months.

| OPPONENT | DATE | UK TIME | VENUE |
|---|---|---|---|
| Croatia | **3 June** | 07.30 | **Niigata, Japan** |
| Ecuador | **9 June** | 07.30 | **Miyagi, Japan** |
| Italy | **13 June** | 12.30 | **Oita, Japan** |

## "Central American super-power under pressure"

# MEXICO

Historically, Mexico has always been the best team of the CONCACAF federation and will be appearing at the World Cup Finals for the 12th time in Japan/Korea. Surprisingly for such a regionally dominant team, they've made very little impact on the tournament itself, reaching the last eight on only two occasions – both when they were hosting the Finals. Otherwise, it's been an early bath for the "Tri-Colores".

Mexico's role as the footballing super-power of the region is not what it was. In recent years the USA have developed into serious challengers and Costa Rica, who Mexico finished six points adrift of in qualification, are now finding the talent and discipline to outshine their Central American opponents.

Between January 2000 and the end of January 2002 Mexico played a staggering 53 full internationals competing not only in the World Cup qualifiers but the Gold Cup (twice), Confederations Cup (twice), Copa America, US Cup and a host of friendlies around the world.

Despite the thrashing of Trinidad & Tobago 7-0 (Jared Borguetti scoring a hat-trick), Mexico finished runners-up to Trinidad & Tobago in the semi-final round to qualify for the six team final round, which included Costa Rica, Honduras, Jamaica and USA. In order to qualify they needed to finish in the top three.

Mexico made a poor start, winning just one of their first five games when, following the 3-1 defeat by Honduras, coach Enrique Meza resigned. Meza's record had been poor – 11 defeats and only five wins. His successor, Javier Aguirre, inherited a dispirited team and was given just ten days to turn things round for the must-win game against the USA.

Aguirre made eight changes to the team that had lost to Honduras with striker Borguetti, "El Emperador" Claudio Suarez, the most capped player in the world, and midfielder Gerardo Torrado the only survivors. America played dreadfully and Borgetti's 15th minute goal proved to be enough for a priceless Mexican victory.

Former striker Cuauchtemoc Blanco, who had been ruled out through injury since October 2000, was recalled to the team and scored both goals in a 2-1 win over Jamaica, ending Jamaica's 51-game unbeaten run at home. Blanco's injury had been caused by Trinidad & Tobago's Ansil Elcock's wild tackle and Elcock, perhaps fearing for his own safety, was absent when Mexico beat them 3-0, Blanco scoring the third from the penalty spot.

A 0-0 draw in Costa Rica left Aguirre's team needing to beat Honduras in their last game to qualify. Blanco was in excellent form again scoring twice and setting up another for Juan Francisco Palencia in a deserved 3-0 win. Keeping Blanco fit will be the key to Mexico's progression at the Finals.

### ★ THE LOWDOWN

**Population:** 101.9 million

**Capital:** Mexico City

**Leader:** Vicente Quesada

**Life Expectancy:** Male: 68 yrs Female: 75 yrs

>> Mexico was under Spanish rule for three centuries before finally achieving independence in 1810.

>> In the year 2000, it was estimated that 3,900 hectares of arable land in Mexico was being used for cannabis cultivation.

>> Mexico is one of the most seismologically active regions on Earth.

★ **ASSOCIATION:** Federacion Mexicana de Futbol Asociacion
★ **JOINED FIFA:** 1929
★ **JOINED FOOTBALL CONFEDERATION:** 1961
★ **PLAYERS:** 1,402,300

★ **CLUBS:** 77
★ **WEBSITE:** none
★ **HONOURS:** CONCACAF/Gold Cup – 1965, 1971, 1977, 1993, 1996, 1998

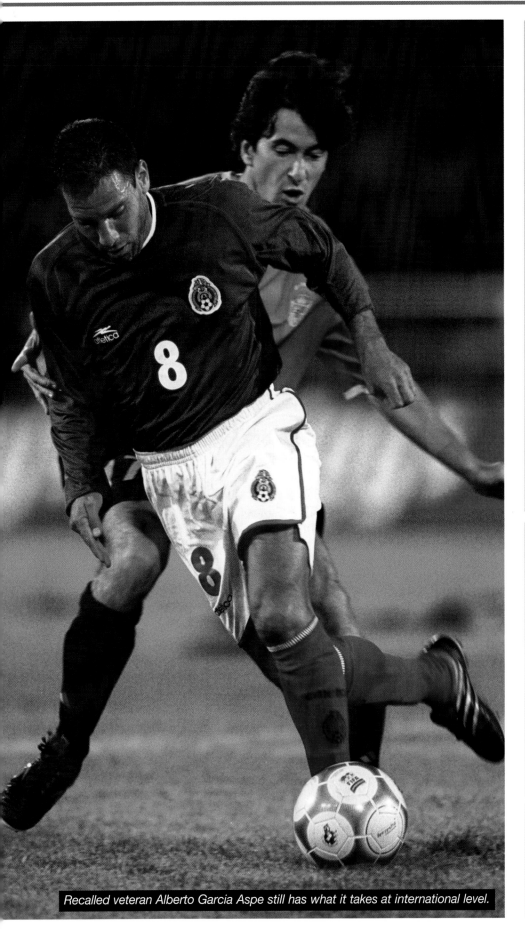

*Recalled veteran Alberto Garcia Aspe still has what it takes at international level.*

## ★ ROAD TO QUALIFICATION

Jul 00 **Panama** (a) > (w) 0-**1** Ramirez, R 86

Jul 00 **Trinidad & Tobago** (a) > (l) 1-**0**

Aug 00 **Canada** (h) > (w) **2**-0
Abundis 38, Fenwick 81 og

Sep 00 **Panama** (h) > (w) **7**-1
Ruiz, V 8 pen, Abundis 36, Zepeda 44, Blanco, C 47 pen, 90, Marquez 54, Ramirez, R 75

Oct 00 **Trinidad & Tobago** (h) > (w) **7**-0
Blanco, C 20, 26 pen, Borquetti 24, 29, 78, Davino 65, Ruiz, V 74 pen

Nov 00 **Canada** (a) > (d) 0-**0**

Feb 01 **United States** (a) > (l) 2-**0**

Mar 01 **Jamaica** (h) > (w) **4**-0
De Nigris 15, 17, Borquetti 83, 87

Apr 01 **Trinidad & Tobago** (a) > (d) 1-**1**
Pardo 61

Jun 01 **Costa Rica** (h) > (l) **1**-2 Abundis 7

Jun 01 **Honduras** (a) > (l) 3-**1** Ruiz, V 86

Jun 01 **United States** (h) > (w) **1**-0
Borquetti 15

Sep 01 **Jamaica** (a) > (w) 1-**2**
Blanco, C 68, 76

Sep 01 **Trinidad & Tobago** (h) > (w) **3**-0
Garcia Aspe 25, Arellano 44, Blanco, C 86

Oct 01 **Costa Rica** (a) > (d) 0-**0**

Nov 01 **Honduras** (h) > (w) **3**-0
Blanco, C 65, 78, Palencia 72

## ★ FINAL GROUP TABLE

| Team | P | W | D | L | F | A | Pts |
|------|---|---|---|---|---|---|-----|
| Costa Rica | 10 | 7 | 2 | 1 | 17 | 7 | 23 |
| Mexico | 10 | 5 | 2 | 3 | 16 | 9 | 17 |
| United States | 10 | 5 | 2 | 3 | 11 | 8 | 17 |
| Honduras | 10 | 4 | 2 | 4 | 17 | 17 | 14 |
| Jamaica | 10 | 2 | 2 | 6 | 7 | 14 | 8 |
| Trinidad & Tob | 10 | 1 | 2 | 7 | 5 | 18 | 5 |

## ★ SEMI-FINAL GROUP TABLE

| Team | P | W | D | L | F | A | Pts |
|------|---|---|---|---|---|---|-----|
| Trinidad & Tob | 6 | 5 | 0 | 1 | 14 | 7 | 15 |
| Mexico | 6 | 4 | 1 | 1 | 17 | 2 | 13 |
| Canada | 6 | 1 | 2 | 3 | 1 | 8 | 5 |
| Panama | 6 | 0 | 1 | 5 | 1 | 16 | 1 |

## ★ RECENT RESULTS

Feb 02 **Yugoslavia** (h) > (l) **1**-2
Mendoza 75

Mar 02 **Albania** (h) > (w) **4**-0
Borquetti 23, Morales 29, Bautista 51, 90

Apr 02 **United States** (a) > (l) 1-**0**

## DID YOU KNOW?

**Mexican goalkeeper Antonio Carbajal played at five different World Cup Finals in 1950, 1954, 1958, 1962 and 1966.**

**The arrival of new coach** Javier Aguirre has brought about a change in tactics and recall for Alberto Garcia Aspe. Previously, Mexico played a very cautious 4-4-2, but Aguirre has introduced a more attacking game. Veteran Garcia Aspe combines with Johan Rodriguez, supported by Ramon Morales and Gerardo Torrado on the wings, to provide the protection the back three need and add speed to counter-attacks. The return of Cuauhtemoc Blanco after injury also sees his role change from forward to playmaker in an attacking midfielder position playing behind a front two. Young forward Jared Borgetti has gained support up front from the experienced Francisco Palencia. These changes have improved Mexico's results, but have not transformed them into a thrilling side. Mexico lacks strength in depth and the return of the old guard of Garcia Aspe and Blanco has really only added experience to a very ordinary Mexican side.

# PROBABLE FORMATION  3-5-2

PEREZ

VIDRIO — BROWN

MARQUEZ

H MORALES — RODRIGUEZ — GARCIA ASPE — TORRADO

BLANCO

PALENCIA — BORGUETTI

## ★ MEN THAT MATTER!

### CUAUHTEMOC BLANCO

Age>> 29
Club>> Valladolid
Scored nine goals (four penalties) from seven appearances (including three as sub) having been kept out by a severe injury sustained in qualifying. He returned in time to help clinch qualification.

### GERARDO TORRADO

Age>> 23
Club>> Sevilla
An attacking midfielder, more of a creative player than a goalscorer. Last year he earned a move from from Mexico's Pumas UNAM to Sevilla.

### FRANCISCO PALENCIA

Age>> 29
Club>> Espanyol
Palencia is an automatic choice for Mexico because of his thrilling pace and occasional goals. Can play as a striking partner for Blanco or Borguetti or as an attacking midfielder.

## ★ PROBABLE SQUAD  ★ QUALIFICATION RECORD

| NAME | POSITION | CLUB | APS/GOALS | GAMES | MINS | Y/C | R/C | GOALS |
|---|---|---|---|---|---|---|---|---|
| Jorge Campos | Goalkeeper | Pumas UNAM, Mexico | 127/0 | 8 | 720 | 0 | 0 | 0 |
| Oscar Perez | Goalkeeper | Cruz Azul, Mexico | 26/0 | 5 | 450 | 0 | 0 | 0 |
| Oswaldo Sanchez | Goalkeeper | Guadalajara, Mexico | 20/0 | 3 | 270 | 0 | 0 | 0 |
| Salvador Carmona | Defender | Toluca, Mexico | 51/0 | 5 | 397 | 2 | 0 | 0 |
| Duilio Davino | Defender | America, Mexico | 66/1 | 7 | 630 | 1 | 0 | 1 |
| Rafael Marquez | Defender | Monaco, France | 31/2 | 11 | 969 | 3 | 1 | 1 |
| Heriberto Morales | Defender | Atletico Morelia, Mexico | 12/0 | 3 | 270 | 1 | 0 | 0 |
| Pavel Pardo | Defender | America, Mexico | 85/2 | 10 | 900 | 3 | 0 | 1 |
| Alberto Rodriguez | Defender | Pachuca, Mexico | 8/0 | 2 | 90 | 0 | 0 | 0 |
| Manuel Vidrio | Defender | Pachuca, Mexico | 22/1 | 5 | 450 | 1 | 0 | 0 |
| Jesus Arellano | Midfielder | Monterrey, Mexico | 35/4 | 7 | 435 | 1 | 1 | 1 |
| Alberto Garcia Aspe | Midfielder | Puebla, Mexico | 102/19 | 5 | 355 | 2 | 0 | 1 |
| Ramon Morales | Midfielder | Guadalajara, Mexico | 6/0 | 4 | 271 | 1 | 0 | 0 |
| Johan Rodriguez | Midfielder | Santos Laguna, Mexico | 12/2 | 4 | 261 | 1 | 1 | 0 |
| Victor Ruiz | Midfielder | Necaxa, Mexico | 16/6 | 10 | 696 | 0 | 0 | 3 |
| Gerardo Torrado | Midfielder | Sevilla, Spain | 24/1 | 4 | 283 | 4 | 0 | 0 |
| German Villa | Midfielder | America, Mexico | 61/0 | 9 | 702 | 3 | 0 | 0 |
| Miguel Zepeda | Midfielder | Cruz Azul, Mexico | 16/2 | 11 | 633 | 0 | 0 | 1 |
| Cuauhtemoc Blanco | Forward | Valladolid, Spain | 68/29 | 7 | 472 | 1 | 0 | 9 |
| Jared Borgetti | Forward | Santos Laguna, Mexico | 23/11 | 8 | 574 | 0 | 0 | 6 |
| Luis Hernandez | Forward | America, Mexico | 79/35 | 9 | 582 | 2 | 0 | 0 |
| Francisco Palencia | Forward | Espanyol, Spain | 66/8 | 14 | 908 | 0 | 0 | 0 |
| Antonio De Nigris | Forward | Monterrey, Mexico | 14/4 | 3 | 185 | 0 | 0 | 2 |

**KEY:** APPS/GOALS = International Appearances/Goals; GAMES=Qualification Games played; MINS=Minutes played; Y/C= Yellow cards R/C=Red cards

# HISTORY AT THE WORLD CUP

1930 1934 1938 1950 1954 1958 1962 1966 1970 1974 1978 1982 1986 1990 1994 1998

**1994 >** Garcia Aspe, Bernal and Luis Garcia all fail in the penalty shoot out against Bulgaria.

**1998 >** Blanco shows his class with two-foot trickery against a mesmerised South Korea,

**1986 >** Hugo Sanchez scores goals and spends plenty of energy trying to win free kicks.

**1930 >** The first-ever World Cup match sees Mexico beaten 4-1 by France in Montevideo.

**1978 >** Mexico suffers surprise elimination at the hands of Honduras and El Salvador.

**1974 >** Mexico suffers shock elimination by Haiti in the CONCACAF section.

## ★ WORLD CUP HISTORY

| | | | |
|---|---|---|---|
| 1930 >> First Round | | 1970 >> Quarter-Finals | |
| 1934 >> Did Not Qualify | | 1974 >> Did Not Qualify | |
| 1938 >> Did Not Enter | | 1978 >> First Round | |
| 1950 >> First Round | | 1982 >> Did Not Qualify | |
| 1954 >> First Round | | 1986 >> Quarter-Finals | |
| 1958 >> First Round | | 1990 >> Banned | |
| 1962 >> First Round | | 1994 >> Second Round | |
| 1966 >> First Round | | 1998 >> Second Round | |

## ★ WORLD CUP RECORDS, STORIES AND WEIRDNESS

**FIRST SUBSTITUTE TO SCORE** >> Mexico's Juan Basaguren was the first substitute to score in a World Cup Final, netting in Mexico's 1970 4-0 win over El Salvador.

**QUICKEST GOAL** >> Mexico were on the wrong end of the fastest goal ever scored in the World Cup, put in by Czechoslovakia's Vaclav Masek after just 16 seconds in 1962.

# GROUP F

| OPPONENT | DATE | UK TIME | VENUE |
|----------|------|---------|-------|
| Argentina | **2 June** | **06.30** | **Ibaraki, Japan** |
| Sweden | **7 June** | **07.30** | **Kobe, Japan** |
| England | **12 June** | **07.30** | **Osaka, Japan** |

## "will the final be Sunday's Sunday?"

# NIGERIA

**N**igeria is the leading country of West Africa and has the largest population of any state on the continent, which has produced upwards of 200 professional footballers playing around the world. The country has an incredible pool of football talent and is widely regarded as Africa's best hope for World Cup success.

The 'Super Eagles' started embarrassingly on the road to World Cup qualification. In the preliminary round they were drawn against World Cup debutantes Eritrea and for the away first leg only 14 players turned up including two goalkeepers. Adding insult to the injured feelings of the Nigerian stars, who just two months earlier had finished African Nations Cup runners-up, the game had to be played on a school field because the stadium was under repair. Embarrassingly, the Nigerians were held to a 0-0 draw. A fortnight later, pride was restored with an easy 4-0 win and a place in the qualifying draw.

Nigeria began in Lagos against Sierra Leone with a team that only featured three regulars in Jay-Jay Okocha, Sunday Oliseh and Nwankwo Kanu. Such was the makeshift nature of the team that both Oliseh and Kanu found themselves playing alongside their younger brothers Azubike and Christopher. Okocha and Benedict Okwuegbu got the goals in a 2-0 win, but the team was criticised for not scoring more.

Defeats in Liberia and Sierra Leone, and a draw away to Ghana, had Nigeria on the back foot facing the prospect of not qualifying. The draw with Ghana was all the more galling since the Nigerians had put out their best team, many of their players called up from Europe leagues, while Ghana opted for local players. It was a game everyone had expected Nigeria to win.

Worse was to follow when Sierra Leone scored their first goal of the qualifiers inflicting a shock defeat on Nigeria. A bout of sustained criticism followed leading five days later to the dismissal of coach Jo Bonfrere, who had, in any case, been under pressure since Nigeria had failed to defend their Olympic title in September 2000. Nigeria, five points adrift of leaders Liberia, needed not only to win their last three games but also hoped Liberia would slip up.

The new coach Shaibi Amodu's first match in charge was against Liberia in Port Harcourt and the players responded with an excellent performance producing a 2-0 win with goals from Nwankwo Kanu and Victor Agali, closing the gap to two points. Then Liberia suffered a surprise 2-1 home defeat by Ghana and although they finished with a 1-0 win over Sierra Leone, Nigeria's 4-0 drubbing of Sudan meant the Super Eagles knew they could fly to the top of the group by beating Ghana in their final game.

All 16,000 tickets at the Liberty Stadium in Port Harcourt were sold out and victory for Nigeria looked even more likely when Ghana were forced to field a makeshift team after several of their foreign-based stars failed to turn up. A minute after kick off and qualification looked certain when 2000 African Player of the Year, Victor Agali, opened the scoring. Tijani Babangida scored twice before the break to set up an untroubled second half and an easy 3-0 win. The result meant Nigeria became the fifth and last of the African nations to qualify for the World Cup Finals – their third appearance at the Finals in succession.

### ★ THE LOWDOWN

**Population:** 126.6 million

**Capital:** Abuja

**Leader:** Olusegun Obasanjo

**Life Expectancy:** Male: 51 yrs Female: 51 yrs

>> Nigeria is Africa's most populous country and is made up of over 250 ethnic groups.

>> On 12th December 1991 the capital was officially transferred from Lagos to Abuja.

>> Although English is the official government language, there are 350 to 400 other languages spoken in Nigeria, with many different dialects!

★ **ASSOCIATION:** Nigeria Football Association
★ **JOINED FIFA:** 1959
★ **JOINED CAF:** 1959
★ **PLAYERS:** 80,190

★ **CLUBS:** 326
★ **WEBSITE:** www.nfaonline.com
★ **HONOURS:** African Nations Cup – 1980, 1994.

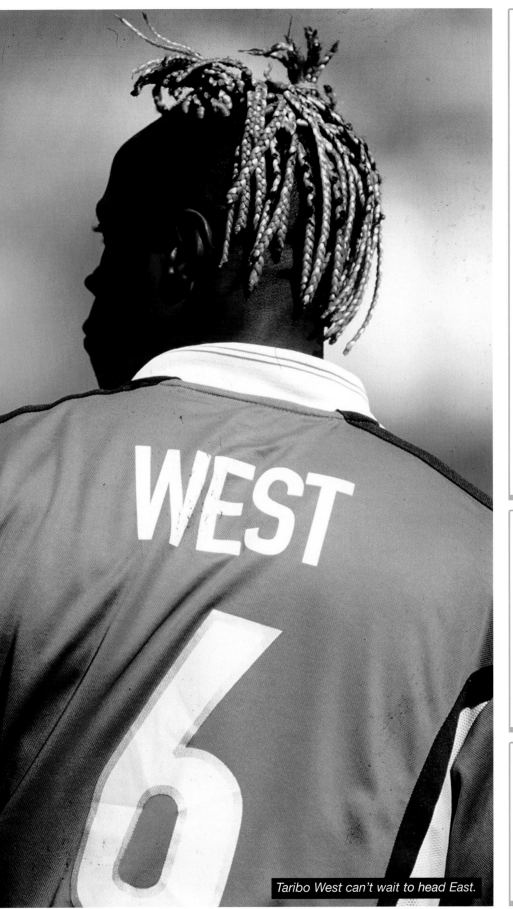

*Taribo West can't wait to head East.*

## ★ ROAD TO QUALIFICATION

Apr 00 **Eritrea** (a) > (d) 0-**0**

Apr 00 **Eritrea** (h) > (w) **4**-0 (agg **4**-0)
Akwuegbu 13, Lawal 20, Akpoborie 65, Kanu, N 89

Jun 00 **Sierra Leone** (h) > (w) **2**-0
Okocha 12, Akwuegbu 79

Jul 00 **Liberia** (a) > (l) 2-**1** Kanu, N 35

Jan 01 **Sudan** (h) > (w) **3**-0
Agali 56, 68, Kanu, N 79

Mar 01 **Ghana** (a) > (d) 0-**0**

Apr 01 **Sierra Leone** (a) > (l) 1-**0**

May 01 **Liberia** (h) > (w) **2**-0
Kanu, N 11, Agali 59

Jul 01 **Sudan** (a) > (w) 0-**4**
Okocha 40, Ayegbeni 47, 87, Aghahowa 78

Jul 01 **Ghana** (h) > (w) **3**-0
Agali 1, Babangida 18, 32

## ★ FINAL GROUP TABLE

| Team | P | W | D | L | F | A | Pts |
|---|---|---|---|---|---|---|---|
| **Nigeria** | 8 | 5 | 1 | 2 | 15 | 3 | 16 |
| Liberia | 8 | 5 | 0 | 3 | 10 | 8 | 15 |
| Sudan | 8 | 4 | 0 | 4 | 8 | 10 | 12 |
| Ghana | 8 | 3 | 2 | 3 | 10 | 9 | 11 |
| Sierra Leone | 8 | 1 | 1 | 6 | 2 | 15 | 4 |

## ★ RECENT RESULTS

Mar 02 **Paraguay** (a) > (d) 1-**1**
Okocha 82 pen

**Nigeria's 4-4-2 formation** is all about providing ample goal chances for strikers Victor Agali and Nwankwo Kanu (or Julius Aghahowa). The midfield is one of Africa's most experienced with right-sided Finidi George, Nigeria's longest serving international, playing in his third World Cup. The hugely exciting Sunday Oliseh supports the attack with help on the left from Garbo Lawal. Defensive midfield duties fall to Austin Okocha, whose presence in front of the back four will be important since the back line, with the exception of Taribo West, is relatively inexperienced at this level. The full backs are Joseph Yobo and Ifeanyi Udeze, who can play on both sides of the field. Partnering West in the centre is Ukrainian-based Isaac Okoronkwo. Ike Shorunmu is Nigeria's first choice goalkeeper.

# PROBABLE FORMATION 4-4-2

SHORUNMU

YOBO · UDEZE

OKORONKWO · WEST

GEORGE · OLISEH · OKOCHA · LAWAL

AGALI · KANU

## ★ MEN THAT MATTER!

### NWANKWO KANU

Age>> 25

Club>> Arsenal

Diagnosed with a serious heart condition in 1996 and written off. Since then Kanu has been showered with numerous club, international and individual honours including African and Olympic titles.

### VICTOR AGALI

Age>> 23

Club>> Schalke

Nigerian Player of the Year in 2000 who made a goal scoring debut against Zambia in an African Nations Cup qualifier in January 2001. Now established as first choice attacker.

### SUNDAY OLISEH

Age>> 27

Club>> Borussia Dortmund

Experienced midfielder who has won the African Nations Cup (1994) and Olympics (1996) and played in Belgium, Germany, Holland and Italy. Scored a stunning World Cup goal against Spain at France 98.

## ★ PROBABLE SQUAD · ★ QUALIFICATION RECORD

| NAME | POSITION | CLUB | APS/GOALS | GAMES | MINS | Y/C | R/C | GOALS |
|------|----------|------|-----------|-------|------|-----|-----|-------|
| Ademole Bankole | Goalkeeper | Crewe Alexandra, England | 0/0 | 0 | 0 | 0 | 0 | 0 |
| Ndubuisi Egbo | Goalkeeper | SK Tirana, Albania | 8/0 | 1 | 90 | 0 | 0 | 0 |
| Ike Shorunmu | Goalkeeper | unattached | 28/0 | 7 | 630 | 0 | 0 | 0 |
| Celestine Babayaro | Defender | Chelsea, England | 23/0 | 1 | 16 | 0 | 0 | 0 |
| Eric Ejiofor | Defender | Maccabi Haifa, Israel | 8/0 | 2 | 170 | 2 | 0 | 0 |
| Emeka Ifejiagwa | Defender | Wolfsburg, Germany | 10/0 | 4 | 260 | 0 | 0 | 0 |
| Isaac Okoronkwo | Defender | Shakhtar Donetsk, Ukraine | 5/0 | 1 | 90 | 0 | 0 | 0 |
| Godwin Okpara | Defender | Standard Liege, Belgium | 19/0 | 4 | 360 | 2 | 0 | 0 |
| Ifeanyi Udeze | Defender | PAOK Salonika, Greece | 9/0 | 6 | 524 | 2 | 0 | 0 |
| Taribo West | Defender | Kaiserslautern, Germany | 33/0 | 7 | 630 | 1 | 0 | 0 |
| Joseph Yobo | Defender | Marseille, France | 7/0 | 4 | 360 | 0 | 0 | 0 |
| Tijani Babangida | Midfielder | Vitesse Arnhem, Holland | 33/5 | 5 | 177 | 0 | 0 | 2 |
| Justice Christopher | Midfielder | Royal Antwerp, Belgium | 4/0 | 2 | 180 | 0 | 0 | 0 |
| Finidi George | Midfielder | Ipswich, England | 57/7 | 7 | 560 | 2 | 0 | 0 |
| Garba Lawal | Midfielder | Roda JC, Holland | 26/3 | 7 | 534 | 0 | 0 | 0 |
| Pascal Ojigwe | Midfielder | Bayer Leverkusen, Germany | 14/1 | 3 | 144 | 0 | 0 | 0 |
| Austin Okocha | Midfielder | Paris Saint-Germain, France | 49/7 | 8 | 720 | 1 | 0 | 2 |
| Sunday Oliseh | Midfielder | Borussia Dortmund, Germany | 50/2 | 8 | 673 | 0 | 0 | 0 |
| Victor Agali | Forward | Schalke, Germany | 8/5 | 6 | 498 | 1 | 0 | 4 |
| Julius Aghahowa | Forward | Shakhtar Donetsk, Ukraine | 9/5 | 4 | 186 | 3 | 0 | 1 |
| Yakubu Aiyegbeni | Forward | Maccabi Haifa, Israel | 7/3 | 3 | 202 | 0 | 0 | 2 |
| Benedict Akwuegbu | Forward | Grazer AK, Austria | 13/5 | 3 | 247 | 1 | 0 | 1 |
| Nwankwo Kanu | Forward | Arsenal, England | 27/6 | 9 | 594 | 0 | 0 | 3 |

**KEY:** APPS/GOALS = International Appearances/Goals; GAMES=Qualification Games played; MINS=Minutes played; Y/C= Yellow cards R/C=Red cards

# HISTORY AT THE WORLD CUP

1930 1934 1938 1950 1954 1958 1962 1966 1970 1974 1978 1982 1986 1990 1994 1998

**1998 >** Sunday Oliseh's half volley proves the winner as Nigeria shock Spain 3-2.

**1994 >** Emmanuel Amunike's goal puts Nigeria within two minutes of beating Italy in the second round.

**1974 >** Nigeria trail Ghana 3-2 in an abandoned game, but Ghana given 2-0 win and out go Nigeria.

**1978 >** Nigeria finish bottom of the final round behind Tunisia and Egypt.

## ★ WORLD CUP HISTORY

| | |
|---|---|
| **1930** >> Did Not Enter | **1970** >> Did Not Qualify |
| **1934** >> Did Not Enter | **1974** >> Did Not Qualify |
| **1938** >> Did Not Enter | **1978** >> Did Not Qualify |
| **1950** >> Did Not Enter | **1982** >> Did Not Qualify |
| **1954** >> Did Not Enter | **1986** >> Did Not Qualify |
| **1958** >> Did Not Enter | **1990** >> Did Not Qualify |
| **1962** >> Did Not Qualify | **1994** >> Second Round |
| **1966** >> Did Not Enter | **1998** >> Second Round |

## ★ WORLD CUP RECORDS, STORIES AND WEIRDNESS

**TOP SCORER**>> Nigeria's best all-time international scorer is Rashidi Yekini.

**TOP SCORER IN QUALIFYING**>> Victor Agali with 4.

**WORLD CUP WEIRDNESS**>> Nigeria alleges that an unknown group is attempting to force the cancellation of its World Cup warm-up matches. A spokesman said that in an attempt to sabotage Nigeria's World Cup build up, a nameless group has "written to those involved in our pre-World Cup matches to inform them we are not interested in the matches anymore"

| OPPONENT | DATE | UK TIME | VENUE |
|---|---|---|---|
| South Africa | **2 June** | 08.30 | **Busan, Korea** |
| Spain | **7 June** | 10.00 | **Jeonju, Korea** |
| Slovenia | **12 June** | 12.30 | **Seogwipo, Korea** |

## "what will Maldini make of his new charges?"

# PARAGUAY

**P**araguay is the team with the goalscoring goalkeeper and had a magnificent coach who was sacked!

José Luis Chilavert, Paraguay's number one goalkeeper and team captain, loves to take free kicks, penalties and corners and is often found roaming the pitch. Remarkably, he scored four times during the qualifiers, including Paraguay's second goal in the 90th minute of a 2-0 win in Colombia. In the next game he converted an 84th minute penalty to complete a 5-1 home thrashing of Peru, contributed a goal in the 5-1 demolition of Bolivia and then converted a penalty in the big clash with Argentina. And how often can it be said of an international goalkeeper that he has had a penalty saved?! On this occasion by Chile's Sergio Vargas, but Chilavert's blushes were also saved by Carlos Paredes's winner in the third minute of injury time. At the start of the 2001-02 season he chose to remain with relegated French club Strasbourg when he could have played easily in the higher league. Sadly he will miss the opening World Cup match against South Africa through suspension.

Now to that magnificent coach: Sergio Markarian, Uruguayan by birth, managed a tough qualification programme by beating Brazil, holding favourites Argentina home and away and earning qualification with two games to spare after Uruguay drew their penultimate match. It was the first time Paraguay had qualified for

successive World Cup Finals – an impressive result from a country whose population only amounts to 5 million.

Paraguay had come through the toughest World Cup qualifying group playing superb football and Markarian, who had coached Paraguay at the 1992 Olympics, was a popular boss. Nevertheless, halfway through qualification, Markarian had quit following criticism of a 2-1 defeat by Ecuador, but there was such a clamour from fans and players alike that he retracted his resignation a week later. Markarian's popularity did not extend, however, to the Paraguayan FA and media and after Paraguay had qualified, the team, perhaps understandably, took their collective feet off the pedal, suffering defeats by Venezuela (1-3) and Colombia (0-4) in their last two games. And that was considered sufficient cause to dismiss Markarian.

Ex-Italy boss Cesare Maldini has been appointed his successor. It will be interesting to see how they get on with the new man who has little time to impose his ideas on a squad with whom he does not share a common language. Under Markarian, Paraguay played to a 4-4-2 system, the formation Maldini favours and which he used to such great effect with Italy at France 98. Retaining it may well be the key to Paraguay's impact on this year's Finals. Four years ago Paraguay reached the second round where they were knocked out by the World Cup's first-ever golden goal.

### ★ THE LOWDOWN

**Population:** 5.7 million

**Capital:** Asuncion

**Leader:** Luis Macchi

**Life Expectancy:** Male: 71 yrs Female: 76 yrs

>> 200 years ago sightseers were not welcome at the Palacio de Gobierno, the royal residence in Paraguay; during the reign of the military dictator Rodriguez de Francia anyone found staring at the building was shot on sight. Things are friendlier now; even a souvenir shop has been opened!

>> Paraguay is a land-locked country surrounded by Argentina, Bolivia and Brazil.

★ **ASSOCIATION:** Asociacion Paraguaya de Futbol

★ **JOINED FIFA:** 1921

★ **JOINED CONEMBOL:** 1921

★ **PLAYERS:** 140,000

★ **CLUBS:** 1,500

★ **WEBSITE:** none.

★ **HONOURS:** Copa America – 1953, 1979.

## ★ ROAD TO QUALIFICATION

Mar 00 **Peru** (a) > (l) 2-**0**

Apr 00 **Uruguay** (h) > (w) **1**-0 Ayala 17

Jun 00 **Ecuador** (h) > (w) **3**-1
Toledo 11, Brizuela 43, 64

Jun 00 **Chile** (a) > (l) 3-**1** Cardozo 71

Jul 00 **Brazil** (h) > (w) **2**-1
Paredes 6, Campos 83

Jul 00 **Bolivia** (a) > (d) 0-0

Aug 00 **Argentina** (a) > (d) 1-**1** Acuna 61

Sep 00 **Venezuela** (h) > (w) **3**-0
Gonzalez, G 30, Cardozo 35, Paredes 44

Oct 00 **Colombia** (a) > (w) 0-**2**
Santa Cruz 4, Chilavert 90

Nov 00 **Peru** (h) > (w) **5**-1
Santa Cruz 15, Del Solar 25 og,
Cardozo 44, Paredes 65, Chilavert 84 pen

Mar 01 **Uruaguay** (a) > (w) 0-**1**
Alvarenga 64

Apr 01 **Ecuador** (a) > (l) 2-**1** Cardozo 26

Jun 01 **Chile** (h) > (w) **1**-0 Paredes 90

Aug 01 **Brazil** (a) > (l) 2-**0**

Sep 01 **Bolivia** (h) > (w) **5**-1
Paredes 33, Cardozo 45, 89, Chilavert 50,
Santa Cruz 69

Oct 01 **Argentina** (h) > (d) **2**-2
Chilavert 51 pen, Morinigo 70

Nov 01 **Venezuela** (a) > (l) 3-**1** Arce 28 pen

Nov 01 **Colombia** (h) > (l) 0-4

## ★ FINAL GROUP TABLE

| Team | P | W | D | L | F | A | Pts |
|------|---|---|---|---|---|---|-----|
| Argentina | 18 | 13 | 4 | 1 | 42 | 15 | 43 |
| Ecuador | 18 | 9 | 4 | 5 | 23 | 20 | 31 |
| Brazil | 18 | 9 | 3 | 6 | 31 | 17 | 30 |
| **Paraguay** | **18** | **9** | **3** | **6** | **29** | **23** | **30** |
| Uruguay | 18 | 7 | 6 | 5 | 19 | 13 | 27 |
| Colombia | 18 | 7 | 6 | 5 | 20 | 15 | 27 |
| Bolivia | 18 | 4 | 6 | 8 | 21 | 33 | 18 |
| Peru | 18 | 4 | 4 | 10 | 14 | 25 | 16 |
| Venezuela | 18 | 5 | 1 | 12 | 18 | 44 | 16 |
| Chile | 18 | 3 | 3 | 12 | 15 | 27 | 12 |

## ★ RECENT RESULTS

Feb 02 **Bolivia** (h) > (d) **2**-2
Cardozo 3, Struway 90

Mar 02 **Nigeria** (h) > (d) **1**-1 Gamarra 24

*José Luis Chilavert, penalty taker, free kick specialist and part-time goalkeeper.*

## DID YOU KNOW?

Cesare Maldini is not the first Italian to take charge of Paraguay. Vessilio Bartoli was given the job almost 50 years ago.

The Paraguay line-up could undergo radical change if new boss Cesare Maldini decides to switch from Paraguay's regular 4-4-2 to a 3-5-2; the formation he used with Italy during France 98. Assuming Maldini opts for no change at this late stage, the back four will consist of full backs Francisco Arce and Denis Canizaand Carlos Gamarra and Celso Ayala in the centre. If Maldini goes for 3-5-2 then Pedro Sarabia will join them. Roberto Acuna is the key player out on the right of midfield – Maldini might want to switch him inside with the tenacious Carlos Paredes in the middle alongside Victor Quintana. Guido Alvarenga provides the speed down the left (or probable wing-back role along with Arce, if the formation is changed). Hugo Brizuela and Roque Santa Cruz provide the little and large in attack. Free roaming goalkeeper José Luis Chilavert (and aspirant goalscorer) misses the first game with Ricardo Tavarelli his probable replacement.

# PROBABLE FORMATION 4-4-2

CHILAVERT

ARCE

CANIZA

GAMARRA

AYALA

ACUNA

QUINTANA

PAREDES

ALVARENGA

SANTA CRUZ

BRIZUELA

## ★ MEN THAT MATTER!

### JOSÉ LUIS CHILAVERT

Age>> 36

Club>> Strasbourg

Suspended from the first match following a spitting incident in the qualifiers. Takes and saves penalties and free kicks and intends to become the first goalkeeper to score at a World Cup.

### CARLOS PAREDES

Age>> 25

Club>> FC Porto

This versatile midfielder can be used as a man-marker or as a creative player. He has been an automatic choice for Paraguay ever since the last World Cup.

### ROBERTO ACUNA

Age>> 30

Club>> Real Zaragoza

Paraguay's most capped international is a major creative influence and presence on the right side of midfield. Played at the last World Cup and missed just two games during qualifying.

## ★ PROBABLE SQUAD  ★ QUALIFICATION RECORD

| NAME | POSITION | CLUB | APS/GOALS | GAMES | MINS | Y/C | R/C | GOALS |
|---|---|---|---|---|---|---|---|---|
| Aldo Bobadilla | Goalkeeper | Cerro Porteno, Paraguay | 3/0 | 2 | 180 | 0 | 0 | 0 |
| Jose Luis Chilavert | Goalkeeper | Strasbourg, France | 67/8 | 14 | 1260 | 5 | 0 | 4 |
| Ricardo Tavarelli | Goalkeeper | Olimpia, Paraguay | 17/0 | 1 | 90 | 0 | 0 | 0 |
| Francisco Arce | Defender | Palmeiras, Brazil | 48/5 | 10 | 880 | 0 | 0 | 1 |
| Celso Ayala | Defender | River Plate, Argentina | 73/6 | 16 | 1431 | 2 | 1 | 1 |
| Denis Caniza | Defender | Santos Laguna, Mexico | 46/1 | 12 | 1080 | 2 | 0 | 0 |
| Paula Da Siva | Defender | Venezia, Italy | 3/0 | 3 | 252 | 0 | 0 | 0 |
| Carlos Gamarra | Defender | AEK Athens, Greece | 73/4 | 13 | 1100 | 0 | 0 | 0 |
| Claudio Rodriguez | Defender | San Lorenzo, Argentina | 4/0 | 4 | 288 | 1 | 0 | 0 |
| Pedro Sarabia | Defender | River Plate, Argentina | 39/0 | 8 | 720 | 0 | 0 | 0 |
| Roberto Acuna | Midfielder | Real Zaragoza, Spain | 76/5 | 15 | 1266 | 4 | 0 | 1 |
| Guido Alvarenga | Midfielder | Leon, Mexico | 15/2 | 7 | 441 | 1 | 0 | 1 |
| Jorge Campos | Midfielder | Universidad Catilica, Chile | 29/3 | 6 | 187 | 0 | 0 | 1 |
| Julio Cesar Enciso | Midfielder | Olimpia, Paraguay | 59/2 | 8 | 546 | 1 | 0 | 0 |
| Diego Gavilan | Midfielder | Newcastle, England | 17/0 | 5 | 254 | 2 | 0 | 0 |
| Gustavo Morinigo | Midfielder | Libertad, Paraguay | 8/1 | 3 | 146 | 2 | 0 | 1 |
| Carlos Paredes | Midfielder | Porto, Portugal | 38/6 | 14 | 1182 | 3 | 0 | 3 |
| Victor Quintana | Midfielder | Olimpia, Paraguay | 18/0 | 13 | 706 | 2 | 1 | 0 |
| Estanislao Struway | Midfielder | Libertad, Paraguay | 67/3 | 13 | 847 | 3 | 0 | 0 |
| Miguel Benitez | Forward | Olimpia, Paraguay | 29/11 | 5 | 73 | 1 | 0 | 0 |
| Hugo Brizuela | Forward | Pachuca, Mexico | 21/3 | 7 | 364 | 1 | 1 | 2 |
| Jose Cardozo | Forward | Toluca, Mexico | 55/15 | 15 | 1218 | 2 | 0 | 6 |
| Roque Santa Cruz | Forward | Bayern Munich, Germany | 21/7 | 12 | 904 | 1 | 0 | 3 |

KEY: APPS/GOALS = International Appearances/Goals; GAMES=Qualification Games played; MINS=Minutes played; Y/C= Yellow cards R/C=Red cards

# HISTORY AT THE WORLD CUP

**1998 >** Jorge Campos battles with Bulgaria's Anatoli Nankov.

**1998 >** Chilavert's free kick against Bulgaria nearly provides the World Cup with its first goalscoring keeper.

**1986 >** South American Footballer of the Year Julio Romero helps Paraguay to the second round.

**1950 >** Paraguay qualifies without playing a game after Ecuador and Peru withdraw.

**1958 >** Paraguay give one of the team's best performances to beat Uruguay 5-0 in qualifying.

**1962 >** Paraguay lose inter-continental play-off to Mexico and miss out on Finals in Chile.

## ★ WORLD CUP HISTORY

| | | | |
|---|---|---|---|
| **1930** >> First Round | | **1970** >> Did Not Qualify | |
| **1934** >> Did Not Enter | | **1974** >> Did Not Qualify | |
| **1938** >> Did Not Enter | | **1978** >> Did Not Qualify | |
| **1950** >> First Round | | **1982** >> Did Not Qualify | |
| **1954** >> Did Not Qualify | | **1986** >> Second Round | |
| **1958** >> First Round | | **1990** >> Did Not Qualify | |
| **1962** >> Did Not Qualify | | **1994** >> Did Not Qualify | |
| **1966** >> Did Not Qualify | | **1998** >> Second Round | |

## ★ WORLD CUP RECORDS, STORIES AND WEIRDNESS

**FIRST OWN GOAL** >> Ramon Gonzales of Paraguay holds the honour of scoring the World Cup's first ever own goal – against the United States in 1930. The USA won 3-0.

| OPPONENT | DATE | UK TIME | VENUE |
|---|---|---|---|
| South Korea | **4 June** | 12.30 | **Busan, Korea** |
| Portugal | **10 June** | 12.30 | **Jeonju, Korea** |
| USA | **14 June** | 12.30 | **Daejeon, Korea** |

## "back to form and a tournament dark horse"

# POLAND

It's easy to forget that Poland were once one of the best sides in world football. By the end of the 1999-2000 season Poland had not won a single match of their eight internationals and had once again failed to qualify for a major tournament. Their new boss Jerzy Engel saw his team score just once in his first five games in charge and few, if any, gave the Poles a hope of reaching the 2002 World Cup Finals.

Then Nigerian-born striker Emmanuel Olisadebe took Polish Citizenship and set about transforming the national team – with a staggering 10 goals in his first 13 internationals. He scored on his debut in a friendly against Romania in Bucharest to earn a 1-1 draw, starting a run of 13 matches without a defeat; the longest unbeaten run by a Polish national side.

Engel's re-vitalised Poland has been built around a well-organised defence and a devastatingly effective counter-attacking game that exploits the pace and power of Olisadebe. The new Poland unveiled itself in Kiev against the Ukraine in front of a 55,000 crowd. Olisadebe gave Poland the lead twice in the 3rd and 33rd minute and midfielder Radoslaw Kaluzny put the result beyond doubt in the 57th. That 3-1 victory ended a 10-match run without a win.

Not that the Polish public thought much of it. Only 7,000 fans turned up for qualifier against the Belarus in which Kaluzny was outstanding, netting a hat-trick in another 3-1 win. A 0-0 draw at home to Wales saw Poland revert to type, but events in Oslo in March 2001 proved once and for all that Poland with Olisadebe was now an attacking, goal scoring side to compare with their illustrious forebears.

Olisadebe found the net twice in six minutes to give Poland a 2-0 lead by the 29th minute. Norway battled back to level terms by the 66th minute and with just nine minutes to go substitute midfielder Bartosz Karwan scored the winner. Four days later Poland thrashed Armenia 4-0, sparking a rush for tickets (the game in Bydgoszcz was sold out in a day) for the friendly with Scotland a month later.

Back on the qualification trail at Cardiff's Millennium Stadium, and Poland trail Wales after just 13 minutes. In the past the Poles would have capitulated but now they come from behind – thanks to goals from Pawel Kryszalowicz and, inevitably, Olisadebe for a 2-1 win. A bad-tempered 1-1 draw in Armenia, which ends in a brawl and the sending off of defender Jacek Bak, earns another point, which means a win at home to Norway would be enough for qualification.

Poland were in the in form team having now gone 12 matches without defeat – a performance that'd not been seen since the mid-seventies during the golden age of Polish soccer when they were semi-finalists at successive World Cups. Poland earned a deserved 3-0 win with goals from Kryszalowicz, Olisadebe and Marcin Zewlakow and magnificent goalkeeping performance by Jerzy Dudek.

Poland are back and will be one of the World Cup's dark horses. Coach Jerzy Engel has a settled pool of 25 players of roughly equal ability including goalkeeper Dudek, who at £4.9 million became Poland's most expensive player ever when he joined Liverpool.

## ★ THE LOWDOWN

**Population:** 38.6 million

**Capital:** Warsaw

**Leader:** Leszek Miller

**Life Expectancy:** Male: 69 yrs
Female: 78 yrs

>> Poland is one of the world's largest producers of silver.

>> Despite a reputation as a country with pollution problems, Poland does have many unspoilt regions of natural beauty. It is home to the last surviving virgin forest of the European mainland, which is inhabited by the largest herd of European bison.

>> In 1989, after over 40 years of communist rule, the Trade Union leader Lech Walesa formed the first post-communist democratic government.

★ **ASSOCIATION:** Polski Zwiazek Pilki Noznej

★ **JOINED FIFA:** 1923

★ **JOINED UEFA:** 1954

★ **PLAYERS:** 317,500

★ **CLUBS:** 5,881

★ **WEBSITE:** www.pzpn.pl

★ **HONOURS:** Olympics – 1972.

*Bartosz Karwan and France's Emmanuel Petit.*

## ★ ROAD TO QUALIFICATION

**Sep 00 Ukraine** (a) > (w) 1-**3**
Olizadebe 3, Nowak 33, Kaluzny 55

**Oct 00 Belarus** (h) > (w) **3**-1
Kaluzny 25, 62, 73

**Oct 00 Wales** (h) > (d) **0**-0

**Mar 01 Norway** (a) > (w) 2-**3**
Olizadebe 23, 30, Karwan 81

**Mar 01 Armenia** (h) > (w) **4**-0
Zewlakow, Mi 15 pen, 81, Olizadebe 41, Karwan 88

**Jun 01 Wales** (a) > (w) 1-**2**
Olizadebe 32, Kryszalowicz 72

**Jun 01 Armenia** (a) > (d) 1-**1** Kaluzny 5

**Sep 01 Norway** (h) > (w) **3**-0
Kryszalowicz 45, Olizadebe 77, Zewlakow, Ma 87

**Sep 01 Belarus** (a) > (l) 4-**1**
Zewlakow, Ma 78

**Oct 01 Ukraine** (h) > (d) **1**-1 Olizadebe 40

## ★ FINAL GROUP TABLE

| Team | P | W | D | L | F | A | Pts |
|---|---|---|---|---|---|---|---|
| Poland | 10 | 6 | 3 | 1 | 21 | 11 | 21 |
| Ukraine | 10 | 4 | 5 | 1 | 13 | 8 | 17 |
| Belarus | 10 | 4 | 3 | 3 | 12 | 11 | 15 |
| Norway | 10 | 2 | 4 | 4 | 12 | 14 | 10 |
| Wales | 10 | 1 | 6 | 3 | 10 | 12 | 9 |
| Armenia | 10 | 0 | 5 | 5 | 7 | 19 | 5 |

## ★ RECENT RESULTS

**Feb 02 Northern Ireland** (h) > (w) **4**-1
Kryszalowicz 6, 64, Kaluzny 12, Zewlakow, Mi 69

**Mar 02 Japan** (h) > (l) **0**-2

## DID YOU KNOW?

Wladyslaw Zmuda made 22 appearances over four World Cups in 1974, 1978, 1982 and 1986.

**Poland play an attack-minded** 4-4-2 system that always looks to release the pace-blessed goalscoring machine Emmanuel Olisadebe. Poland know that given just half a chance, this super-quick and skilful striker will score. Add Olisadebe's partner, the equally quick Pawel Kryszalowicz, and opponents find that they're often hit before they know it. Piotr Swierczewski is the team's experienced midfield playmaker who looks to exploit the pace in attack and on the wings through Bartosz Karwan on the right and Marek Kozminski on the left. Radoslaw Kaluzny anchors the midfield but will show his goalscoring abilities from free kicks and corners. The two Tomaszs, Hajto and Waldoch, are the uncompromising centre backs with Tomasz Klos and the excellent Michal Zewlakow at full back. And once past them, there's Liverpool's Jerzy Dudek in goal.

## PROBABLE FORMATION 4-4-2

DUDEK

KLOS — Michael ZEWLAKOW

HAJTO — WALDOCH

KARWAN — KALUZNY — SWIERCZEWSKI — KOZMINSKI

KRYSZALOWICZ — OLISADEBE

## ★ MEN THAT MATTER!

### EMMANUAL OLISADEBE

Age>> 23
Club>> Panathiniakos
Nigerian-born striker regarded as one of the most talented players in the world. Boasts an enviable international strike rate — his first 13 games reaped 10 goals including eight in the qualifiers.

### JERZY DUDEK

Age>> 29
Club>> Liverpool
Poland's most expensive player, and goalkeeper, after Liverpool signed him from Feyenoord for £4.9 million. Magnificent during qualifying particularly against Norway where Poland clinched their place in the Finals.

### MICHAEL ZEWLAKOW

Age>> 26
Club>> Mouscron
A gifted attack-minded left back who was the only Polish player ever-present during qualifiers. He is also a formidable free-kick specialist adding to Poland's thriving array of attacking options.

## ★ PROBABLE SQUAD | ★ QUALIFICATION RECORD

| NAME | POSITION | CLUB | APS/GOALS | GAMES | MINS | Y/C | R/C | GOALS |
|------|----------|------|-----------|-------|------|-----|-----|-------|
| Jerzy Dudek | Goalkeeper | Liverpool, England | 19/0 | 10 | 835 | 0 | 0 | 0 |
| Radoslaw Majdan | Goalkeeper | Goztepe, Turkey | 2/0 | 0 | 0 | 0 | 0 | 0 |
| Adam Matysek | Goalkeeper | Zaglebie, Poland | 33/0 | 1 | 65 | 0 | 0 | 0 |
| Jacek Bak | Defender | Lens, France | 33/1 | 4 | 194 | 0 | 0 | 0 |
| Tomasz Hajto | Defender | Schalke, Germany | 41/5 | 7 | 546 | 2 | 0 | 0 |
| Tomasz Klos | Defender | Kaiserslautern, Germany | 34/1 | 9 | 804 | 1 | 0 | 0 |
| Mariusz Kukielka | Defender | Amica Wronki, Poland | 8/0 | 1 | 90 | 0 | 0 | 0 |
| Tomasz Waldoch | Defender | Schalke, Germany | 68/2 | 6 | 540 | 0 | 0 | 0 |
| Michal Zewlakow | Defender | Mouscron, Belgium | 21/1 | 10 | 888 | 0 | 0 | 2 |
| Jacek Zielinski | Defender | Legia Warsaw, Poland | 48/1 | 5 | 450 | 0 | 0 | 0 |
| Arkadiusz Bak | Midfielder | Birmingham, England | 8/0 | 4 | 360 | 1 | 0 | 0 |
| Tomasz Iwan | Midfielder | Austria Wien, Austria | 37/4 | 5 | 327 | 1 | 0 | 0 |
| Jacek Krynowek | Midfielder | Nurnberg, Germany | 15/2 | 5 | 182 | 1 | 0 | 0 |
| Radoslaw Kaluzny | Midfielder | Energie Cottbus, Germany | 26/9 | 7 | 578 | 3 | 0 | 5 |
| Bartosz Karwan | Midfielder | Legia Warsaw, Poland | 15/3 | 7 | 467 | 0 | 0 | 2 |
| Marek Kozminski | Midfielder | Brescia, Italy | 38/1 | 8 | 632 | 1 | 0 | 0 |
| Jacek Krzynowek | Midfielder | Nurnberg, Germany | 19/1 | 4 | 150 | 0 | 0 | 0 |
| Piotr Swierczewski | Midfielder | Marseille, France | 62/1 | 9 | 795 | 2 | 0 | 0 |
| Tomasz Zdebel | Midfielder | Genclerbirligi, Turkey | 9/0 | 3 | 71 | 1 | 0 | 0 |
| Pawel Kryszalowicz | Forward | Eintracht Frankfurt, Germany | 19/3 | 8 | 507 | 1 | 0 | 2 |
| Emmanuel Olisadebe | Forward | Panathinaikos, Greece | 13/10 | 9 | 707 | 0 | 0 | 7 |
| Radoslav Gilewicz | Forward | Tirol Innsbruck, Austria | 9/0 | 3 | 106 | 0 | 0 | 0 |
| Maciej Zurawski | Forward | Wisla Krakow, Poland | 7/0 | 0 | 0 | 0 | 0 | 0 |

**KEY:** APPS/GOALS = International Appearances/Goals; GAMES=Qualification Games played; MINS=Minutes played; Y/C= Yellow cards R/C=Red cards

# HISTORY AT THE WORLD CUP

**1930 1934 1938 1950 1954 1958 1962 1966 1970 1974 1978 1982 1986 1990 1994 1998**

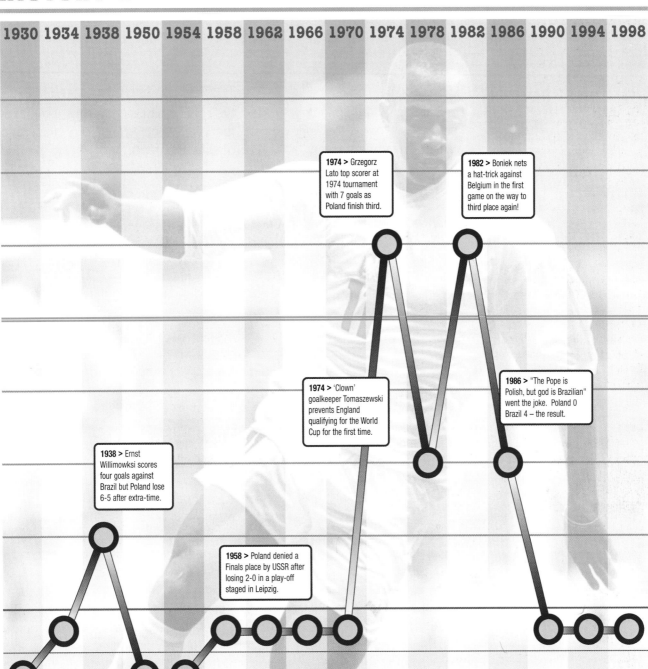

**1974 >** Grzegorz Lato top scorer at 1974 tournament with 7 goals as Poland finish third.

**1982 >** Boniek nets a hat-trick against Belgium in the first game on the way to third place again!

**1974 >** 'Clown' goalkeeper Tomaszewski prevents England qualifying for the World Cup for the first time.

**1986 >** "The Pope is Polish, but god is Brazilian" went the joke. Poland 0 Brazil 4 – the result.

**1938 >** Ernst Willimowksi scores four goals against Brazil but Poland lose 6-5 after extra-time.

**1958 >** Poland denied a Finals place by USSR after losing 2-0 in a play-off staged in Leipzig.

## ★ WORLD CUP HISTORY

| 1930 >> Did Not Enter | 1970 >> Did Not Qualify |
|---|---|
| 1934 >> Did Not Qualify | 1974 >> Third Place |
| 1938 >> First Round | 1978 >> Second Round |
| 1950 >> Did Not Enter | 1982 >> Third Place |
| 1954 >> Did Not Enter | 1986 >> Second Round |
| 1958 >> Did Not Qualify | 1990 >> Did Not Qualify |
| 1962 >> Did Not Qualify | 1994 >> Did Not Qualify |
| 1966 >> Did Not Qualify | 1998 >> Did Not Qualify |

## ★ WORLD CUP RECORDS, STORIES AND WEIRDNESS

**MOST APPEARANCES IN FINALS** >> Grzegorz Lato with 20 appearances is 4th on the all-time list.

**MOST GOALS** >> Along with Deyna and Szarmach, Grzegorz Lato was one of the stars of the Polish side which took third place in the 1974 World Cup. Lato scored 7 times in the 1974 finals and totalled 10 in all his World Cup appearances.

**MOST GOALS IN A MATCH** >> Ernst Willimowski with 4 against Brazil in 1938.

| OPPONENT | DATE | UK TIME | VENUE |
|---|---|---|---|
| USA | **5 June** | 10.00 | **Suwon, Korea** |
| Poland | **10 June** | 12.30 | **Jeonju, Korea** |
| South Korea | **14 June** | 12.30 | **Incheon, Korea** |

## "flair wrapped in an enigma"

# PORTUGAL

Portugal are an enigmatic side blessed with one of the world's most talented and expensive midfield partnerships. European Footballer of the Year and highly influential Luis Figo, Portugal's most capped player with 80 appearances, is worth a staggering £37.5 million to Real Madrid and his partner Rui Costa is a £28 million Serie A midfielder with AC Milan. Both players performed gloriously at Euro 2000 as the creative engine of Portugal's free flowing, exciting side.

At Euro 2000 Portugal reached the semi-finals playing some fantastic football, most notably against Kevin Keegan's England. The Portuguese came from 2-0 down to win 3-2 in their opening game, beat Romania with an injury-time winner from Francisco Da Costa and outclassed Germany with a Sergio Conceicao hat-trick before defeating Turkey 2-0 in the quarter-finals.

Their thrilling run came to an end at the semi-final stage when they were knocked out by a golden goal, France's Zinedane Zidane converting from the penalty spot after Abel Xavier was adjudged, by the linesman, to have handled Sylvain Wiltord 's shot. While France celebrated, Portugal's too vigorous protests led to the dismissal of Nuno Gomes and later suspensions for Abel Xavier.

More controversy was to follow when Portuguese defender Fernando Couto tested positive for banned substance nandrolone while playing with Lazio. He received a worldwide 10-month ban (later reduced to four months).

Back on the field Portugal continued to play their entertaining brand of football, winning their World Cup qualifying group and seeing to the elimination of Holland in the process. The Portuguese took four points off the Dutch, winning in Eindhoven with two goals from Sergio Conceicao and Pauleta. In the return fixture, the Dutch looked to have taken their revenge, establishing a two-goal lead. But a late goal from Pauleta and a last minute penalty from Figo forced the draw.

Against the Republic of Ireland, Portugal drew 1-1 both home and away. Their main rivals dealt with, Portugal were left with an easy last few qualification furlongs and in flew the goals; against Cyprus 6-0, Moldova 3-0 (a Figo hat-trick), Andorra 7-1 (Nuno Gomes 4 goals), Cyprus again 3-1 and Estonia 5-0. They deservedly topped the group.

Portugal have only ever been occasional World Cup participants. In 1966, the Eusebio-inspired team reached the semi-finals, losing to England at Wembley. In the heat of Mexico in 1986, defeats by Poland and Morocco, after they'd beaten England, led to a first round exit. The Portuguese have certainly got better since then and have added strength and resilience (in players like Nuno Frechaut, Jorge Costa and Petit) to their undoubtedly skilful game. Now they are much less likely to be pushed aside.

On their day, as they have shown frequently over the past two years, Portugal can be flair personified and just about impossible to deal with. An unpredictable World Cup dark horse that could surprise us all.

## ★ THE LOWDOWN

**Population:** 10 million

**Capital:** Lisbon

**Leader:** Antonio Gutteres

**Life Expectancy:** Male: 72 yrs Female: 79 yrs

>> Portugal is one of the oldest European nations and Portuguese is the most commonly spoken language in South America.

>> At over 1000 metres, Guarda in central Portugal is claimed by its inhabitants to be the highest city in Europe.

>> Bobby Robson, the former England and current Newcastle United Manager, has managed Portugal's two biggest football clubs – F C Porto and Sporting Lisbon.

- ★ **ASSOCIATION:** Federacao Portuguese de Futebol
- ★ **JOINED FIFA:** 1928
- ★ **JOINED UEFA:** 1954
- ★ **PLAYERS:** 79,300
- ★ **CLUBS:** 204
- ★ **WEBSITE:** www.fpf.pt
- ★ **HONOURS:** None

Luis Figo – the world's best player.

## ★ ROAD TO QUALIFICATION

**Sep 00 Estonia** (a) > (w) 1-**3**
Rui Costa 15, Figo 49, Sa Pinto 56

**Oct 00 Rep of Ireland** (h) > (d) **1**-1
Conceicao 57

**Oct 00 Holland** (a) > (w) 0-**2**
Conceicao 10, Pauleta 44

**Feb 01 Andorra** (h) > (w) **3**-0
Figo 1, 49, Pauleta 35

**Mar 01 Holland** (h) > (d) 2-2
Pauleta 85, Figo 90 pen

**Jun 01 Rep of Ireland** (a) > (d) 1-**1** Figo 79

**Jun 01 Cyprus** (h) > (w) **6**-0
Pauleta 36, 71, Barbosa 55, 59,
Pinto 76, 81

**Sep 01 Andorra** (a) > (w) 1-**7**
Nuno Gomes 36, 40, 45, 90, Pauleta 39,
Rui Jorge 45, Conceicao 58

**Sep 01 Cyprus** (a) > (w) 1-**3**
Nuno Gomes 47, Pauleta 64, Conceicao 71

**Oct 01 Estonia** (h) > (w) **5**-0
Pinto 29, Nuno Gomes 49, 65, Pauleta 59,
Figo 79

## ★ FINAL GROUP TABLE

| Team | P | W | D | L | F | A | Pts |
|---|---|---|---|---|---|---|---|
| Portugal | 10 | 7 | 3 | 0 | 33 | 7 | 24 |
| Rep of Ireland | 10 | 7 | 3 | 0 | 23 | 5 | 24 |
| Netherlands | 10 | 6 | 2 | 2 | 30 | 9 | 20 |
| Estonia | 10 | 2 | 2 | 6 | 10 | 26 | 8 |
| Cyprus | 10 | 2 | 2 | 6 | 13 | 31 | 8 |
| Andorra | 10 | 0 | 0 | 10 | 5 | 36 | 0 |

## ★ RECENT RESULTS

**Feb 02 Spain** (a) > (d) 1-**1** Costa 28

**Mar 02 Finland** (h) > (l) **1**-4 Conceicao 40

## DID YOU KNOW?

**In Portugal's first World Cup they reached the semi-finals. They were due to play England at Goodison Park, where the Portuguese had been based, but the tie was switched to Wembley.**

Impressively, Portugal scored 33 goals in ten qualifying games – amazing when you consider that the Portuguese play with only one recognised striker, Pauleta. But what Pauleta had in support would make any lone forward green with envy. A quality five-man midfield that can quickly get forward in numbers led by central play-maker Rui Costa of Milan. To Rui Costa's right is FIFA World Player of the Year Luis Figo. To his left is the pacy Nuno Capucho. Just hanging slightly back from that trio is the defensive midfield pairing of Beto and Petit, with the latter encouraged to join the attack whenever possible. The experienced defenders, Fernando Couto, Jorge Costa and Rui Jorge, are joined by new boy Frechaut to complete a back four. While Vitor Baia has been out injured, Ricardo has been first choice goalkeeper and could well retain his place.

## PROBABLE FORMATION 4-4-2

RICARDO

FERNANDO COUTO — JORGE COSTA

FRECHAUT — RUI JORGE

FIGO — BETO — RUI COSTA — PETIT

NUNO CAPUCHO

PAULETA

## ★ MEN THAT MATTER!

### LUIS FIGO

Age>> 29

Club>> R. Madrid

The FIFA World Player of the Year signed by Real Madrid for £37.5 million. He was outstanding for Portugal at Euro 2000 and throughout Portugal's qualifying group.

### RUI COSTA

Age>> 30

Club>> AC Milan

Rui Costa is an attacking midfielder worth £28 million of Milan's money. His influence alongside Figo cannot be underestimated often producing an exciting and unexpected piece of play. An exquisite penalty taker too!

### PAULETA

Age>> 29

Club>> Bordeaux

Pauleta was Portugal's top scorer during qualifying with eight goals. His agility, speed and accuracy finally earned his place in the starting line-up.

## ★ PROBABLE SQUAD ★ QUALIFICATION RECORD

| NAME | POSITION | CLUB | APS/GOALS | GAMES | MINS | Y/C | R/C | GOALS |
|------|----------|------|-----------|-------|------|-----|-----|-------|
| Quim | Goalkeeper | Sp Braga, Portugal | 12/0 | 5 | 450 | 1 | 0 | 0 |
| Ricardo | Goalkeeper | Boavista, Portugal | 7/0 | 5 | 450 | 0 | 0 | 0 |
| Pereira | Goalkeeper | Boavista, Portugal | 7/0 | 0 | 0 | 0 | 0 | 0 |
| Beto | Defender | Sp Lisbon, Portugal | 16/1 | 6 | 540 | 0 | 0 | 0 |
| Fernando Couto | Defender | Lazio, Italy | 80/6 | 6 | 496 | 1 | 0 | 0 |
| Fernando Meira | Defender | Stuttgart, Germany | 7/0 | 4 | 145 | 0 | 0 | 0 |
| Nuno Frechaut | Defender | Boavista, Portugal | 7/0 | 5 | 400 | 0 | 0 | 0 |
| Manuel Dimas | Defender | Sp Lisbon, Portugal | 44/0 | 2 | 178 | 1 | 0 | 0 |
| Jorge Costa | Defender | Charlton, England | 44/2 | 7 | 566 | 1 | 0 | 0 |
| Rui Jorge | Defender | Sp Lisbon, Portugal | 18/1 | 8 | 646 | 1 | 0 | 1 |
| Nuno Capucho | Midfielder | Porto, Portugal | 28/2 | 8 | 379 | 0 | 0 | 0 |
| Luis Figo | Midfielder | Real Madrid, Spain | 80/27 | 9 | 810 | 2 | 0 | 6 |
| Paulo Bento | Midfielder | Porto, Portugal | 30/0 | 3 | 100 | 0 | 0 | 0 |
| Paulo Sousa | Midfielder | Panathinaikos, Greece | 50/0 | 2 | 114 | 0 | 0 | 0 |
| Petit | Midfielder | Boavista, Portugal | 7/0 | 5 | 417 | 1 | 0 | 0 |
| Rui Costa | Midfielder | Milan, Italy | 67/20 | 8 | 717 | 0 | 0 | 1 |
| Sergio Conceicao | Midfielder | Internazionale, Italy | 39/9 | 6 | 508 | 0 | 0 | 4 |
| Pedro Barbosa | Midfielder | Sp Lisbon, Portugal | 20/5 | 2 | 143 | 0 | 0 | 2 |
| Joao Pinto | Forward | Sp Lisbon, Portugal | 74/23 | 8 | 455 | 0 | 0 | 3 |
| Nuno Gomes | Forward | Fiorentina, Italy | 27/13 | 6 | 280 | 0 | 0 | 7 |
| Pauleta | Forward | Bordeaux, France | 30/12 | 10 | 740 | 0 | 0 | 8 |
| Ricardo Sa Pinto | Forward | Sp Lisbon, Portugal | 45/10 | 4 | 188 | 0 | 0 | 1 |
| Sabrosa Simao | Forward | Benfica, Portugal | 11/1 | 6 | 182 | 0 | 0 | 0 |

**KEY:** APPS/GOALS = International Appearances/Goals; GAMES=Qualification Games played; MINS=Minutes played; Y/C= Yellow cards R/C=Red cards

# HISTORY AT THE WORLD CUP

1930 1934 1938 1950 1954 1958 1962 1966 1970 1974 1978 1982 1986 1990 1994 1998

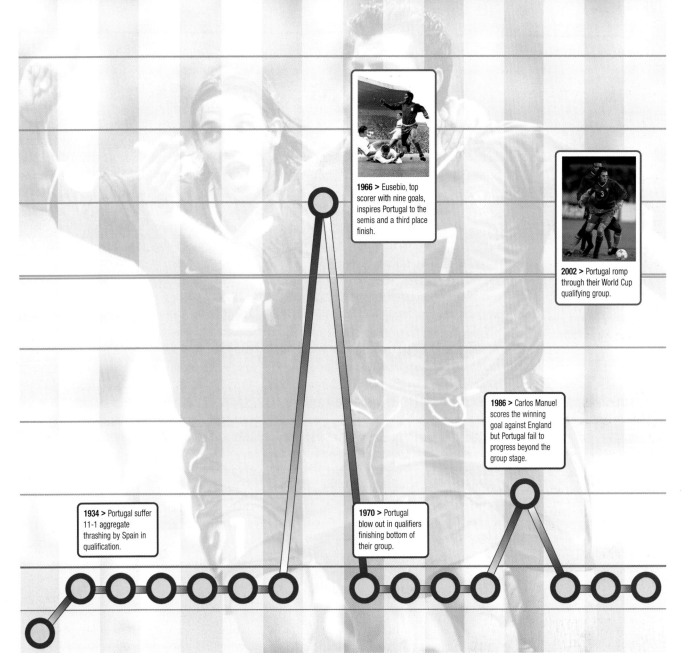

**1966 >** Eusebio, top scorer with nine goals, inspires Portugal to the semis and a third place finish.

**2002 >** Portugal romp through their World Cup qualifying group.

**1986 >** Carlos Manuel scores the winning goal against England but Portugal fail to progress beyond the group stage.

**1934 >** Portugal suffer 11-1 aggregate thrashing by Spain in qualification.

**1970 >** Portugal blow out in qualifiers finishing bottom of their group.

## ★ WORLD CUP HISTORY

| | | | |
|---|---|---|---|
| 1930 >> Did Not Enter | 1970 >> Did Not Qualify |
| 1934 >> Did Not Qualify | 1974 >> Did Not Qualify |
| 1938 >> Did Not Qualify | 1978 >> Did Not Qualify |
| 1950 >> Did Not Qualify | 1982 >> Did Not Qualify |
| 1954 >> Did Not Qualify | 1986 >> First Round |
| 1958 >> Did Not Qualify | 1990 >> Did Not Qualify |
| 1962 >> Did Not Qualify | 1994 >> Did Not Qualify |
| 1966 >> Third Place | 1998 >> Did Not Qualify |

## ★ WORLD CUP RECORDS, STORIES AND WEIRDNESS

**MOST GOALS** >> Eusebio won the first of his 64 caps in 1961, but will be best remembered for his contribution to the 1966 World Cup. "The Black Pearl" was quite brilliant, scoring some outstanding goals. Nine goals made him the tournament's top scorer and he managed to net four in Portugal's remarkable fight-back against North Korea

# GROUP H

| OPPONENT | DATE | UK TIME | VENUE |
|----------|------|---------|-------|
| Tunisia | **5 June** | 07.30 | **Kobe, Japan** |
| Japan | **9 June** | 12.30 | **Yokohama, Japan** |
| Belgium | **14 June** | 07.30 | **Shizuoka, Japan** |

## "old bears hope for a quarter-final place"

# RUSSIA

### ★ THE LOWDOWN

**Population:** 145.4 million

**Capital:** Moscow

**Leader:** Vladimir Putin

**Life Expectancy:** Male: 62 yrs Female: 73 yrs

>> Russia is just about 1.8 times the size of the United States of America.

>> Tourists beware; permafrost covers much of Siberia, there is volcanic activity in the Kuril Islands and earthquakes and volcanic eruptions on the Kamachatka Peninsula.

>> Vodka – Russians traditionally drink their vodka neat, chilled, but without ice, during meals. Well, it's rude not to!

The Russian national side is an ageing team. The fragmentation of the Soviet Union in the early 90s meant Russia having to create a new side without a host of players from the former Soviet Republics and since that time Russia's national side has largely remained the same. Players such as Valeri Karpin, Alexander Mostovoi, Victor Onopko, Dmitri Khlestov, Vladimir Beschastnykh and Omari Tetradze were wearing the Russian shirt in 1992 and are still.

As younger players they qualified for both World Cup 94 and Euro 96, although failing to progress beyond the group stage of either tournament. But it must be said that as the squad has got older their threat has lessened and Russia failed to qualify for either France 98 or Euro 2000.

Euro 96 coach Oleg Romantsev was recalled to manage the Russian side (he retains his day job as coach of the country's dominant club, Spartak Moscow) and immediately expressed a wish to return to the old Soviet-style system of a national side based around one club – Spartak Moscow. But things aren't what they were and even the Russian League has seen an influx of foreign players – as has Spartak themselves. So, as it is all over Europe, young home-grown talent has been hard to find.

Romantsev has been forced to abandon the 'Spartak as Russia' plan, but continues a policy of selecting predominantly Russian-based players, which has led to a Russian squad mainly selected from the Russian League with many players such as Beschastnykh, Sergei Ovchinnikov, Alexander Panov and Tetradze returning home. About a quarter of the potential squad still play abroad, mostly in Spain, but all are playing regularly for their clubs.

Much needed new blood has managed to squeeze its way into the side, notably midfielders Rolan Gusev (aged 24) and Marat Izmailov (aged 19) resulting in a switch from a short passing game to a set up that encourages wing play and long passing, although this has not been an overwhelmingly successful ploy – yet.

Russia won their qualifying group grinding out results against modest and downright weak opposition. At home they scored but a single goal against the mighty Faroe Islands and it needed a first international goal from Sergei Semak late in the game to beat Luxembourg 2-1. To Russia's credit they did take four points off a very disappointing Yugoslavia side and did the double over Switzerland. They had needed just a point to qualify in their final game at home to the Swiss and with their best performance of the competition ran out 4-0 winners – Beschastnykh scoring a hat trick with Yegor Titov netting the fourth.

Russia has set the target of reaching at least the quarter-finals in Japan/Korea, but with a defence lacking pace and over reliance on goalkeeper Ruslan Nigmatullin – who does not yet bear comparison with the most successful Russian footballer of all time, Lev Yashin – that may be over ambitious. They're a team that tries to make the best of what it has got but lacks the all round strengths that tougher, more skilful teams will bring to the tournament.

★ **ASSOCIATION:** Football Union of Russia

★ **JOINED FIFA:** 1992

★ **JOINED UEFA:** 1992

★ **PLAYERS:** 785,000

★ **CLUBS:** 43,700

★ **WEBSITE:** www.rfs.ru

★ **HONOURS:** Olympics* – 1956,1988.
European Championships* – 1960
*As USSR

*Rising midfield star Marat Izmailov in full flight.*

## ★ ROAD TO QUALIFICATION

Sep 00 **Switzerland** (a) > (w) 0-**1**
Beschastnykh 74

Oct 00 **Luxembourg** (h) > (w) **3**-0
Buznikin 20, Khokhlov 58, Titov 90

Mar 01 **Slovenia** (h) > (d) **1**-1 Khlestov 8

Mar 01 **Faroe Islands** (h) > (w) **1**-0
Mostovoi 20

Apr 01 **Yugoslavia** (a) > (w) 0-**1**
Beschastnykh 72

Jun 01 **Yugoslavia** (h) > (d) **1**-1 Kovtun 25

Jun 01 **Luxembourg** (a) > (w) 1-**2**
Alenitchev 16, Semak 76

Sep 01 **Slovenia** (a) > (l) 2-**1** Titov 72

Sep 01 **Faroe Islands** (a) > (w) 0-**3**
Beschastnykh 19, 30, Shirko 88

Oct 01 **Switzerland** (h) > (w) **4**-0
Beschastnykh 14 pen, 19, 39, Titov 82

## ★ FINAL GROUP TABLE

| Team | P | W | D | L | F | A | Pts |
|------|---|---|---|---|---|---|-----|
| **Russia** | 10 | 7 | 2 | 1 | 18 | 5 | 23 |
| Slovenia | 10 | 5 | 5 | 0 | 17 | 9 | 20 |
| Yugoslavia | 10 | 5 | 4 | 1 | 22 | 8 | 19 |
| Switzerland | 10 | 4 | 2 | 4 | 18 | 12 | 14 |
| Faroe Islands | 10 | 2 | 1 | 7 | 6 | 23 | 7 |
| Luxembourg | 10 | 0 | 0 | 10 | 4 | 28 | 0 |

## ★ RECENT RESULTS

Feb 02 **Rep of Ireland** (a) > (l) 2-**0**

Mar 02 **Estonia** (a) > (l) 2-**1**
Beschastnykh 18

## DID YOU KNOW?

**World Cup squads have featured brothers on more than one occasion, but Victor and Vyacheslav Chanov share a unique place in football history. Both were selected for the 1982 Soviet Union squad — as goalkeepers!**

Russia's 4-4-2 formation boasts an excellent last line of defence in goalkeeper Ruslan Nigmatullin and an outstanding front line led by striker Vladimir Beschastnykh, who will be partnered by the experienced Alexander Mostovoi. In midfield Russia have two brilliant playmakers in Yegor Titov and rising star Marat Izmailov. It's questionable whether they can or will play together, in which case Dmitri Khoklov is the likely choice. Khoklov can also play in the striker role where he would take Mostovoi's place. While Valeri Karpin is an automatic choice on the right of midfield, the left is problematic. CSKA's Rolan Gusev or Porto's Dmitri Alenichev are the likely candidates. Behind them is Yuri Kovtun at left back. Yuri Drozdov man-marks with more subtlety than Kovtun on the right. In the centre of defence Victor Onopko, Russia's old war-horse, is joined by Igor Chugainov. Yuri Nikiforov, a former forward, is an alternative in the middle of the back four.

## PROBABLE FORMATION  4-4-2

NIGMATULIN

DROZDOV · KOVTUN

ONOPKO · CHUGAINOV

KARPIN · IZMAILOV · TITOV · GUSEV

MOSTOVOI · BESCHASTNYKH

## ★ MEN THAT MATTER!

### RUSLAN NIGMATULLIN

Age>> 27

Club>> Verona

The 2001 Russian Player of the Year who has the reputation as one of the best goalkeepers around after his outstanding performances during qualifying conceding only five goals in ten games.

### VLADIMIR BESCHASTNYKH

Age>> 28

Club>> Moscow Spartak

Beschastnykh is Russia's main striker with seven goals in qualifying. At 18 years, four months and 16 days he was the youngest Russian player ever to make his debut in August 1992 against Mexico.

### MARAT IZMAILOV

Age>> 19

Club>> Lokomotiv Moscow

Izmailov is Russia's teenage sensation who blazed on to the scene at the back end of last year. He can play in attack or as a playmaker. Wanted by both Under-21 and Senior Russian sides.

## ★ PROBABLE SQUAD · ★ QUALIFICATION RECORD

| NAME | POSITION | CLUB | APS/GOALS | GAMES | MINS | Y/C | R/C | GOALS |
|------|----------|------|-----------|-------|------|-----|-----|-------|
| Alexander Filimonov | Goalkeeper | Kyiv Dynamo, Ukraine | 15\0 | 0 | 0 | 0 | 0 | 0 |
| Ruslan Nigmatullin | Goalkeeper | Verona, Italy | 15\0 | 10 | 900 | 0 | 0 | 0 |
| Sergei Goncharov | Goalkeeper | Moscow Spartak, Russia | 0\0 | 0 | 0 | 0 | 0 | 0 |
| Alexei Smertin | Defender | Bordeaux, France | 23\0 | 6 | 454 | 0 | 0 | 0 |
| Igor Chugainov | Defender | Uralan Elista, Russia | 24\0 | 1 | 90 | 0 | 0 | 0 |
| Omari Tetradze | Defender | Alaniya Vladikavkaz, Russia | 36\1 | 4 | 270 | 0 | 0 | 0 |
| Victor Onopko | Defender | Oviedo, Spain | 90\6 | 10 | 900 | 1 | 0 | 0 |
| Vyacheslav Dayev | Defender | CSKA Moscow, Russia | 3\0 | 2 | 155 | 1 | 0 | 0 |
| Yuri Drozdov | Defender | Lokomotiv Moscow, Russia | 10\0 | 5 | 295 | 3 | 0 | 0 |
| Yuri Kovtun | Defender | Moscow Spartak, Russia | 42\2 | 8 | 720 | 1 | 0 | 1 |
| Yuri Nikiforov | Defender | PSV Eindhoven, Holland | 48\6 | 4 | 360 | 1 | 0 | 0 |
| Alexander Mostovoi | Midfielder | Celta Vigo, Spain | 41\9 | 7 | 630 | 4 | 0 | 1 |
| Dmitri Alenichev | Midfielder | Porto, Portugal | 41\6 | 8 | 561 | 1 | 0 | 1 |
| Dmitri Khokhlov | Midfielder | Real Sociedad, Spain | 35\3 | 10 | 718 | 1 | 0 | 1 |
| Marat Izmailov | Midfielder | Lokomotiv Moscow, Russia | 4\0 | 3 | 224 | 1 | 0 | 0 |
| Andrei Karyaka | Midfielder | Kryliya Sovetov, Russia | 3\0 | 1 | 7 | 0 | 0 | 0 |
| Rolan Gusev | Midfielder | CSKA Moscow, Russia | 10\0 | 5 | 324 | 0 | 0 | 0 |
| Sergei Semak | Midfielder | CSKA Moscow, Russia | 29\1 | 7 | 153 | 0 | 0 | 1 |
| Valeri Karpin | Midfielder | Celta Vigo, Spain | 65\16 | 8 | 720 | 2 | 0 | 0 |
| Yegor Titov | Midfielder | Moscow Spartak, Russia | 30\4 | 10 | 856 | 0 | 0 | 3 |
| Maxim Buznikin | Forward | Lokomotiv Moscow, Russia | 8\5 | 4 | 268 | 0 | 0 | 1 |
| Vladimir Beschastnykh | Forward | Moscow Spartak, Russia | 61\23 | 10 | 640 | 0 | 0 | 7 |
| Alexander Panov | Forward | Dinamo Moscow, Russia | 16\4 | 1 | 42 | 0 | 0 | 0 |

**KEY:** APPS/GOALS = International Appearances/Goals; GAMES=Qualification Games played; MINS=Minutes played; Y/C= Yellow cards R/C=Red cards

# HISTORY AT THE WORLD CUP

**1966 >** Goalkeeper Lev Yashin is in excellent form as USSR reach the semis and finish fourth.

**1970 >** USSR is knocked out by controversial Uruguay winning goal claiming ball was out of play.

**1986 >** Igor Belanov scores a hat-trick but still ends up on the losing side against Belgium.

**1974 >** USSR refuses to play at the National Stadium in Chile where a massacre had taken place.

**1994 >** Oleg Salenko becomes the first player to score five goals in a World Cup match (against Cameroon 6-1).

## ★ WORLD CUP HISTORY

| | |
|---|---|
| 1930 >> Did Not Enter | 1970 >> Quarter-Finals |
| 1934 >> Did Not Enter | 1974 >> Did Not Qualify |
| 1938 >> Did Not Enter | 1978 >> Did Not Qualify |
| 1950 >> Did Not Enter | 1982 >> Second Round |
| 1954 >> Did Not Enter | 1986 >> Second Round |
| 1958 >> Quarter-Finals | 1990 >> First Round |
| 1962 >> Quarter-Finals | 1994 >> First Round |
| 1966 >> Fourth Place | 1998 >> Did Not Qualify   *1930-1990 as Soviet Union |

## ★ WORLD CUP RECORDS, STORIES AND WEIRDNESS

**MOST GOALS IN A TOURNAMENT** >> Centre-forward Oleg Salenko took his tally to 6 at USA '94, scoring 5 against the hapless Cameroons. Salenk would not have been playing in the Cameroon game at all if his compatriot Yuran had not squabbled with Russian manager, Sadyrin.

# GROUP E

| OPPONENT | DATE | UK TIME | VENUE |
|----------|------|---------|-------|
| Germany | **1 June** | 12.30 | **Sapporo, Korea** |
| Cameroon | **6 June** | 10.00 | **Saitama, Japan** |
| Ireland | **11 June** | 12.30 | **Yokohama, Japan** |

## "Pride of the Gulf"

# SAUDI ARABIA

Saudi Arabia deservedly qualified from Asian Group A for their third successive World Cup appearance. With five appearances in a row in the final of the Asian Cup since 1984, winning the title a record-equalling three times, Saudi Arabia have been the continent's best international side for the last 20 years. Best side in the Gulf they may be, but it was not until their last qualification game that the Saudis booked their place in the Finals – ahead of rivals Iran.

They started poorly with a home draw against Bahrain and a 2-0 defeat by the Iranians, results which led to the dismissal of head coach. Slobodan Santrac, and Nasser Al-Johar's re-appointment to the job. Al-Johar has been assured that after an unbeaten run in World Cup qualifying and winning the 2002 Gulf Cup he will be in charge at the World Cup Finals. Not a promise to be taken lightly. Since Eduardo Vingada guided the Saudis to the Asian Cup title in 1996, there have been no fewer than eight changes of head coach, with Otto Pfister and Nasser Al Johar both holding the position twice

From now on the Saudis would always be playing catch-up. With a play-off looking likely, the Saudis faced Thailand while Iran travelled to Bahrain. Luck was finally with the Saudis as they romped to a 4-1 win with goals from Abdullah Bin Shehan, Abdullah Al-Dosary, Sami Al-Jaber and Ibrahim Al-Haib. Meanwhile the Iranians experienced their first defeat – going down 3-1 to Bahrain. The Saudis leapfrogged over the Iranians in the table to qualify.

In an earlier group Saudi Arabia had demonstrated their unarguable superiority, scoring, in six games, 30 goals without reply. Talal Al-Meshal scored nine of those goals including hat-tricks against Bangladesh and Vietnam. Sami Al-Jaber, who will become the first Arab player to appear in three World Cups, also scored a hat-trick against Vietnam.

In their two previous World Cup appearances the Saudis were under foreign coaches. In 1994 it was Argentine Jorge Solari and in 1998, Brazilian Carlos Alberto Parreira. At USA 94 Saudi Arabia made an impressive debut beating Morocco 2-1, in the World Cup's first ever all-Arab clash, and Belgium 1-0, to progress to the second round, where they lost to in form Sweden. A Saudi fan was so impressed with his team's showing that he gave each squad member a Volvo. A generous but ultimately redundant gesture as the Saudi FA had already handed the entire squad a Mercedes each as a reward for qualifying.

At France 98, the Saudis managed just a point thanks to a 2-2 draw with South Africa in a group that included France and Denmark. "We was robbed" might be the timeless refrain of losing teams, but in the case of the Saudis it turned out to be the literal and annoying truth – as they discovered on return to their hotel which had been broken in to while they were busy playing their opening game against Denmark.

The Saudis find themselves in a tough group once again, featuring an improving Germany, a difficult Republic of Ireland side and the African Champions Cameroon. But if experience has its rewards then, with goalkeeper Mohammed Al-Deayea, defenders Mohammed Al Khlawi and Abdullah Zubromawi and forward Sami Al-Jaber all set to appear in their third World Cup Finals, we can expect to see the Pride of the Gulf competing with the best.

---

### ★ THE LOWDOWN

**Population:** 22.7 million

**Capital:** Riyadh

**Leader:** King Fahd bin Abd al-Aziz Al Saud

**Life Expectancy:** Male: 66 yrs Female: 69 yrs

>> Money from petrol sales makes up 75% of the Saudi budget revenue. It has the world's largest oil reserves — a quarter of all known deposits.

>> The Monarch, which is hereditary, is both the Chief of State and Head of Government and there are no elections.

>> Saudi Arabia is the world's largest producer and user of desalinated water – seawater minus the salt – mmm nice!

★ **ASSOCIATION:** Saudi Arabian Football Federation
★ **JOINED FIFA:** 1959
★ **JOINED AFC:** 1972
★ **PLAYERS:** 9,600

★ **CLUBS:** 120
★ **WEBSITE:** None.
★ **HONOURS:** Asian Championship – 1984, 1988, 1996.

*Sami Al-Jaber gallops to his third World Cup Finals appearance.*

## ★ ROAD TO QUALIFICATION

Feb 01 **Mongolia** (h) > (w) **6**-0
Al Shelhoub 10, 26, Al Dossary 22,
Sulimani 30, 59, Al Otabi 70

Feb 01 **Bangladesh** (a) > (w) 0-**3**
Al Meshal 30, 88, Al-Jaber 63

Feb 01 **Vietnam SR** (h) > (w) **5**-0
Al Meshal 18, 89, Al-Jaber 30, 60, 90

Feb 01 **Mongolia** (a) > (a) 0-**6**
Al-Jaber 20, Al Shelhoub 24, Al Meshal 24,
Al Dossary 40, 86, Al-Khilaiwi 76

Feb 01 **Bangladesh** (h) > (w) **6**-0
Harthi 5, Al Meshal 28, 29, 43, Al Dossary
32, 38

Feb 01 **Vietnam SR** (a) > (w) 0-**4**
Al Meshal 31, 71, 80, Al Dossary 89

Aug 01 **Bahrain** (h) > (d) **1**-1 Al Dossary 83

Aug 01 **Iran** (a) > (l) **2**-0

Aug 01 **Iraq** (h) > (w) **1**-0 Al Dossary 45

Sep 01 **Thailand** (a) > (w) **1**-3
Al-Jaber 47, Bin Shehan 63, Al Dossary 70

Sep 01 **Bahrain** (a) > (w) 0-**4**
Al Dossary 26, Bin Shehan 28,
Al Shahrani, A 39, Al-Jaber 88

Sep 01 **Iran** (h) > (d) **2**-2
Al-Shahrani, I 20, Al Yami 59

Oct 01 **Iraq** (a) > (w) **1**-2 Bin Shehan 1, 80

Oct 01 **Thailand** (h) > (w) **4**-1
Bin Shehan 41, Al Dosary, A 50,
Al-Jaber 67, Al Harbi 73

## ★ 2ND RND GROUP TABLE

| Team | P | W | D | L | F | A | Pts |
|---|---|---|---|---|---|---|---|
| Saudi Arabia | 8 | 5 | 2 | 1 | 17 | 8 | 17 |
| Iran | 8 | 4 | 3 | 1 | 10 | 7 | 15 |
| Bahrain | 8 | 2 | 4 | 2 | 8 | 9 | 10 |
| Iraq | 8 | 2 | 1 | 5 | 9 | 10 | 7 |
| Thailand | 8 | 0 | 4 | 4 | 5 | 15 | 4 |

## ★ 1ST RND GROUP TABLE

| Team | P | W | D | L | F | A | Pts |
|---|---|---|---|---|---|---|---|
| Saudi Arabia | 6 | 6 | 0 | 0 | 30 | 0 | 18 |
| Vietnam SR | 6 | 3 | 1 | 2 | 9 | 9 | 10 |
| Bangladesh | 6 | 1 | 2 | 3 | 5 | 15 | 5 |
| Mongolia | 6 | 0 | 1 | 5 | 2 | 22 | 1 |

## ★ RECENT RESULTS

Feb 02 **Brazil** (h) > (l) 0-1

Feb 02 **Denmark** (h) > (l) 0-1

Mar 02 **Uruguay** (h) > (w) 3-2
Al Dossary 8, 18, Al Shahrani 17

## DID YOU KNOW?

**Saudi Arabia was the first team to sack their coach at France 98. Brazilian Carlos Alberto Parreira was fired following defeats by Denmark and France.**

**Saudi Arabia played to a** 4-4-2 formation during France 98 and, while failing to win a single game, showed that with their pace they could, at times, outwit their opponents. In the interim, the Saudis have experimented with 3-5-2 line up – with some success – but coach Nasser Al-Johar is likely to stick with 4-4-2, opting for a more conservative strategy. Goalkeeper Mohammed Al-Deayea retains his place and has an experienced back four in front of him. However, it is a defence that is susceptible to set pieces. The return from injury of Nawaf Al-Temyat is a boost to a midfield that can be overrun, although it did hold its own against Romania and Brazil earlier this year. Sami Al-Jaber and Mohammed Al-Shlhoob will be looking to find the net when they can and not rely on penalties as the team did four years ago.

# PROBABLE FORMATION 4-4-2

AL-DEAYEA

SULIMANI    AL-HARBI

AL-KHILAIWI    ZUBROMAWI

AL-GHAMDI    S AL-DOSARI    AL-TEMYAT    AL-MESHAL

AL-JABER    AL-SHLHOOB

## ★ MEN THAT MATTER!

### SAMI AL-JABER

Age>> 29
Club>> Al Hilal
Sami Al-Jaber, who made his international debut in 1990, will be one of the first Arab Players to play in three World Cups. He scored a penalty against South Africa in 1998.

### NAWAF AL-TEMYAT

Age>> 27
Club>> Al-Hilal
One of Saudi Arabia's most successful players who has won almost every domestic trophy. In 2000 he was voted Asia's Player of the Year. One of the national side's most influential players.

### MOHAMMED AL-DEAYEA

Age>> 29
Club>> Al-Hilal
Al-Deayea is regarded as Asia's best goalkeeper who will be playing in his third World Cup Finals and looks set to establish the Saudi Arabian all-time appearance record.

## ★ PROBABLE SQUAD · ★ QUALIFICATION RECORD

| NAME | POSITION | CLUB | APS/GOALS | GAMES | MINS | Y/C | R/C | GOALS |
|------|----------|------|-----------|-------|------|-----|-----|-------|
| **Tisir Al-Antaif** | Goalkeeper | Al Ahli, Saudi Arabia | - | 1 | 44 | 0 | 0 | 0 |
| **Mohammed Al-Deayea** | Goalkeeper | Al Hilal, Saudi Arabia | - | 8 | 592 | 0 | 0 | 0 |
| **Mohammed Babkr** | Goalkeeper | Al Nassr, Saudi Arabia | - | 7 | 624 | 2 | 0 | 0 |
| **Ahmed Dukhi Al-Dosari** | Defender | Al Hilal, Saudi Arabia | - | 12 | 1034 | 0 | 0 | 0 |
| **Ahmed Khalil Al-Dosari** | Defender | Al Hilal, Saudi Arabia | - | 7 | 546 | 0 | 0 | 0 |
| **Mohammed Al-Jahani** | Defender | Al Ahli, Saudi Arabia | - | 3 | 224 | 0 | 0 | 0 |
| **Mohammed Al-Khilaiwi** | Defender | Al Ittihad, Saudi Arabia | - | 12 | 659 | 1 | 0 | 1 |
| **Saleh Al-Saqri** | Defender | Al Ittihad, Saudi Arabia | - | 5 | 233 | 2 | 1 | 0 |
| **Hussain Sulimani** | Defender | Al Ahli, Saudi Arabia | - | 13 | 1133 | 1 | 0 | 2 |
| **Abdullah Zubromawi** | Defender | Al Hilal, Saudi Arabia | - | 11 | 896 | 0 | 0 | 0 |
| **Saad Al-Dosari** | Midfielder | Al Ahli, Saudi Arabia | - | 6 | 532 | 1 | 0 | 0 |
| **Omar Al-Ghamdi** | Midfielder | Al Hilal, Saudi Arabia | - | 9 | 551 | 1 | 0 | 0 |
| **Ibrahim Al-Harbi** | Midfielder | Al Nassr, Saudi Arabia | - | 11 | 679 | 0 | 0 | 1 |
| **Abdullah Al-Shahrani** | Midfielder | Al Shabab, Saudi Arabia | - | 4 | 320 | 0 | 0 | 0 |
| **Ibrahim Al-Shahrani** | Midfielder | Al Ahli, Saudi Arabia | - | 9 | 540 | 2 | 0 | 1 |
| **Mohammed Al-Shlhoob** | Midfielder | Al Hilal, Saudi Arabia | - | 6 | 471 | 0 | 0 | 3 |
| **Nawaf Al-Temyat** | Midfielder | Al Hilal, Saudi Arabia | - | 5 | 375 | 0 | 1 | 0 |
| **Mohammed Hawsawi** | Midfielder | Al Ittihad, Saudi Arabia | - | 9 | 646 | 3 | 0 | 0 |
| **Obaid Al-Dosari** | Forward | Al Ahli, Saudi Arabia | - | 12 | 950 | 1 | 0 | 10 |
| **Sami Al-Jaber** | Forward | Al Hilal, Saudi Arabia | - | 12 | 954 | 1 | 0 | 8 |
| **Talal Al-Meshal** | Forward | Al Ahli, Saudi Arabia | - | 6 | 457 | 0 | 0 | 11 |
| **Marzouk Al-Otaibi** | Forward | Al Ittihad, Saudi Arabia | - | 8 | 314 | 0 | 0 | 1 |
| **Al Hassan Al-Yami** | Forward | Al Ittihad, Saudi Arabia | - | 4 | 146 | 1 | 0 | 1 |

**KEY:** APPS/GOALS = International Appearances/Goals; GAMES=Qualification Games played; MINS=Minutes played; Y/C= Yellow cards R/C=Red cards

# HISTORY AT THE WORLD CUP

1930 1934 1938 1950 1954 1958 1962 1966 1970 1974 1978 1982 1986 1990 1994 1998

**1998 >** Captain Youssef Al-Thyniyan accuses boss Carlos Alberto Parreira of 'cowardly tactics' as Saudis go out.

**1994 >** Saeed Owairan scores the goal of the tournament with the winner against Belgium.

## ★ WORLD CUP RECORDS, STORIES AND WEIRDNESS

**COACHING RECORD** >> Saudi Arabia have shared the services of Brazilian coach Carlos Alberto Parreira (1998) with three other countries – a World Cup coaching record Parreira shares with Yugoslavian Bora Milutinovic.

# GROUP A

| OPPONENT | DATE | UK TIME | VENUE |
|----------|------|---------|-------|
| France | **31 May** | 12.30 | **Seoul, Korea** |
| Denmark | **6 June** | 07.30 | **Daegu, Korea** |
| Uruguay | **11 June** | 07.30 | **Suwon, Korea** |

## ★ THE LOWDOWN

**Population:** 10.2 million

**Capital:** Dakar

**Leader:** Madior Boye

**Life Expectancy:** Male: 61 yrs Female: 64 yrs

>> Senegal is the western most country on the African Continent.

>> Dances are not allowed during the farming season.

>> Yela is the name given to the music of women. Apparently it mimics the sound they make when pounding grain. It's said that this sound was the primary influence on the development of reggae in the Caribbean – thank goodness they weren't using a multi-chef!

## "welcome to the high table of soccer"

# SENEGAL

Senegal's President Abdoulaye Wade cut short a state visit to Europe in order to bestow the prestigious National Order of the Lion upon the "Lions of Teranga" in recognition of the national side's qualification for their first ever World Cup Finals. Senegal's veteran German coach, Peter Schnittger, had laughed out loud when the qualifying draw was made as his side had been grouped with past African World Cup representatives Algeria, Egypt and Morocco along with Namibia. Arguably the toughest group in the continental qualifiers, it looked beyond Senegal's abilities. In fact after two drawn games, Schnittger stepped down to make way for French coach Bruno Metsu.

A third draw in Morocco, thanks to goalkeeper Tony Sylva, was followed by two impressive home wins. Lone striker El Hadji Ousseynou Diouf scored successive hat-tricks against Namibia (4-0) and Algeria (3-0). However, defeat by Egypt allowed Morocco to take a six-point lead. Senegal then faced Morocco, who needed just a single point to qualify from their final fixture, but sensationally, Senegal's Diouf scored the only goal of the game.

This result meant Morocco topped the table with 15 points. Senegal and Egypt were locked on 12 points, but the Egyptians had the superior goal difference. Egypt were to visit Algeria and Senegal travelled to Namibia. The task looked daunting; Senegal would have to win by a three-goal greater margin than Egypt to qualify.

By half-time Senegal led 3-0 thanks to goals from Pape Thiaw (2) and, inevitably, Diouf, his eighth of the qualifiers. It was goalless at the break between Algeria and Egypt. Then on the hour the Egyptians were awarded a controversial penalty, which they converted. In response the Algerian crowd began throwing missiles, forcing the Egyptians to quit the field, and delaying the game by 15 minutes. Meanwhile, back in Namibia, Senegal had increased their lead to 5-0. Then Algeria equalised, making the whole of Senegal desperate for the final whistle to blow in Annaba, hoping against hope that Egypt wouldn't find the net again. They didn't and Senegal were on their way to Japan/Korea.

Senegal's success owes as much to Peter Schnittger as it does to Bruno Metsu. Schnittger had been involved with African soccer since 1968 and in 1995 he began working on a development programme for Senegalese soccer and the national team. FA President Oumar Seck toured Europe searching for players to strengthen the squad – players like Khalilou Fadiga who was on the point of becoming a Belgian citizen when Seck stepped in.

The strategy which has so lifted Senegalese football involves picking a squad with players who turn out, almost exclusively, for European clubs, mostly French, and who are playing regular first team football. Metsu has also stuck with a consistent selection. He knows his best side and tinkers very rarely with the starting line-up. The results speak for themselves – earlier this year Senegal reached the African Nations Cup Final for the first time losing to Cameroon in a penalty shoot-out. It was Metsu's 19th match in charge and only his third defeat.

However, Senegal's experience is almost exclusively African, so we should welcome them to a place at soccer's high table, where they'll no doubt bring much charm and laughter, while it lasts.

★ **ASSOCIATION:** Federation Senegalaise de Football

★ **JOINED FIFA:** 1962

★ **JOINED CAF:** 1963

★ **PLAYERS:** 4,000

★ **CLUBS:** 75

★ **WEBSITE:** None.

★ **HONOURS:** None.

*Henri Camara chasing World Cup glory.*

## ★ ROAD TO QUALIFICATION

Apr 00 **Benin** (a) > (d) 1-**1** N'Diaye 15

Apr 00 **Benin** (h) > (w) **1**-0 Ba 63 (agg **2**-1)

Jun 00 **Algeria** (a) > (d) 1-**1** Diop 16

Jul 00 **Egypt** (h) > (d) **0**-0

Feb 01 **Morocco** (a) > (d) 0-**0**

Mar 01 **Namibia** (h) > (w) **4**-0
Diouf 24, 44, 52, Camara, H 64

Apr 01 **Algeria** (h) > (w) **3**-0
Diouf 2, 47, 75

May 01 **Egypt** (a) > (l) 1-**0**

Jul 01 **Morocco** (h) > (w) **1**-0 Diouf 17

Jul 01 **Namibia** (a) > (w) 0-**5**
Thiaw 15, 30, Diouf 23, Fadiga 79,
N'Diaye 81

## ★ FINAL GROUP TABLE

| Team | P | W | D | L | F | A | Pts |
|---|---|---|---|---|---|---|---|
| **Senegal** | **8** | **4** | **3** | **1** | **14** | **2** | **15** |
| Morocco | 8 | 4 | 3 | 1 | 8 | 3 | 15 |
| Egypt | 8 | 3 | 4 | 1 | 16 | 7 | 13 |
| Algeria | 8 | 2 | 2 | 4 | 11 | 14 | 8 |
| Namibia | 8 | 0 | 2 | 6 | 3 | 26 | 2 |

## ★ RECENT RESULTS

Mar 02 **Bolivia** (h) > (w) **2**-1
Diop 44, Niang 64

**105**

## DID YOU KNOW?

Senegal's French coach Bruno Metsu has taken his commitment to his adopted home to a new level by marrying a Senegalese woman.

Senegal play a French style 4-4-2 formation, which is appropriate since nearly all the squad play in the French League. Senegal are a skilful passing side, capable of producing a tournament upset. In Monaco's Tony Sylva they've unearthed a decent goalkeeper. Captain Aliou Cisse of Montpellier plays as centre back alongside Rennes' Lamine Diatta with Sochaux's Omar Daf as right back – he can also play on the left – a position that should be occupied by Lens' Pape Sarr or Ferdinand Coly. In midfield Salif Alassane Diao and Pape Bouba Diop play in the centre with Makhtar N'Diaye of Rennes (or Moussa N'Diaye of Sedan) and Khalilou Fadiga, a strong source of creativity, providing the width. In attack is another Lens player El Hadji Diouf who has a real knack for getting goals with Henri Camara, who can also play in midfield, or Pape Thiaw as his partner up front.

# PROBABLE FORMATION  4-4-2

SYLVA

DAF | COLY

DIATTA | A CISSE

Makhtar N'DIAYE | DIAO | PB DIOP | FADIGA

DIOUF | H CAMARA

## ★ MEN THAT MATTER!

### EL HADJI DIOUF

Age>> 21
Club>> Lens
Averages a goal a game at international level, Diouf has shone on the international scene since his debut against Benin in April 2000. Scored successive hat-tricks against Algeria and Namibia.

### KHALILOU FADIGA

Age>> 25
Club>> Auxerre
Born in Senegal, raised in France, a success in Belgium and almost became a Belgian international until snapped by the Senegalese FA. He can play as an attacking midfielder or a forward.

### FERDINAND COLY

Age>> 28
Club>> Lens
Defender Coly has impressed over the past two years. He can play on either flank of defence or midfield and won plaudits for his performances in the 2002 African Nations Cup.

## ★ PROBABLE SQUAD  ★ QUALIFICATION RECORD

| NAME | POSITION | CLUB | APS/GOALS | GAMES | MINS | Y/C | R/C | GOALS |
|---|---|---|---|---|---|---|---|---|
| Oumar Diallo | Goalkeeper | Olympique Khourigba, Senegal | 42/0 | 3 | 270 | 0 | 0 | 0 |
| Samuel Monin | Goalkeeper | Raith, Scotland | 1/0 | 0 | 0 | 0 | 0 | 0 |
| Tony Sylva | Goalkeeper | Monaco, France | 13/0 | 4 | 360 | 1 | 0 | 0 |
| Habib Beye | Defender | Strasbourg, France | 5/0 | 2 | 92 | 0 | 0 | 0 |
| Aliou Cisse | Defender | Montpellier, France | 18/0 | 6 | 484 | 3 | 0 | 0 |
| Ferdinand Coly | Defender | Lens, France | 14/0 | 5 | 450 | 2 | 0 | 0 |
| Omar Daf | Defender | Sochaux, France | 30/0 | 7 | 630 | 2 | 0 | 0 |
| Lamine Diatta | Defender | Rennes, France | 17/1 | 5 | 450 | 0 | 0 | 0 |
| Pape Sarr | Defender | Lens, France | 21/1 | 5 | 450 | 2 | 1 | 0 |
| Salif Diao | Midfielder | Sedan, France | 18/2 | 4 | 347 | 0 | 0 | 0 |
| Pape Bouba Diop | Midfielder | Lens, France | 10/2 | 1 | 13 | 0 | 0 | 0 |
| Pape Malick Diop | Midfielder | Lorient, France | 25/2 | 1 | 90 | 0 | 0 | 0 |
| Khalilou Fadiga | Midfielder | Auxerre, France | 23/2 | 6 | 520 | 0 | 0 | 1 |
| Makhtar N'Diaye | Midfielder | Rennes, France | 10/0 | 0 | 0 | 0 | 0 | 0 |
| Sylvain N'Diaye | Midfielder | Lille, France | 4/0 | 0 | 0 | 0 | 0 | 0 |
| Alassane Ndour | Midfielder | Saint-Etienne, France | 6/0 | 1 | 6 | 0 | 0 | 0 |
| Henri Camara | Forward | Sedan, France | 34/7 | 6 | 478 | 0 | 0 | 1 |
| El Hadji Diouf | Forward | Lens, France | 19/12 | 7 | 630 | 1 | 0 | 8 |
| Moussa N'Diaye | Forward | Sedan, France | 37/4 | 5 | 323 | 0 | 0 | 1 |
| Pape Thiaw | Forward | Strasbourg, France | 12/5 | 3 | 143 | 0 | 0 | 2 |
| Amara Traore | Forward | Gueugnon, France | 11/2 | 1 | 12 | 0 | 0 | 0 |
| Ousmane Diop Papa | Forward | Xanthi, Greece | 3/0 | 3 | 189 | 1 | 0 | 0 |
| Souleymane Camara | Forward | Monaco, France | 7/1 | 0 | 0 | 0 | 0 | 0 |

KEY: APPS/GOALS = International Appearances/Goals; GAMES=Qualification Games played; MINS=Minutes played; Y/C= Yellow cards R/C=Red cards

# HISTORY AT THE WORLD CUP

1930 1934 1938 1950 1954 1958 1962 1966 1970 1974 1978 1982 1986 1990 1994 1998

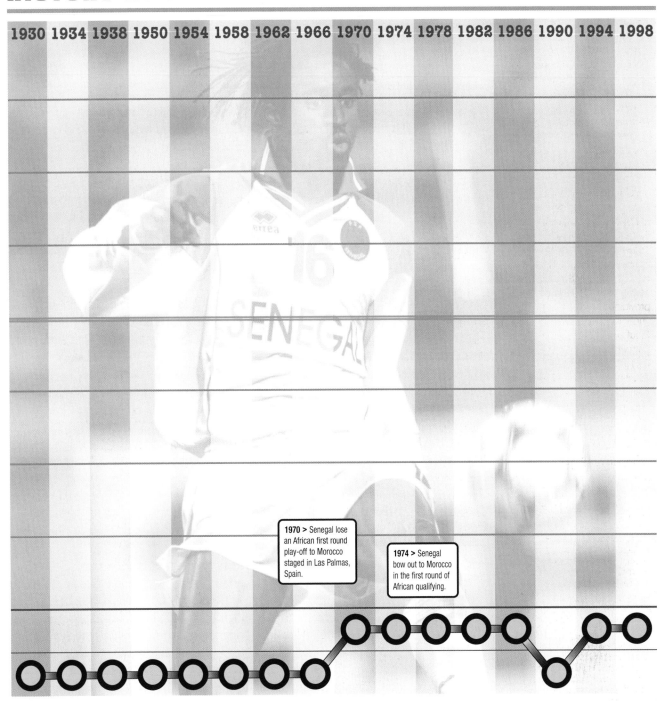

**1970 >** Senegal lose an African first round play-off to Morocco staged in Las Palmas, Spain.

**1974 >** Senegal bow out to Morocco in the first round of African qualifying.

## ★ WORLD CUP HISTORY

| | | | |
|---|---|---|---|
| **1930** >> Did Not Enter | | **1970** >> Did Not Qualify | |
| **1934** >> Did Not Enter | | **1974** >> Did Not Qualify | |
| **1938** >> Did Not Enter | | **1978** >> Did Not Qualify | |
| **1950** >> Did Not Enter | | **1982** >> Did Not Qualify | |
| **1954** >> Did Not Enter | | **1986** >> Did Not Qualify | |
| **1958** >> Did Not Enter | | **1990** >> Did Not Enter | |
| **1962** >> Did Not Enter | | **1994** >> Did Not Qualify | |
| **1966** >> Did Not Enter | | **1998** >> Did Not Qualify | |

## ★ WORLD CUP RECORDS, STORIES AND WEIRDNESS

**APPEARANCES IN THE COMPETITION** >> Senegal currently occupy 100th position in the ranking of all countries that have played in the World Cup – qualifiers and finals. They've appeared in a total of 21 matches (including qualifiers), winning 5, drawing 5 and losing 11 with a –7 goal difference.

# GROUP B

| OPPONENT | DATE | UK TIME | VENUE |
|---|---|---|---|
| Spain | **2 June** | **12.30** | **Gwangju, Korea** |
| South Africa | **8 June** | **07.30** | **Daegu, Korea** |
| Paraguay | **12 June** | **12.30** | **Seogwipo, Korea** |

## "*surprise qualifiers, worth watching on their day*"

# SLOVENIA

### ★ THE LOWDOWN

**Population:** 1.9 million

**Capital:** Ljubljana

**Leader:** Janez Drnovsek

**Life Expectancy:** Male: 71 yrs Female: 79 yrs

>> Slovenia succeeded in establishing its independence from Yugoslavia in 1991.

>> There are over 300 waterfalls in Slovenia, the highest is 130 metres! There are over 7000 caves in the country and the longest is 19 miles!

>> During the eighteenth century, Slovenes would paint pictures of Saints on their beehives; these are so rare now they've become collector's items.

Part of Yugoslavia until 1991, this small nation of two million souls has defied all the odds to reach their first World Cup Finals; but how exactly does a team that are held by the Faroe Islands to a 2-2 draw in their opening qualifying match and go on to win only one of their first five games manage to qualify at all?

Slovenia, the surprise qualifiers of Euro 2000, shocked the football world again by booking a place in Japan/Korea at the expense of Yugoslavia, Switzerland and Romania. From the start they were never expected to get through one of Europe's tightest groups and it certainly looked as if they were playing to the script when they threw away a two-goal lead with just two minutes to play against the part-time fishermen of the Faroe Islands.

Their first five games delivered just one win – a narrow 2-1 victory over Luxembourg – and four draws against Switzerland (coming from behind twice), Russia (an Aleksandr Knavs goal), Yugoslavia (injury time equaliser from Zlatko Zahovic) and the aforementioned opener against the Faroe Islands. Slovenia might have been undefeated up until now, but not even a second, predictable win over Luxembourg was going to make them contenders – was it?

A turning point of sorts came on the trip to Basle in early June 2001 with a 1-0 win over Switzerland. 26-year-old first-half substitute Sebastjan Cimerotic scored the winner, netting his first international goal.

Three months later in the Slovenian capital Ljubljana, coach Srecko Katanec's team defeated Russia with a dramatic and controversial injury time penalty – awarded by English ref Graham Poll. Midfielder Milenko Acimovic coolly scored from the spot for a 2-1 win that gave Slovenia a realistic chance of a play-off place. An impressive 1-1 draw in Yugoslavia followed, which left Slovenia needing only a win over the Faroe Islands to clinch the play-off spot behind Russia.

Two first-half goals from Nastja Ceh were never considered enough, remembering what had happened 13 months earlier, but when substitute Senad Tiganj, on his debut, netted the third goal in the 82nd minute, Slovenia knew the play-off spot was theirs.

They had been in a play-off situation before – successfully booking their place for Euro 2000 – but this time they were considered the underdogs going up against an experienced Romanian team. In the event they proved to be the better team, winning 3-2 on aggregate with goals from Acimovic, Osterc (first leg) and Rudonja (second leg).

While they may have actually remained unbeaten throughout qualifying, Slovenia are regarded as the weakest of the European teams destined for Japan/Korea. Although they scored in every one of the qualifying games, keeping a clean sheet is something of a Slovenian rarity. They're an erratic, often unpredictable team as much within a game as between matches. During their Euro 2000 clash with Yugoslavia they played thrilling football, storming to a 3-0 lead and then threw it away allowing Yugoslavia to score three goals in the last quarter of the game. That breathless performance was in stark contrast to their goalless drudge of a game with Norway.

The chances are that the world will see all shades of Slovenian football at the World Cup Finals, with a side battling against its own inconsistencies as much as their opponents. But they'll be well worth watching – just in case it's one of their good days.

- ★ **ASSOCIATION:** Nogometna Zveza Slovenije
- ★ **JOINED FIFA:** 1993
- ★ **JOINED UEFA:** 1992
- ★ **PLAYERS:** 20,200
- ★ **CLUBS:** 375
- ★ **WEBSITE:** www.nzs.si
- ★ **HONOURS:** None

## ★ ROAD TO QUALIFICATION

Sep 00 **Faroe Islands** (a) > (d) 2-2
Udovic 25, Osterc 87

Oct 00 **Luxembourg** (a) > (w) 1-**2**
Zahovic 39, Milinovic 40

Oct 00 **Switzerland** (h) > (d) 2-2
Siljak 44, Acimovic 77

Mar 01 **Russia** (a) > (d) 1-1 Knavs 22

Mar 01 **Yugoslavia** (h) > (d) **1**-1
Zahovic 90

Jun 01 **Luxembourg** (h) > (w) 2-0
Zahovic 35, 66 pen

Jun 01 **Switzerland** (a) > (w) 0-**1**
Cimirotic 83

Sep 01 **Russia** (h) > (w) **2**-1
Osterc 62, Acimovic 90 pen

Sep 01 **Yugoslavia** (a) > (d) 1-**1**
Milinovic 10

Oct 01 **Faroe Islands** (h) > (w) **3**-0
Ceh 13, 31, Tiganj 82

Nov 01 **Romania** (h) > (w) **2**-1
Acimovic 41, Osterc 73

Nov 01 **Romania** (a) > (d) 1-**1** (agg **3**-2)
Rudonja 57

## ★ FINAL GROUP TABLE

| Team | P | W | D | L | F | A | Pts |
|---|---|---|---|---|---|---|---|
| Russia | 10 | 7 | 2 | 1 | 18 | 5 | 23 |
| **Slovenia** | **10** | **5** | **5** | **0** | **17** | **9** | **20** |
| Yugoslavia | 10 | 5 | 4 | 1 | 22 | 8 | 19 |
| Switzerland | 10 | 4 | 2 | 4 | 18 | 12 | 14 |
| Faroe Islands | 10 | 2 | 1 | 7 | 6 | 23 | 7 |
| Luxembourg | 10 | 0 | 0 | 10 | 4 | 28 | 0 |

## ★ RECENT RESULTS

Feb 02 **Honduras** (n) > (l) 1-**5**
Zahovic 52 pen

Feb 02 **China PR** (n) > (d) 0-0
*(Slovenia won 4-3 on pens)*

Mar 02 **Croatia** (a) > (d) 0-**0**

*Desperate to add glamour to their squad, Slovenia recruit a rather bemused Hugh Grant.*

### DID YOU KNOW?

**Coach Srecko Katanec was a Slovenian international making five appearances after previously playing 31 times for Yugoslavia including the 1990 World Cup.**

Slovenia has stuck with the same strategy and largely the same personnel that entertained fans at Euro 2000 but only produced two draws and a defeat. In the interim Marko Simeunovic has displaced Malden Dabanovic as Slovenia's number one goalkeeper. The three-man defence has Marinko Galic as sweeper with Zelijko Milinovic and Aleksandr Knavs either side of him. Ales Ceh and Miran Pavlin are the defensive midfielders while Amir Karic on the left and Saso Gajser on the right will provide the width. Zlatko Zahovic almost acts as a third striker, playing just behind the front two. This shadowing position has brought Zahovic and Slovenia many goals, but it's a ploy that most opponents now anticipate. The front two consist of main striker Milan Osterc and partner Mladen Rudonja. While Slovenia has a settled side, it is growing long in the tooth and lacks the pace of former years.

## PROBABLE FORMATION 3-4-2-1

SIMEUNOVIC

MILINOVIC KNAVS

GALIC

GAJSER A CEH PAVLIN KARIC

ZAHOVIC RUDONJA

OSTERC

---

### ★ MEN THAT MATTER!

#### MILAN OSTERC

Age>> 26

Club>> Hapoel Tel Aviv

Previously used as a supersub to good effect, Osterc has established himself as a first choice forward with Slovenia after scoring vitals goals against Russia and, in the play-offs, Romania.

#### MLADEN RUDONJA

Age>> 30

Club>> Primorje Ajdovscina

Rudonja has become the strike partner to Milan Osterc. A decent forward he faces pressure from Milenko Acimovic. Rudonja has good control and can play on left side of midfield.

#### ZLATKO ZAHOVIC

Age>> 31

Club>> Benfica

At Euro 2000 Slovenia were seen as a one-man team — with Zahovic being that man. He still continues to score but now plays just behind the front two.

### ★ PROBABLE SQUAD ★ QUALIFICATION RECORD

| NAME | POSITION | CLUB | APS/GOALS | GAMES | MINS | Y/C | R/C | GOALS |
|---|---|---|---|---|---|---|---|---|
| Mladen Dabanovic | Goalkeeper | Lokeren, Belgium | 19/0 | 3 | 186 | 0 | 0 | 0 |
| Dejan Nemec | Goalkeeper | Brugge, Belgium | 0/0 | 0 | 0 | 0 | 0 | 0 |
| Marko Simeunovic | Goalkeeper | Maribor, Slovenia | 41/0 | 10 | 894 | 0 | 0 | 0 |
| Spasoje Bulajic | Defender | Koln, Germany | 15/1 | 4 | 270 | 0 | 0 | 0 |
| Marinko Galic | Defender | No Club, Slovenia | 62/0 | 7 | 630 | 0 | 0 | 0 |
| Aleksander Knavs | Defender | Kaiserslautern, Germany | 35/2 | 9 | 810 | 1 | 0 | 1 |
| Zeljko Milinovic | Defender | JEF United, Japan | 33/3 | 11 | 990 | 2 | 0 | 2 |
| Goran Sankovic | Defender | Slavia Prague, Czech Republic | 1/0 | 1 | 27 | 0 | 0 | 0 |
| Muamer Vugdalic | Defender | Maribor, Slovenia | 11/0 | 6 | 540 | 2 | 0 | 0 |
| Milenko Acimovic | Midfielder | Red Star Belgrade, Yugoslavia | 36/9 | 9 | 522 | 2 | 0 | 3 |
| Ales Ceh | Midfielder | Grazer AK, Austria | 69/1 | 12 | 1080 | 3 | 0 | 2 |
| Nastja Ceh | Midfielder | Brugge, Belgium | 2/2 | 1 | 50 | 0 | 0 | 0 |
| Sasa Gajser | Midfielder | Gent, Belgium | 17/1 | 5 | 398 | 4 | 0 | 0 |
| Amir Karic | Midfielder | Maribor, Slovenia | 40/1 | 8 | 567 | 4 | 0 | 0 |
| Dzoni Novak | Midfielder | Unterhaching, Germany | 66/2 | 11 | 990 | 3 | 0 | 0 |
| Miran Pavlin | Midfielder | Porto, Portugal | 42/4 | 11 | 916 | 3 | 0 | 0 |
| Zoran Pavlovic | Midfielder | No Club, Slovenia | 18/0 | 8 | 294 | 0 | 0 | 0 |
| Rajko Tavcar | Midfielder | Nurnberg, Germany | 5/0 | 1 | 35 | 0 | 0 | 0 |
| Zlatko Zahovic | Midfielder | Benfica, Portugal | 61/31 | 8 | 687 | 2 | 0 | 4 |
| Sebastjan Cimirotic | Forward | Lecce, Italy | 11/1 | 6 | 288 | 1 | 0 | 1 |
| Milan Osterc | Forward | Hapoel Tel Aviv, Israel | 38/8 | 11 | 601 | 1 | 0 | 3 |
| Mladen Rudonja | Forward | Portsmouth, England | 55/1 | 10 | 721 | 0 | 0 | 1 |
| Senad Tiganj | Forward | Olimpija Ljubljana, Slovenia | 1/1 | 1 | 20 | 0 | 0 | 1 |

**KEY:** APPS/GOALS = International Appearances/Goals; GAMES=Qualification Games played; MINS=Minutes played; Y/C= Yellow cards R/C=Red cards

# HISTORY AT THE WORLD CUP

1930 1934 1938 1950 1954 1958 1962 1966 1970 1974 1978 1982 1986 1990 1994 1998

**1998 >** Slovenia fail to win a single game of their first World Cup qualifying campaign.

## ★ WORLD CUP HISTORY

| | | | |
|---|---|---|---|
| **1930** >> Did Not Enter | | **1970** >> Did Not Enter | |
| **1934** >> Did Not Enter | | **1974** >> Did Not Enter | |
| **1938** >> Did Not Enter | | **1978** >> Did Not Enter | |
| **1950** >> Did Not Enter | | **1982** >> Did Not Enter | |
| **1954** >> Did Not Enter | | **1986** >> Did Not Enter | |
| **1958** >> Did Not Enter | | **1990** >> Did Not Enter | |
| **1962** >> Did Not Enter | | **1994** >> Did Not Enter | |
| **1966** >> Did Not Enter | | **1998** >> Did Not Qualify | |

## ★ WORLD CUP RECORDS, STORIES AND WEIRDNESS

**MOST GOALS** >> Slovenia's best all-time World Cup scorer is Zlatko Zahovic with 6.

**FIFA RANKING** >> Their current position is 27 and their best has been 26th.

# GROUP B

| OPPONENT | DATE | UK TIME | VENUE |
|----------|------|---------|-------|
| Paraguay | **2 June** | 08.30 | **Busan, Korea** |
| Slovenia | **8 June** | 07.30 | **Daegu, Korea** |
| Spain | **12 June** | 12.30 | **Daejeon, Korea** |

## "the Bafana Bafana seek second round glory"

# SOUTH AFRICA

It's been a decade since South Africa re-entered the international sporting fold – after years of isolation in response to her apartheid policies – and South Africa coach Carlos Queiroz has made it clear how he wants his team to celebrate the anniversary at this summer's World Cup. He wants the Bafana Bafana to reach the second round. At France 98, in their first World Cup appearance, defeat by France and draws with Denmark and Saudi Arabia saw them make a first round exit.

Queiroz's team has been in a period of transition for the last couple of years; younger players like Delron Buckley, Siyabonga Nomvete and captain Shaun Bartlett are proving their international mettle and the large number of players previously used by the national side has been cut in a bid to become more consistent.

Queiroz took over the reins of the national team in the shadow of one of the World Cup's worst ever human disasters. After defeating Lesotho 3-0 on aggregate with two pretty drab performances in the preliminary round, South Africa opened their qualifying programme proper away to Zimbabwe at the National Sports Stadium in Harare. Delron Buckley gave the visitors a sixth minute lead and thereafter South Africa controlled the game. In the 82nd minute Buckley struck again to secure the points.

However, South Africa's goal celebrations provoked a hail of missiles from the crowd. The crowd's venom was directed both towards the South African players and the Zimbabwean bench. In a bid to quell the disturbances the Zimbabwean Police fired teargas into the crowd causing a stampede that led to the deaths of 13 fans. On the pitch players and officials were forced to lie face down to avoid the clouds of teargas engulfing them. A decision was taken to abandon the game and later FIFA ruled that the result – 2-0 – would stand.

It was six months before South Africa would return to World Cup action when they produced wins over Burkina Faso and Malawi – albeit in a less than convincing fashion. South African World Cup hopes were boosted, as were the hopes of Zimbabwe, when one of the main rivals, Guinea, were expelled from the competition. Zimbabwe's hopes were short lived as South Africa beat them 2-1 thanks to first-half goals from Shaun Bartlett and Benni McCarthy. This big, decisive clash attracted just 15,000 fans at the Soccer City Stadium in Johannesburg. Just a month earlier South Africa had been struck by its own stadium disaster in which 43 people had died.

A 1-1 draw away to Burkina Faso earned South Africa the point they needed to qualify for their second successive Finals.

Since South Africa returned to the international football family it's been a colourful decade for "The Boys". Crowned African Champions in 1996, and successful qualification for two World Cups Finals, such was the confidence in the South African game that they applied to host, and were hot favourites to get, the 2006 World Cup Finals. However, they ultimately lost out to Germany because the Oceania representative refused to follow his Confederation's instructions to vote for South Africa and went home.

## ★ THE LOWDOWN

**Population:** 43.5 million

**Capital:** Pretoria

**Leader:** Thabo Mbeki

**Life Expectancy:** Male: 47 yrs Female: 48 yrs

>> There are eleven official languages used in South Africa, including Afrikaans, English, Zulu, Venda and Swazi.

>> The National Flag includes six different colours: red, blue, green, black, yellow and white.

>> South Africa is the world's largest producer of platinum and gold.

★ **ASSOCIATION:** South African Football Association
★ **JOINED FIFA:** 1992
★ **JOINED CAF:** 1992
★ **PLAYERS:** 1,039,900

★ **CLUBS:** 51,944
★ **WEBSITE:** www.safa.org.za
★ **HONOURS:** African Nations Cup – 1996.

## ★ ROAD TO QUALIFICATION

Apr 00 **Lesotho** (a) > (w) 0-**2**
Bartlett 40, Pule 71

Apr 00 **Lesotho** (h) > (w) **1**-0 (agg **3**-0)
Bartlett 48

Jul 00 **Zimbabwe** (a) > (w) 0-**2**
Buckley 6, 82

Jan 01 **Burkina Faso** (h) > (w) **1**-0
Bartlett 17

Feb 01 **Malawi** (a) > (w) 1-**2**
Masinga 25, Nomvethe 81

May 01 **Zimbabwe** (h) > (w) **2**-1
Bartlett 18, McCarthy 40

Jul 01 **Burkina Faso** (a) > (d) 1-**1**
Zuma 24

Jul 01 **Malawi** (h) > (w) **2**-0
Booth 5, August 54

## ★ FINAL GROUP TABLE

| Team | P | W | D | L | F | A | Pts |
|---|---|---|---|---|---|---|---|
| **South Africa** | 6 | 5 | 1 | 0 | 10 | 3 | 16 |
| Zimbabwe | 7 | 4 | 0 | 3 | 7 | 8 | 12 |
| Guinea | 3 | 2 | 1 | 0 | 7 | 3 | 7 |
| Burkina Faso | 7 | 1 | 2 | 4 | 9 | 11 | 5 |
| Malawi | 7 | 0 | 2 | 5 | 5 | 13 | 2 |

## ★ RECENT RESULTS

Jan 02 **Burkina Faso** (n) > (d) **0**-0

Jan 02 **Ghana** (n) > (d) **0**-0

Jan 02 **Morocco** (n) > (w) **3**-1
Zuma 41, Mngomeni 48, Nomvethe 50

Feb 02 **Mali** (n) > (l) 2-**0**

Mar 02 **Georgia** (a) > (l) 4-**1** Buckley 69

*His country hopes for exactly what it says on the shirt.*

**113**

## DID YOU KNOW?

**South Africa will celebrate a decade back in the international fold when they participate in the World Cup Finals after the end of their period of isolation because of their apartheid policies.**

South Africa's 3-5-2 line up has brought them much success on the African continent in the last few years, but they certainly lost their way at the 2002 African Nations Cup – suggesting that without the right personnel they may well struggle at the World Cup. Hans Vonk has displaced Andre Arendse as first choice goalkeeper. The back three are likely to be Aaraon Mokoena, Pierre Issa and Frank Schoeman, although Mbulelo Mabizela and Bradley Carnell make strong cases for inclusion. Playmaker John Moshoeu, absent from the African Nations Cup, is seen as a vital player who will be supported by Thano Mngomeni and Delron Buckley. South Africa has an abundance of decent wide men at the moment with Manchester United's Quinton Fortune and FC Copenhagen's Sibusiso Zuma providing plenty of creativity if brought into the game. In attack, Benni McCarthy and Shaun Bartlett look the likely pairing, but Siyabonga Nomvete could break them up.

## PROBABLE FORMATION 3-5-2

VONK

A MOKOENA    SCHOEMAN

ISSA

ZUMA    MNGOMENI    BUCKLEY    FORTUNE

MOSHOEU

McCARTHY    BARTLETT

## ★ MEN THAT MATTER!

### SUBUSISO ZUMA

Age>> 26
Club>> FC Copenhagen
Right-winger and excellent crosser of the ball who has finally established himself in the side after making his debut in October 1998 against Angola. Voted Denmark's 2000-01 Player of the Year.

### BENNI MCCARTHY

Age>> 24
Club>> Celta Vigo/ FC Porto (loan)
Benni McCarthy has had a tough time at club level but has been consistently selected for his country. He scored the vital winning goal in the 2-1 win over Zimbabwe in the qualifiers.

### SHAUN BARTLETT

Age>> 29
Club>> Charlton Athletic
Shaun Bartlett has played football in Africa, Europe, America and Britain. He made his international debut in 1995 and he was South Africa's main goalscorer during the qualifiers.

## ★ PROBABLE SQUAD / ★ QUALIFICATION RECORD

| NAME | POSITION | CLUB | APS/GOALS | GAMES | MINS | Y/C | R/C | GOALS |
|------|----------|------|-----------|-------|------|-----|-----|-------|
| Andre Arendse | Goalkeeper | Santos , South Africa | 49/0 | 2 | 180 | 0 | 0 | 0 |
| Bryan Baloyi | Goalkeeper | Kaizer Chiefs, South Africa | 17/0 | 1 | 90 | 0 | 0 | 0 |
| Hans Vonk | Goalkeeper | Heerenveen, Holland | 27/0 | 1 | 90 | 1 | 0 | 0 |
| Aaron Mokoena | Defender | Germinal Beerschot, Belgium | 20/0 | 3 | 270 | 1 | 0 | 0 |
| Bradley Carnell | Defender | Stuttgart, Germany | 19/0 | 2 | 180 | 0 | 0 | 0 |
| David Kannemeyer | Defender | Kaizer Chiefs, South Africa | 9/0 | 2 | 180 | 0 | 0 | 0 |
| Frank Schoeman | Defender | Farum, Denmark | 14/0 | 3 | 270 | 1 | 0 | 0 |
| Pierre Issa | Defender | Watford, England | 40/0 | 4 | 360 | 2 | 0 | 0 |
| Cyril Nzama | Defender | Kaizer Chiefs, South Africa | 17/1 | 2 | 180 | 1 | 0 | 0 |
| Alfred Phiri | Midfielder | Samsunspor, Turkey | 10/2 | 2 | 94 | 2 | 0 | 0 |
| Delron Buckley | Midfielder | Bochum, Germany | 29/4 | 3 | 226 | 0 | 0 | 2 |
| John Moshoeu | Midfielder | Bursaspor, Turkey | 63/6 | 1 | 90 | 0 | 0 | 0 |
| Helman Mkhalele | Midfielder | Goztepe, Turkey | 63/7 | 3 | 169 | 0 | 0 | 0 |
| Quinton Fortune | Midfielder | Manchester United, England | 38/0 | 2 | 146 | 1 | 0 | 0 |
| Eric Tinkler | Midfielder | Barnsley, England | 46/1 | 1 | 90 | 0 | 0 | 0 |
| Teboho Mokoena | Midfielder | St Gallen, Switzerland | 9/0 | 2 | 107 | 0 | 0 | 0 |
| Jacob Lekcetho | Midfielder | Lokomotiv Moscow, Russia | 13/0 | 1 | 90 | 0 | 0 | 0 |
| Matthew Booth | Midfielder | Mamelodi Sundowns, South Africa | 13/2 | 1 | 90 | 0 | 0 | 1 |
| Benedict McCarthy | Forward | Porto, Portugal | 40/17 | 4 | 240 | 0 | 0 | 1 |
| Bradley August | Forward | Santos, South Africa | 14/3 | 2 | 98 | 0 | 0 | 1 |
| Shaun Bartlett | Forward | Charlton, England | 60/23 | 4 | 352 | 0 | 0 | 2 |
| Siyabongo Nomvete | Forward | Udinese, Italy | 29/5 | 4 | 152 | 0 | 0 | 1 |
| Sibusiso Zuma | Forward | Copenhagen, Denmark | 22/3 | 4 | 316 | 0 | 0 | 0 |

**KEY:** APPS/GOALS = International Appearances/Goals; GAMES=Qualification Games played; MINS=Minutes played; Y/C= Yellow cards R/C=Red cards

# HISTORY AT THE WORLD CUP

1930 1934 1938 1950 1954 1958 1962 1966 1970 1974 1978 1982 1986 1990 1994 1998

**1998 >** Shaun Bartlett's last minute penalty salvages a draw with the Saudis as the Africans suffer internal problems.

**1974-90 >** South Africa are subject to a worldwide sports ban because of apartheid.

**1954-74 >** South Africa are suspended from FIFA.

## ★ WORLD CUP HISTORY

| | | | |
|---|---|---|---|
| 1930 | >> Did Not Enter | 1970 | >> Suspended |
| 1934 | >> Did Not Enter | 1974 | >> Suspended |
| 1938 | >> Did Not Enter | 1978 | >> Did Not Enter |
| 1950 | >> Did Not Enter | 1982 | >> Did Not Enter |
| 1954 | >> Suspended | 1986 | >> Did Not Enter |
| 1958 | >> Suspended | 1990 | >> Did Not Enter |
| 1962 | >> Suspended | 1994 | >> Did Not Qualify |
| 1966 | >> Suspended | 1998 | >> First Round |

## ★ WORLD CUP RECORDS, STORIES AND WEIRDNESS

**MOST SENDINGS OFF IN A MATCH** >> Denmark against South Africa in 1998 saw three players sent off.

## GROUP D

| OPPONENT | DATE | UK TIME | VENUE |
|----------|------|---------|-------|
| Poland | **4 June** | 12.30 | **Busan, Korea** |
| USA | **10 June** | 07.30 | **Daegu, Korea** |
| Portugal | **14 June** | 12.30 | **Incheon, Korea** |

### "looking for their first win"

# SOUTH KOREA

World Cup co-hosts South Korea are undeniably one of Asia's strongest teams. They've qualified for the last four World Cup Finals and were the first Asian side to play in the Finals – back in 1954. However, in all of their 14 World Cup matches, the South Koreans have yet to record a win. And they carry the added burden of knowing that in no previous World Cups have the hosts failed to reach the second round. Oh, how they would love to emulate the heroic achievement of their northern counterparts who, in 1966, reached the quarter-finals.

No need to qualify as co-hosts of course, they were placed in the top group of seeds for the draw (normally they'd be in the bottom group), but the draw itself was far from kind. Two improving European teams, Poland and Portugal, stand in the way of a second round place, as do the United States.

South Korean fans are not entirely optimistic about their team's chances and recognising that they'd come as far as they were likely to without outside help, appointed former Holland national team coach Guus Hiddink in January 2001. He was put in charge of a squad with several talented players, most of whom play their club football at home or in Japan. The Dutchman is the first non-Korean to coach the national side and was given 17 months to sort them out. Lined up were a series of tournaments including the Carlsberg Cup in Hong Kong, the Emirates Cup in Dubai, a tournament in Egypt and the co-hosting of the Confederations Cup and, earlier this year, the Gold Cup in the USA along with a host of friendly internationals.

Hiddink's first step was to adopt the playing system used by Korea's leading clubs, such as the highly successful Suwon Bluewings, which roughly equates to a 4-5-1 formation. This would mean that the national squad would have to switch from a three-man to a four-man defence. The change in organisation led to problems and the defence stuttered, especially against strong European opposition. Both France and the Czech Republic thrashed the Koreans 5-0.

The midfield, however, showed improvement thanks to the arrival of youngster Song Chong-gug alongside wide-man Lee Young-pyo and free-kick specialist Park Ji-sung. This five-man midfield supports a single striker such as Choi Yong-soo or the new wonder boy of South Korean football Lee Dong-gook, who led his country to the Asian Under-19 title 1999 and was top scorer at the 2000 Asian Championships – where South Korea finished fourth.

At the Confederations Cup, Korea had a bad case of the *deja vus*, showing the sort of form we can expect to see in the Finals. Despite beating both Mexico and Australia, they unluckily bowed out at the group stage. At the Gold Cup, however, they were semi-finalists beating Mexico in a penalty shoot-out, with two saves from goalkeeper Lee Woon-jae along the way.

Even when you add up the value of Hiddink's experience, home advantage and massive support of a football-mad nation, the Koreans are going to find it difficult. At the last World Cup Hiddink, wearing his Dutch hat, handed out a 5-0 thrashing to the Koreans and they would be wise to limit their ambitions to securing their first World Cup Finals win. Asian soccer also has vested interest in a breakthrough Korean performance as the continent seeks to increase its numbers in future World Cup Finals.

★ **ASSOCIATION:** Korea Football Association

★ **JOINED FIFA:** 1948

★ **JOINED AFC:** 1954

★ **PLAYERS:** 20,050

★ **CLUBS:** 476

★ **WEBSITE:** www.kfa.or.kr

★ **HONOURS:** Asian Championship – 1956, 1960

*Kim Do-hoon chasing a World Cup dream.*

## GROUP D

### DID YOU KNOW?
Boss Bora Militinovic is 'Mister World Cup'. This will be his fifth World Cup Finals with a different team each time — Mexico (1986), Costa Rica (1990), USA (1994) and Nigeria (1998).

South Korea's prospects of making an impact at the World Cup are not particularly good. Although their players are technically adept, shortcomings in other aspects of their game, particularly their relative lack of physical presence, make them vulnerable. Dutch coach Guus Hiddink has opted for a 4-4-2 formation that is hugely dependent on keeper Lee Woon-jae and South Korea's best known player, Hong Myung-bo, providing last ditch protection of the goalmouth. In midfield, despite the presence of the popular Song Chong-gug and sweeper captain Hong Myung-bo, the Koreans will find it hard to cope. A bold attacking partnership of Lee Dong-gook, the Michael Owen of Korean football, and the highly paid Kim Do-hoon offers some hope for goals. Getting the ball to these two will be a major problem.

## PROBABLE FORMATION 4-4-2

LEE WOON-JAE

KIM TAE-YOUNG    LEE MIN-SUNG

HONG MYUNG-BO    LEE LIM-SAENG

CHOI SUNG-YONG    SONG CHONG-GUG    LEE YONG-PYU    CHOI TAE-UK

KIM DO-HOON    LEE DONG-GOOK

## ★ MEN THAT MATTER!

### HONG MYUNG-BO

Age>> 33
Club>> Kashiwa Reysol
South Korea's most capped player is regarded as the best sweeper in Asia. This will be Hong's fourth successive World Cup.

### LEE YOUNG-PYO

Age>> 25
Club>> Anyang Cheetahs

After impressing in the Korean's Olympic Under-23 team he was promoted to the senior team. Lee Young-pyo can play on the left of midfield and equally carve out chances through the middle.

### SONG CHONG-GUG

Age>> 23
Club>> Pusan Icons
Song Chong-gug, who impressed at the 2001 Confederations Cup, is the new boy wonder of South Korean football. He plays in midfield and is quick off the mark allowing him to create chances.

## ★ PROBABLE SQUAD    ★ QUALIFICATION RECORD

| NAME | POSITION | CLUB | APS/GOALS | GAMES | MINS | Y/C | R/C | GOALS |
|---|---|---|---|---|---|---|---|---|
| Lee Woon-jae | Goalkeeper | Sangmoo, South Korea | 25/0 | - | - | - | - | - |
| Kim Byung-ji | Goalkeeper | Pohang Steelers, South Korea | 54/0 | - | - | - | - | - |
| Kim Yong-dae | Goalkeeper | Yonsei University, South Korea | 12/0 | - | - | - | - | - |
| Hong Myung-bo | Defender | Pohang Steelers, South Korea | 122/9 | - | - | - | - | - |
| Kang Chul | Defender | Chunnam Dragons, South Korea | 53/1 | - | - | - | - | - |
| Kim Tae-young | Defender | Chunnam Dragons, South Korea | 68/3 | - | - | - | - | - |
| Lee Lim-saeng | Defender | Puchon SK, South Korea | 24/0 | - | - | - | - | - |
| Lee Min-sung | Defender | Sangmoo, South Korea | 54/2 | - | - | - | - | - |
| Sim Jae-won | Defender | Eintracht Frankfurt, Germany | 18/2 | - | - | - | - | - |
| Song Chong-gug | Defender | Pusan Icons, South Korea | 18/1 | - | - | - | - | - |
| Choi Sung-yong | Midfielder | Suwon Bluewings, South Korea | 54/1 | - | - | - | - | - |
| Choi Tai-uk | Midfielder | Anyang Cheetahs, South Korea | 11/3 | - | - | - | - | - |
| Ha Seok-ju | Midfielder | Pohang Steelers, South Korea | 91/23 | - | - | - | - | - |
| Kim Nam-il | Midfielder | Chunnam Dragons, South Korea | 12/1 | - | - | - | - | - |
| Lee Young-pyo | Midfielder | Anyang Cheetahs, South Korea | 39/3 | - | - | - | - | - |
| Song Chong-gug | Midfielder | Pusan Icons, South Korea | 19/1 | - | - | - | - | - |
| Yoo Sang-chul | Midfielder | Kashiwa Reysol, Japan | 90/16 | - | - | - | - | - |
| Yoon Jong-hwan | Midfielder | Cerezo Osaka, Japan | 33/2 | - | - | - | - | - |
| Ahn Jung-hwan | Forward | Perugia, Italy | 14/2 | - | - | - | - | - |
| Choi Yong-soo | Forward | JEF United Ichihara, Japan | 54/27 | - | - | - | - | - |
| Hwang Sun-hong | Forward | Kashiwa Reysol, Japan | 92/47 | - | - | - | - | - |
| Kim Do-hoon | Forward | Chonbuk, South Korea | 57/20 | - | - | - | - | - |
| Lee Dong-gook | Forward | Pohang Steelers, South Korea | 25/9 | - | - | - | - | - |

KEY: APPS/GOALS = International Appearances/Goals; GAMES=Qualification Games played; MINS=Minutes played; Y/C= Yellow cards R/C=Red cards

# HISTORY AT THE WORLD CUP

1930 1934 1938 1950 1954 1958 1962 1966 1970 1974 1978 1982 1986 1990 1994 1998

**1998 >** Yoo Sang-chul's equaliser against Belgium earns South Korea their only World Cup point.

**1994 >** Hong Myung-bo and Seo Jung-won earn the Koreans a shock 2-2 draw with Spain.

**1990 >** South Korea commit 86 fouls – more than anyone else – in their first round matches.

**1978 >** South Korea finish runners-up to Iran in the Asian qualifiers.

**1954 >** Goalkeeper Hong is beaten 16 times in two games by Hungary (9-0) and Turkey (7-0).

**1962 >** South Korea lose inter-continental play-off to Yugoslavia denying Asia a place in the Finals.

**1974 >** South Korea take Australia to a play-off but miss out by a single goal in Hong Kong.

**1986 >** Kim Jong-boo is on target against Bulgaria as Koreans win their first ever World Cup point.

**1958 >** South Korea are refused entry to the World Cup because FIFA say they have not applied properly.

**1970 >** South Korea finish runners-up to Australia in Asia-Oceania qualifying group.

## ★ WORLD CUP HISTORY

| | |
|---|---|
| **1930** >> Did Not Enter | **1970** >> Did Not Qualify |
| **1934** >> Did Not Enter | **1974** >> Did Not Qualify |
| **1938** >> Did Not Enter | **1978** >> Did Not Qualify |
| **1950** >> Did Not Enter | **1982** >> Did Not Qualify |
| **1954** >> First Round | **1986** >> First Round |
| **1958** >> Did Not Enter | **1990** >> First Round |
| **1962** >> Did Not Qualify | **1994** >> First Round |
| **1966** >> Did Not Enter | **1998** >> First Round |

## ★ WORLD CUP RECORDS, STORIES AND WEIRDNESS

**BIGGEST DEFEAT** >> South Korea were thrashed 9-0 by Hungary in Zurich in 1954. Between them Kocis and Hungarian great Puskas scored 5.

# GROUP B

| OPPONENT | DATE | UK TIME | VENUE |
|---|---|---|---|
| Slovenia | **2 June** | 12.30 | **Gwangju, Korea** |
| Paraguay | **7 June** | 10.00 | **Jeonju, Korea** |
| South Africa | **12 June** | 12.30 | **Daejeon, Korea** |

## "perennial under-achievers?"

# SPAIN

Spain qualified with ease for the World Cup Finals – as they always do. Unbeaten, scoring 21 goals, shared between 11 different players, in eight games. There was never any doubt that Spain would be in the Finals. The remaining doubt is whether this time they will do anything about their poor record in major tournaments. It takes a Spaniard with a long memory to recall the heady days when his country achieved their best finish in a World Cup Finals, a fourth place all the way back in the 1950 World Cup Brazil.

At France '98 Spain bowed out at the group stage after suffering an opening 3-2 defeat by Nigeria and then held to a 0-0 draw by Paraguay. At Euro 2000 Spain reached the quarter-finals where they were defeated 2-1 by France, but it could have been different but for Raul's last minute penalty miss.

Spain's relative lack of international success is all the more surprising when you look at their domestic game. They boast one of the strongest and richest leagues in the world, attracting many top stars from abroad and, significantly, most of the national squad play for Spanish clubs.

Some sort of breakthrough was thought to have been achieved when Spain, as hosts, lifted the 1992 Olympic Soccer Gold Medal. However, few of the Olympic winning team really established themselves in the national side and ten years on Spain have still to truly thrive at major tournaments.

Undoubtedly, this is a country brimming with football talent. Their star player is Raul who, since making his debut in October 1996 at the age of 19, carries the weight of expectation of fans and media alike for both club and country. He's been ever present in the side since Euro 2000 and is rarely missing from the Real Madrid line up.

Calculations show that over the past two seasons Raul has played more football than any other Spanish player.

Other established figures include goalkeeper Jose Canizares, Luis Enrique (both featured in the Olympic team) and midfielder Fernando Hierro. New coach Jose Antonio Camacho, a former Real Madrid defender, has also been keen to introduce young players into the side, notably, Diego Tristan, who scored on each occasion he started a qualifying game, and midfielder Vicente who had an outstanding debut in the 4-0 home thrashing of Austria.

The Spanish have always blended youth and experience exceedingly well. And whatever system they adopt, the more flamboyant attacking style promoted by Camacho or the cautious defence-packed midfield system of his predecessor, they have always won competitive games. Friendlies are a different matter, usually accorded a lower priority, and it's no surprise that Spain's only defeats since Euro 2000 have been in friendlies by Germany, Holland and England. On the other hand, they've beaten World Cup holders France and World Cup co-hosts Japan, also in friendlies.

Spanish clubs thrive in European competition with Real Madrid European Champions League winners in 2000, and Valencia Champions League runners-up in 2000 and 2001. Alaves too were UEFA Cup finalists last season. Inexplicably, tournament soccer remains a problem for the Spanish national side. Their form, seeding and FIFA Ranking suggest that Spain ought to be serious contenders for a World Cup final, but past experience tips them as an also ran. An indefinable something prevents them making a serious impact on the world stage, despite the multi-million Euros of talent on show.

### ★ THE LOWDOWN

**Population:** 40 million

**Capital:** Madrid

**Leader:** Jose Maria Aznar

**Life Expectancy: Male:** 75 yrs Female: 82 yrs

>> Take a trip to Pamplona on 7th July if you want to see the Festival of San Fermin. Basically, this involves hundreds of men running for their lives, chased by dozens of bulls through the streets of the town. Now that's entertainment!

>> Whilst Spain managed to avoid active participation in either of the World Wars, it did suffer a devastating civil war between 1936-39 and only became truly democratic 27 years ago.

★ **ASSOCIATION:** Real Federacion Espanola De Futbol
★ **JOINED FIFA:** 1904
★ **JOINED UEFA:** 1954
★ **PLAYERS:** 408,200

★ **CLUBS:** 10,240
★ **WEBSITE:** www.futvol.com
★ **HONOURS:** European Championship – 1964; Olympics – 1992.

Gaizka Mendieta – style, skill and steel personified. Dodgy barnet though.

## ★ ROAD TO QUALIFICATION

**Sep 00 Bosnia** (a) > (w) 1-**2**
Gerard 39, Etxeberria 72

**Oct 00 Israel** (h) > (w) **2**-0
Gerard 22, Hierro 54

**Oct 00 Austria** (a) > (d) 1-**1** Baraja 27

**Mar 01 Liechtenstein** (h) > (w) **5**-0
Helguera 21, Mendieta 37, 82,
Hierro 55 pen, Raul 68

**Jun 01 Bosnia** (h) > (w) **4**-1
Hierro 27, Javi Moreno 76, Raul 89,
Diego Tristan 90

**Jun 01 Israel** (a) > (d) 1-**1** Raul 63

**Sep 01 Austria** (h) > (w) **4**-0
Diego Tristan 45, Morientes 79, 84,
Mendieta 90

**Sep 01 Liechtenstein** (a) > (w) 0-**2**
Raul 19, Nadal 82

## ★ FINAL GROUP TABLE

| Team | P | W | D | L | F | A | Pts |
|---|---|---|---|---|---|---|---|
| Spain | 8 | 6 | 2 | 0 | 21 | 4 | 20 |
| Austria | 8 | 4 | 3 | 1 | 10 | 8 | 15 |
| Israel | 8 | 3 | 3 | 2 | 11 | 7 | 12 |
| Bosnia | 8 | 2 | 2 | 4 | 12 | 12 | 8 |
| Liechtenstein | 8 | 0 | 0 | 8 | 0 | 23 | 0 |

## ★ RECENT RESULTS

**Feb 02 Portugal** (h) > (d) **1**-1 Morientes 41
**Mar 02 Holland** (a) > (l) 1-**0**

## DID YOU KNOW?

Spain's biggest international win was 12-1 over Malta in an European Championship qualifier in December 1983. Santillana and Rincon both scored four times in the game.

**Oh, how they flatter to deceive,** Spain – the perennial under-achievers of international football. Will it be different this time? Well coach Jose Antonio Camacho has yet again a world beating squad at his disposal. A team that starts with goalkeeper Jose Santiago Canizares, runs through centre back Fernando Hierro and midfielder Josep Guadiola and finishes with world class striker Raul Gonzalez Blanco. Four experienced players on whom Spain relies to make things happen – and during qualifying they did just that. Hierro is partnered with Nadal in the centre of defence with Sergi left back and new boy Manuel Pablo, who has made the right back position his own since making his debut in August 2000. Guardiola is still supported by the familiar Luis Enrique on the left while Ivan Helguera and Gaizka Mendieta complete a midfield quartet of style, steel and skill. Raul, still carrying the expectations of the Spanish supporters, has had the pressure taken off him up front with the arrival of the revelation that is Diego Tristan.

## PROBABLE FORMATION 4-4-2

CANIZARES

MANUEL PABLO — HIERRO — NADAL — SERGI

MENDIETA — HELGUERA — GUARDIOLA — LUIS ENRIQUE

RAUL — TRISTAN

## ★ MEN THAT MATTER!

### RAUL GONZALEZ

Age>> 24
Club>> Real Madrid
Raul is the golden boy of Spanish football who missed a crucial penalty against France at Euro 2000. He won the European Champions League winner with Real Madrid in 1998 and 2000.

### FERNANDO HIERRO

Age>> 34
Club>>Real Madrid
Captain and Spain's most capped outfield player will be playing in his fourth World Cup in a 13-year international career. He has experienced defeat just seven times in 83 appearances with Spain.

### DIEGO TRISTAN

Age>> 26
Club>> Deportivo La Coruna
>> Inspired by Spain's 1986 World Cup hero Emilio Butragueno, Tristan broke into the Spanish side after banging in the goals for La Coruna following an £8 million move.

## ★ PROBABLE SQUAD / ★ QUALIFICATION RECORD

| NAME | POSITION | CLUB | APS/GOALS | GAMES | MINS | Y/C | R/C | GOALS |
|------|----------|------|-----------|-------|------|-----|-----|-------|
| Santiago Canizares | Goalkeeper | Valencia, Spain | 33/0 | 3 | 270 | 0 | 0 | 0 |
| Iker Casillas | Goalkeeper | Real Madrid, Spain | 12/0 | 5 | 450 | 0 | 0 | 0 |
| Jose F'cisco Molina | Goalkeeper | Deportivo La Coruna, Spain | 8/0 | 0 | 0 | 0 | 0 | 0 |
| Fernandez Abelardo | Defender | Barcelona, Spain | 54/3 | 3 | 270 | 0 | 0 | 0 |
| Agustin Aranzabal | Defender | Real Sociedad, Spain | 24/0 | 2 | 180 | 0 | 0 | 0 |
| Fernando Hierro | Defender | Real Madrid, Spain | 83/27 | 13 | 1047 | 0 | 0 | 3 |
| Miguel Angel Nadal | Defender | Mallorca, Spain | 56/3 | 5 | 404 | 0 | 0 | 1 |
| Manuel Pablo | Defender | Deportivo La Coruna, Spain | 12/0 | 7 | 630 | 1 | 0 | 0 |
| Carles Puyol | Defender | Barcelona, Spain | 6/0 | 2 | 97 | 0 | 0 | 0 |
| Barjuan Sergi | Defender | Barcelona, Spain | 56/1 | 4 | 360 | 1 | 0 | 0 |
| Ruben Baraja | Midfielder | Valencia, Spain | 9/2 | 4 | 263 | 2 | 0 | 1 |
| Luis Enrique | Midfielder | Barcelona, Spain | 57/12 | 4 | 235 | 1 | 0 | 0 |
| Josep Guardiola | Midfielder | Brescia, Italy | 47/5 | 3 | 233 | 0 | 0 | 0 |
| Ivan Helguera | Midfielder | Real Madrid, Spain | 20/2 | 6 | 397 | 2 | 0 | 1 |
| Gaizka Mendieta | Midfielder | Lazio, Italy | 31/7 | 7 | 517 | 0 | 0 | 3 |
| Juan Carlos Valeron | Midfielder | Deportivo La Coruna, Spain | 18/0 | 3 | 210 | 0 | 0 | 0 |
| Rodriguez Vicente | Midfielder | Valencia, Spain | 4/0 | 1 | 84 | 0 | 0 | 0 |
| Javi Moreno | Forward | AC Milan, Italy | 5/1 | 3 | 195 | 0 | 0 | 1 |
| Fernando Morientes | Forward | Real Madrid, Spain | 17/13 | 2 | 109 | 0 | 0 | 2 |
| Pedro Munitis | Forward | Real Madrid, Spain | 21/2 | 4 | 219 | 2 | 0 | 0 |
| Gonzalez Raul | Forward | Real Madrid, Spain | 49/23 | 8 | 671 | 0 | 0 | 4 |
| Diego Tristan | Forward | Deportivo La Coruna, Spain | 6/2 | 4 | 210 | 0 | 0 | 2 |
| Ismael Urzaiz | Forward | Athl Bilbao, Spain | 25/8 | 3 | 200 | 0 | 0 | 0 |

**KEY:** APPS/GOALS = International Appearances/Goals; GAMES=Qualification Games played; MINS=Minutes played; Y/C= Yellow cards R/C=Red cards

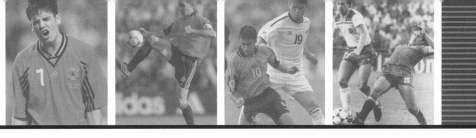

# HISTORY AT THE WORLD CUP

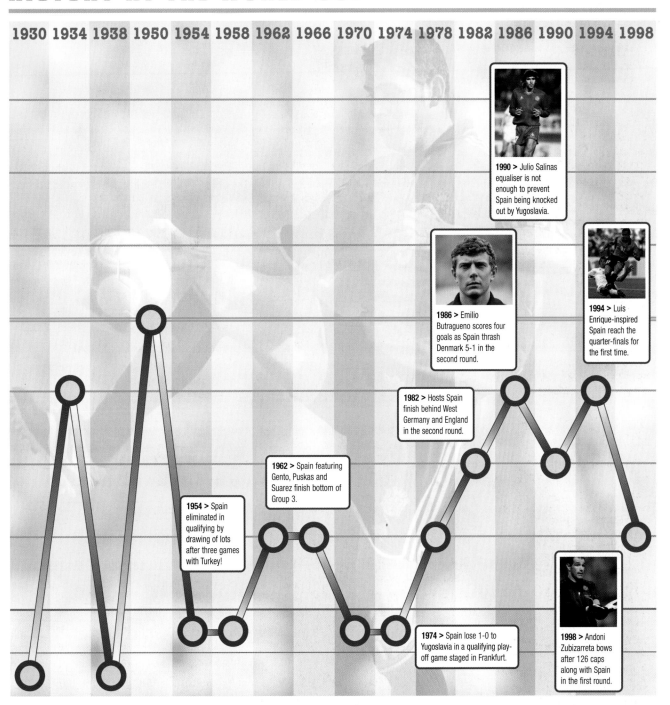

**1930 1934 1938 1950 1954 1958 1962 1966 1970 1974 1978 1982 1986 1990 1994 1998**

**1990 >** Julio Salinas equaliser is not enough to prevent Spain being knocked out by Yugoslavia.

**1986 >** Emilio Butragueno scores four goals as Spain thrash Denmark 5-1 in the second round.

**1994 >** Luis Enrique-inspired Spain reach the quarter-finals for the first time.

**1982 >** Hosts Spain finish behind West Germany and England in the second round.

**1962 >** Spain featuring Gento, Puskas and Suarez finish bottom of Group 3.

**1954 >** Spain eliminated in qualifying by drawing of lots after three games with Turkey!

**1974 >** Spain lose 1-0 to Yugoslavia in a qualifying play-off game staged in Frankfurt.

**1998 >** Andoni Zubizarreta bows after 126 caps along with Spain in the first round.

## ★ WORLD CUP HISTORY

| | | | |
|---|---|---|---|
| **1930** >> Did Not Enter | | **1970** >> Did Not Qualify | |
| **1934** >> Quarter-Final | | **1974** >> Did Not Qualify | |
| **1938** >> Did Not Enter | | **1978** >> First Round | |
| **1950** >> Fourth Place | | **1982** >> Second Round | |
| **1954** >> Did Not Qualify | | **1986** >> Quarter-Final | |
| **1958** >> Did Not Qualify | | **1990** >> Second Round | |
| **1962** >> First Round | | **1994** >> Quarter-Final | |
| **1966** >> irst Round | | **1998** >> First Round | |

## ★ WORLD CUP RECORDS, STORIES AND WEIRDNESS

**MOST GOALS IN A MATCH** >> Emilio Butragueño put 4 past Denmark in 1986.

**SHOCKING RESULT** >> Spain against Denmark 5-1 in 1986: In the first round Denmark had been cruising, winning all their matches, including thrashing South American champions Uruguay 6-1 and West Germany 2-0. They even took the lead in their second round game against Spain, but then the wheels fell off. Butragueño scored four of Spain's five goals in this astonishing game.

| OPPONENT | DATE | UK TIME | VENUE |
|----------|------|---------|-------|
| England | **2 June** | 10.30 | **Saitama, Japan** |
| Nigeria | **7 June** | 07.30 | **Kobe, Japan** |
| Argentina | **12 June** | 07.30 | **Miyagi, Japan** |

## "the Swedes, not to everyone's taste"

# SWEDEN

The current Swedish side is arguably short on world class players and is considered a workmanlike side that makes up for a lack of flair with good organisation, hard work, and team play. It's a hard side to beat that ploughed its way, doggedly, through qualifying – topping a group, luckily for Sweden, devoid of any of the more powerful European sides. It was better than Azerbaijan, Macedonia and Moldova, but in no way superior to Slovakia or Turkey.

Sweden have developed a reputation as a cautious, goal-shy outfit that scores few goals but, fortunately, concedes even less. This was evident at Euro 2000 where they failed to win a single game. Top striker Kennet Andersson, who before retiring from the game had run up a tally of 31 goals in 71 appearances, failed to score at the tournament. The Swedes were also reliant on Henrik Larsson who had barely recovered from a long-term injury.

A defeat by Iceland in a friendly – Sweden's first loss to the Icelanders in 49 years – coupled with a narrow World Cup win over Azerbaijan and draws with Turkey and Slovakia, had the Swedish media baying for the heads of joint coaches Tommy Söderberg and Lars Lagerbäck. Under Söderberg/Lagerbäck Sweden had averaged less than a goal a game and the 0-0 draw with Slovakia meant they'd gone some 14 matches since scoring more than one goal in a game.

Sweden ploughed on beating Macedonia 1-0 by a single Anders Svensson goal. The Southampton player had also scored the winner against Azerbaijan in the opening qualifying game.

Substitute Marcus Allback was the saviour in Moldova. The Heerenveen forward came on in the 81st minute and scored twice in the last two minutes of the match to give Sweden a 2-0 win in a game they had fielded an experimental and disastrous midfield system. Allback scored both goals in the 2-0 home win over Slovakia in a game that Lagerbäck described as Sweden's most important result yet.

Four days later, and to everyone's amazement, they thrashed Moldova 6-0. Henrik Larsson, Europe's Golden Boot Winner with his 53 goals in all competitions for Celtic, who had been widely criticised for his lack of goalscoring at international level, netted four times – albeit with a hat-trick of penalties. The 2-1 victory over Macedonia set up a daunting trip to Istanbul to decide who would automatically qualify and who would be condemned to the play-offs.

Turkey's Hakan Sukur beat goalkeeper Thomas Hedman in the 51st minute giving Turkey a deserved lead – they'd dominated the game – and the play-offs beckoned for the Swedes. Henrik Larsson stole an equaliser in the 87th minute then, dramatically, Andreas Andersson scored in the dying seconds to snatch a 2-1 win and qualification for the World Cup.

The majority of the current Swedish squad play outside the country and the two biggest names in the side are Celtic's phenomenal striker Henrik Larsson and defender and captain Patrik Andersson. Larsson is one of the world's best marksmen. Andersson won the UEFA Champions League with Bayern Munich in 2001 before moving to Barcelona last summer. The emergence of Zlatan Ibrahimovic in the latter stages of qualification suggested that he could have an important role to play in the new side. The 19 year-old left Malmö FF in 2001 for Dutch giants Ajax Amsterdam, becoming the most expensive Swedish footballer in history.

Sweden's last World Cup appearance was in 1994 when they reached the semi-finals and ultimately secured third place. Whether the current side can repeat such endeavours will depend, for the most part, on the performance of these three players.

★ **ASSOCIATION:** Svenska Fotbollfoerbundet

★ **JOINED FIFA:** 1904

★ **JOINED UEFA:** 1954

★ **PLAYERS:** 485,000

★ **CLUBS:** 3,250

★ **WEBSITE:** www.svenskfotbol.se

★ **HONOURS:** Olympics – 1948.

Captain Patrik Andersson steadies the Swedish ship.

## ★ ROAD TO QUALIFICATION

**Sep 00 Azerbaijan** (a) > (w) 0-**1**
Svensson, A 9

**Oct 00 Turkey** (h) > (d) **1**-1 Larsson 65

**Oct 00 Slovakia** (a) > (d) 0-**0**

**Mar 01 Macedonia** (h) > (w) **1**-0
Svensson, A 43

**Mar 01 Moldova** (a) > (w) 0-**2**
Allback 89, 90

**Jun 01 Slovakia** (h) > (w) **2**-0
Allback 45, 51

**Jun 01 Moldova** (h) > (w) **6**-0
Larsson 38 pen, 58, 68 pen, 79,
Alexandersson, D 74, Andersson 77

**Sep 01 Macedonia** (a) > (w) 1-**2**
Larsson 28, Andersson, P 33

**Sep 01 Turkey** (a) > (w) 1-**2**
Larsson 87, Andersson, A 90

**Oct 01 Azerbaijan** (h) > (w) **3**-0
Svensson, A 52, Larsson 60 pen,
Ibrahimovic 69

## ★ FINAL GROUP TABLE

| Team | P | W | D | L | F | A | Pts |
|---|---|---|---|---|---|---|---|
| Sweden | 10 | 8 | 2 | 0 | 20 | 3 | 26 |
| Turkey | 10 | 6 | 3 | 1 | 18 | 8 | 21 |
| Slovakia | 10 | 5 | 2 | 3 | 16 | 9 | 17 |
| Macedonia | 10 | 1 | 4 | 5 | 11 | 18 | 7 |
| Moldova | 10 | 1 | 3 | 6 | 6 | 20 | 6 |
| Azerbaijan | 10 | 1 | 2 | 7 | 4 | 17 | 5 |

## ★ RECENT RESULTS

**Feb 02 Greece** (a) > (d) 2-**2**
Svensson, A 31, Selakovic 64

**Mar 02 Switzerland** (h) > (d) **1**-1
Allback 29

125

## DID YOU KNOW?

**Sweden's first official international was an 11-3 victory over Norway in Gothenburg in July 1908.**

Sweden's squad lacks depth and this tends to be reflected in the dour way the team plays. With no real flair players, Sweden are a dogged yet reliable side. Patrik Andersson and Johan Mjallby are the breakwaters of defence with Olaf Mellberg and Teddy Lucic sandwiching them as full backs. Mellberg and Lucic are not creative when moving forward but solid in their defensive duties. Sweden's midfield has undergone enormous change. Tobias Linderoth is the defensive anchor looking to supply the flanks where Niclas Alexandersson and Freddy Ljungberg seek to find ways round defences. Anders Svensson is a lively attack-minded midfielder, but lacks consistency at international level. Celtic's goal-machine Henrik Larsson is still the man the Swedes look to for goals, but in Marcus Allback they might have discovered a new star.

## PROBABLE FORMATION 4-4-2

HEDMAN

MELLBERG LUCIC

P ANDERSSON MJALLBY

ALEXANDERSSON LINDEROTH A SVENSSON LJUNGBERG

ALLBACK LARSSON

## ★ MEN THAT MATTER!

### MARCUS ALLBACK

Age>> 28

Club>> Heerenveen

Marcus Allback has stepped out of the shadow of Kennet Andersson and begun finding the net regularly for Sweden. His goals against Moldova and Slovakia were vital in qualifying.

### HENRIK LARSSON

Age>> 30

Club>> Celtic

An extraordinary goalscoring machine for his Scottish club with 35 goals in 2001, he scored a hat-trick of penalties against Moldova.

### PATRIK ANDERSSON

Age>> 30

Club>> Barcelona

Captain of the national side and a rock in defence. Andersson's transfer to Spanish giants Barcelona from German giants Bayern Munich reflect his reputation as one of Europe's top defenders.

## ★ PROBABLE SQUAD   ★ QUALIFICATION RECORD

| NAME | POSITION | CLUB | APS/GOALS | GAMES | MINS | Y/C | R/C | GOALS |
|---|---|---|---|---|---|---|---|---|
| Magnus Hedman | Goalkeeper | Coventry, England | 42/0 | 10 | 900 | 0 | 0 | 0 |
| Mattias Asper | Goalkeeper | Real Sociedad, Spain | 0/0 | 0 | 0 | 0 | 0 | 0 |
| Magnus Kihlstedt | Goalkeeper | Copenhagen, Denmark | 6/0 | 0 | 0 | 0 | 0 | 0 |
| Christoffer Andersson | Defender | Helsingborgs, Sweden | 12/0 | 3 | 169 | 0 | 0 | 0 |
| Patrik Andersson | Defender | Barcelona, Spain | 94/3 | 10 | 844 | 1 | 0 | 1 |
| Karl Corneliusson | Defender | AIK Stockholm, Sweden | 9/1 | 3 | 215 | 1 | 0 | 0 |
| Pontus Kamark | Defender | IFK Gothenburg, Sweden | 57/0 | 2 | 151 | 0 | 0 | 0 |
| Jozo Matovac | Defender | Helsingborg, Sweden | 3/0 | 2 | 180 | 0 | 0 | 0 |
| Olof Mellberg | Defender | Aston Villa, England | 19/0 | 8 | 720 | 0 | 0 | 0 |
| Kleber Saarenpaa | Defender | AaB Aalborg, Denmark | 12/0 | 5 | 311 | 0 | 0 | 0 |
| Niclas Alexandersson | Midfielder | Everton, England | 55/6 | 7 | 565 | 0 | 0 | 1 |
| Daniel Andersson | Midfielder | Venezia, Italy | 32/1 | 8 | 228 | 0 | 0 | 1 |
| Tobias Linderoth | Midfielder | Everton, England | 15/1 | 6 | 512 | 1 | 0 | 0 |
| Fredrik Ljungberg | Midfielder | Arsenal, England | 30/2 | 9 | 810 | 1 | 0 | 0 |
| Haken Mild | Midfielder | Wimbledon, England | 74/8 | 5 | 219 | 0 | 0 | 0 |
| Johan Mjallby | Midfielder | Celtic, Scotland | 31/4 | 5 | 427 | 0 | 0 | 0 |
| Stefan Schwarz | Midfielder | Sunderland, England | 69/6 | 2 | 170 | 0 | 0 | 0 |
| Anders Svensson | Midfielder | Southampton, England | 23/7 | 9 | 450 | 1 | 0 | 2 |
| Magnus Svensson | Midfielder | Brondby, Denmark | 24/1 | 3 | 248 | 0 | 0 | 1 |
| Marcus Allback | Forward | Heerenveen, Holland | 15/6 | 6 | 433 | 0 | 0 | 4 |
| Zlatan Ibrahimovic | Forward | Ajax, Holland | 4/1 | 1 | 24 | 0 | 0 | 1 |
| Henrik Larsson | Forward | Celtic, Scotland | 64/21 | 10 | 900 | 0 | 0 | 8 |
| Yksel Osmanovski | Forward | Bordeaux, France | 14/2 | 3 | 110 | 0 | 0 | 0 |

**KEY:** APPS/GOALS = International Appearances/Goals; GAMES=Qualification Games played; MINS=Minutes played; Y/C= Yellow cards R/C=Red cards

# HISTORY AT THE WORLD CUP

1930 1934 1938 1950 1954 1958 1962 1966 1970 1974 1978 1982 1986 1990 1994 1998

**1933 >** Sweden beat Estonia 4-1 in first World Cup qualifier to be played in Europe.

**1958 >** Sweden host and reach their First World Cup Final.

**1990 >** Stefan Schwarz and co suffer three 2-1 defeats by Brazil, Scotland and Costa Rica.

**1938 >** Wetterstrom scores four goals as Sweden thrash Cuba 8-0 in the quarter-finals.

**1994 >** Tomas Brolin shines as Sweden finish in third place beating Bulgaria 4-0 in the play-off.

**1950 >** Goals from Jeppson (2) and Andersson see Sweden inflict upon Italy their first World Cup defeat.

**1962 >** Sweden, with superior goal difference, fail to qualify after play-off with Switzerland.

## ★ WORLD CUP RECORDS, STORIES AND WEIRDNESS

**MOST GOALS IN A MATCH** >> Gustav Wetterström scored 4 against Cuba in 1938.

**PENALTY SUCCESS** >> Sweden has converted 5 of the 6 penalties it has been awarded at World Cup Finals, a performance bettered only by three other nations.

| OPPONENT | DATE | UK TIME | VENUE |
|----------|------|---------|-------|
| Russia | **5 June** | 07.30 | **Kobe, Japan** |
| Belgium | **10 June** | 10.00 | **Oita, Japan** |
| Japan | **14 June** | 07.30 | **Osaka, Japan** |

## "'Les Aigles de Carthage' impress in qualifying"

# TUNISIA

Tunisia impressed with the way they qualified for their third appearance at a World Cup Finals. During France 98 they found themselves in a tough group with Colombia, England and Romania – against whom they secured an impressive 1-1 draw. All in all they had generally acquitted themselves well on the world stage. Many of the players at France 98 will be back again to compete at Japan/Korea as the Tunisians have kept the core of a side – originally assembled at under-23 level – to compete at the 1996 Atlanta Olympics.

"Les Aigles de Carthage", who had finished fourth at the 2000 African Nations Cup under Italian coach Francesco Scoglio, dismissed Mauritania 5-1 on aggregate in the preliminary round and kicked off the group stage away against main rivals Ivory Coast.

Midfielder Zoubier Beya was in magnificent form setting up both goals for Imed Mhedhebi and Kais Ghodhbane in the 12th and 19th minutes respectively. What would have been a fantastic start to the group was tempered by poor defensive play that allowed the home side to recover and achieve an unlikely 2-2 draw. The Ivory Coast fans were even less happy with their team than the Tunisian supporters were with theirs and both teams found themselves holed up in the stadium while the police used tear gas to disperse the crowd.

It needed a sterling performance in their next game against Madagascar when Hassan Gabsi was sent off in the first half. Ten-man Tunisia battled on, Beya putting them ahead on the stroke of half time. That was all that was needed as the Tunisians defended well, keeping the Madagascans at arms' length.

Immediately after, Tunisia's qualification hopes were undermined when coach Scoglio quit. The Italian had been offered a job by club side Genoa and wanted to split his time between Italy and Tunisia. The Tunisian FA decided this was not an option and so Scoglio stepped down to be replaced by German Eckhard Krautzen. Krautzen continued Scoglio's good work, winning 2-1 in Congo and thrashing the Democratic Republic of Congo (formerly Zaire) 6-0 at home.

Two goals in the last five minutes from Ali Zitouni and Imed Mhadhebi clinched a 2-0 win in Madagascar followed by a 1-1 draw with Ivory Coast, now the only team who could stop them qualifying.

Tunisia then disposed of Congo 6-0 at home with goals from Badra, Zitouni, Beya (2), Mhadbi and Jelassi, virtually assuring qualification. In their last game, Tunisia travelled to the Stade de Martyrs in the Congo Democratic Republic and, in a brilliantly controlled performance, inflicted upon the home side their worst-ever home defeat. Khaled Badra put Tunisia ahead after 14 minutes with Zoubier Beya netting twice just after the break for a deserved 3-0 win. A result that unfortunately led to rioting among the unhappy Congo Democratic Republic supporters.

However, not all is entirely well with the North Africans. In reality Tunisia are an ageing side who lack sufficient depth in their squad to deal with injuries, as was demonstrated by their poor performance at the 2002 African Nations Cup where they not only failed to win, but failed to score. German coach Krautzen has also gone to be replaced by ex-France and Morocco coach Henri Michel.

## ★ THE LOWDOWN

**Population:** 9.7 million

**Capital:** Tunis

**Leader:** Mohammed Ghannouchi

**Life Expectancy:** Male: 72 yrs
Female: 75 yrs

>> Agriculture makes up the basis of the Tunisian economy; it accounts for 23% of the labour force.

>> Until 1815 piracy made up a large part of the national income, until, that is, the U.S. Navy attacked Tunis and put a stop to it.

>> In the south the fierce "Sirocco" winds can take the temperatures into the mid-40 degrees centigrade — better wear a hat and take plenty of liquids!

★ **ASSOCIATION:** Federation Tunisienne de Football
★ **JOINED FIFA:** 1960
★ **JOINED CAF:** 1960
★ **PLAYERS:** 18,300
★ **CLUBS:** 215
★ **WEBSITE:** www.ftf.com.tn
★ **HONOURS:** None

Genoa's Khaled Badra shows why none shall pass.

## ★ ROAD TO QUALIFICATION

**Apr 00 Mauritania** (a) > (w) 1-**2**
Jaidi 65, Gabsi 76

**Apr 00 Mauritania** (h) > (w) **3**-0 (agg **5**-1)
Bilal 16 og, Jaziri 25, Mhadhebi 49

**Jun 00 Ivory Coast** (a) > (d) 2-2
Imed 13, Kais 20

**Jul 00 Madagascar** (h) > (w) **1**-0 Baya 45

**Jan 01 Congo** (a) > (w) 1-**2**
Zitouni, A 38, Jaziri 58

**Feb 01 Congo DR** (h) > (w) **6**-0
Zitouni, A 8, 90, Jaziri 26, 64, Konzari 30, Baya 84

**Apr 01 Ivory Coast** (h) > (d) **1**-1 Jaziri 49

**May 01 Madagascar** (a) > (w) 0-**2**
Zitouni, A 85, Mhadhebi 90

**Jun 01 Congo** (h) > (w) **6**-0
Badra 28 pen, Zitouni, A 38, Baya 44, 61, Mhadhebi 58, Jelassi 90

**Jul 01 Congo DR** (a) > (w) 0-**3**
Badra 14, Baya 50, 54

## ★ FINAL GROUP TABLE

| Team | P | W | D | L | F | A | Pts |
|---|---|---|---|---|---|---|---|
| Tunisia | 8 | 6 | 2 | 0 | 23 | 4 | 20 |
| Ivory Coast | 8 | 4 | 3 | 1 | 18 | 8 | 15 |
| Congo DR | 8 | 3 | 1 | 4 | 7 | 16 | 10 |
| Madagascar | 8 | 2 | 0 | 6 | 5 | 15 | 6 |
| Congo | 8 | 1 | 2 | 5 | 5 | 15 | 5 |

## ★ RECENT RESULTS

Mar 02 **South Korea** (h) > (d) **0**-0

Mar 02 **Norway** (h) > (d) **0**-0

## DID YOU KNOW?

**Tunisia caused a shock in their first World Cup match in 1978 by beating Mexico 3-1 after going a goal down.**

Tunisia are reliant upon their first choice strikers Ali Zitouni and Adel Sellimi as became painfully obvious when both were absent from Tunisia's disastrous African Nations Cup – at which Tunisia failed to score a single goal. Sellimi, who has had a falling out with boss Henri Michel, is not guaranteed his place. Considering the current dearth of Tunisian talent, Sellimi's absence could again prove critical. If he does not travel to Japan/Korea then Jamel Zabi is his likely replacement. Tunisia are an ageing team, but age brings wisdom – of a sort. They are a defensively strong side and notoriously difficult to beat. Khaled Badra, Mounir Boukadida, Radhi Jaidi and Hatem Trabelsi are an experienced quartet, three of whom play their club soccer in Europe. The midfield is solid if neither blessed with flair nor an ability to surprise. Watch for Imed Mhadhebi, the player most likely to try and do something special.

## PROBABLE FORMATION   4-4-2

EL OUAER

BADRA   H TRABELSI

BOUKADIDA   JAIDI

BAYA   BOUZAIENE   NAFTI   MHADHEBI

ZITOUNI   SELLIMI

## ★ MEN THAT MATTER!

### KHALED BADRA

Age>> 29

Club>> Genoa

Tough, reliable defender who played for Tunisia at France 98 after making his mark at the Atlanta Olympics two years earlier. Highly-rated by ex-Tunisia boss Scoglio who signed him for Genoa.

### MHADHEBI

Age>> 26

Club>> Genoa

Featured in all but one of the qualifiers, scoring 4 goals which earned him a move to Genoa from Etoile Sahel at the beginning of the season.

### CHOKRI EL OAUER

Age>> 35

Club>> Esperence

El Oauer is a controversial goalkeeper who was banned from club competition after faking injury in an African Champions League. He will captain Tunisia and has played in five African Nations Cups.

## ★ PROBABLE SQUAD     ★ QUALIFICATION RECORD

| NAME | POSITION | CLUB | APS/GOALS | GAMES | MINS | Y/C | R/C | GOALS |
|---|---|---|---|---|---|---|---|---|
| Hassen Bejaoui | Goalkeeper | CA Bizerte, Tunisia | 0/0 | 0 | 0 | 0 | 0 | 0 |
| Chokri al-Ouaer | Goalkeeper | Esperance, Tunisia | 101/0 | 6 | 540 | 0 | 0 | 0 |
| Ahmed Jaouachi | Goalkeeper | US Monastir, Tunisia | 0/0 | 0 | 0 | 0 | 0 | 0 |
| Khaled Badra | Defender | Esperance, Tunisia | 71/9 | 8 | 720 | 1 | 0 | 2 |
| Mounir Boukadida | Defender | Waldhof Mannheim, Germany | 51/3 | 3 | 149 | 0 | 0 | 0 |
| Raouf Bouzaiene | Defender | Genoa, Italy | 40/0 | 8 | 586 | 1 | 0 | 0 |
| Radhi Jaidi | Defender | Esperance, Tunisia | 41/3 | 7 | 630 | 1 | 0 | 0 |
| Hamdi Marzouki | Defender | Africain, Tunisia | 4/0 | 1 | 22 | 0 | 0 | 0 |
| Emir Mkademi | Defender | Etoile Sahel, Tunisia | 6/0 | 0 | 0 | 0 | 0 | 0 |
| Hatem Trabelsi | Defender | Ajax, Holland | 26/0 | 3 | 111 | 0 | 0 | 0 |
| Walid Azaiez | Defender | Esperance, Tunisia | 18/2 | 1 | 90 | 0 | 0 | 0 |
| Zoubeir Baya | Midfielder | Besiktas, Turkey | 76/18 | 8 | 692 | 1 | 0 | 6 |
| Slim Ben Achour | Midfielder | Martigues, France | 2/0 | 0 | 0 | 0 | 0 | 0 |
| Riadh Bouazizi | Midfielder | Bursaspor, Turkey | 45/2 | 3 | 241 | 0 | 0 | 0 |
| Hassen Gabsi | Midfielder | Genoa, Italy | 47/16 | 6 | 459 | 3 | 1 | 0 |
| Kaies Ghodhbane | Midfielder | Etoile Sahel, Tunisia | 62/3 | 6 | 267 | 1 | 0 | 0 |
| Mehdi Nafti | Midfielder | Racing Santander, Spain | 2/0 | 0 | 0 | 0 | 0 | 0 |
| Bessam Daassi | Forward | Stade Tunisien, Tunisia | 4/2 | 0 | 0 | 0 | 0 | 0 |
| Ziad Jaziri | Forward | Etoile Sahel, Tunisia | 23/8 | 5 | 380 | 1 | 0 | 3 |
| Imed Mhadhebi | Forward | Genoa, Italy | 30/9 | 7 | 228 | 1 | 0 | 2 |
| Adel Sellimi | Forward | Freiberg, Germany | 2/0 | 2 | 162 | 0 | 1 | 0 |
| Jamel Zabi | Forward | CA Bizerte, Tunisia | 4/3 | 0 | 0 | 0 | 0 | 0 |
| Ali Zitouni | Forward | Esperance, Tunisia | 24/9 | 8 | 533 | 1 | 0 | 5 |

**KEY:** APPS/GOALS = International Appearances/Goals; GAMES=Qualification Games played; MINS=Minutes played; Y/C= Yellow cards R/C=Red cards

# HISTORY AT THE WORLD CUP

1930 1934 1938 1950 1954 1958 1962 1966 1970 1974 1978 1982 1986 1990 1994 1998

**1998 >** Skander Souayah's penalty in the draw with Romania is Tunisia's only goal of the competition.

**1978 >** Tunisia hold West Germany to a 0-0 draw after beating Mexico.

**1970 >** Tunisia go out on a toss of a coin after a third, drawn play-off game with Morocco.

**1962 >** Tunisia go out after lots are drawn with Morocco in the African qualifiers.

**1974 >** Tunisia are knocked out by Ivory Coast in the second round of African qualifying.

## ★ WORLD CUP HISTORY

| | |
|---|---|
| 1930 >> Did Not Enter | 1970 >> Did Not Qualify |
| 1934 >> Did Not Enter | 1974 >> Did Not Qualify |
| 1938 >> Did Not Enter | 1978 >> First Round |
| 1950 >> Did Not Enter | 1982 >> Did Not Qualify |
| 1954 >> Did Not Enter | 1986 >> Did Not Qualify |
| 1958 >> Did Not Enter | 1990 >> Did Not Qualify |
| 1962 >> Did Not Qualify | 1994 >> Did Not Qualify |
| 1966 >> Did Not Enter | 1998 >> First Round |

## ★ WORLD CUP RECORDS, STORIES AND WEIRDNESS

**SHORTEST WORLD CUP CAREER** >> Tunisia's Khemais Labidi played just two minutes against Mexico in 1978 as they ran out 3-1 winners. He was never seen on the world stage again.

# GROUP C

| OPPONENT | DATE | UK TIME | VENUE |
|----------|------|---------|-------|
| Brazil | **3 June** | **10.00** | **Ulsan, Korea** |
| Costa Rica | **9 June** | **10.00** | **Incheon, Korea** |
| China | **13 June** | **07.30** | **Seoul, Korea** |

## *"will it be Turkish delight in Korea?"*

# TURKEY

Turkey are back at the World Cup after a 48-year absence. Turkish soccer has been improving at international level in recent years; they qualified for both Euro 96 and Euro 2000, and while losing all their group games in England, reached the quarter-final stage in Amsterdam. At club level Galatasaray became the first Turkish club to win a European trophy when they beat Arsenal to lift the UEFA Cup.

The national team has been largely unchanged since Euro 2000 with Inter Milan's Hakan Sukur, who began his career at Galatasaray and is the most accomplished Turkish player of all time, still leading the attack and Fenerbahçe keeper Rüstü Recber in goal with a midfield of Okan Buruk and Tugay Kerimoglu at its heart. New coach Senol Gunes has brought on a significant young talent in German-born Yiliray Basturk. A dynamic and creative player who livens up the Turkish team whenever he is on the field.

Not that coach Senol Gunes has the universal backing of the Turkish media. Turkey's six-team qualifying group came down to a three-horse race between the Turks, Slovakia and Sweden. They started well with wins over Moldova and Azerbaijan sandwiching a dramatic 1-1 draw in Sweden, where Tayfur Havatcu converted an injury time penalty equaliser – an impressive result as they had to field a seriously under strength side owing to injuries, suspensions and Hakan Sukur playing on despite food poisoning.

A 1-1 home draw with rivals Slovakia was followed by wins over Macedonia and Azerbaijan. In the return fixture Turkey were almost blown away by Macedonia in Bursa. Turkey found themselves 2-0 down inside just 20 minutes in front of 25,000 of their own supporters. It needed an unlikely hat-trick from Aston Villa's defender Alpay and the sending off of opponent Krstev to salvage a point in a thrilling 3-3 draw.

Hakan Sukur's first-half winner in Slovakia, however, assured Turkey of at least a play-off place. With a home fixture against Sweden to come, automatic qualification seemed probable. Hakan Sukur gave Turkey a 51st minute lead against the Swedes and they were within two minutes of victory when Henrik Larsson equalised. Andreas Andersson scored the winner for Sweden in the last minute of the game and Turkey were suddenly condemned to the play-offs. Unsurprisingly, coach Senol Gunes was subjected to another barrage of criticism.

In the play-offs Turkey were drawn against Austria. Senol Gunes was able to silence his critics with a 6-0 aggregate win including a 5-0 second leg thrashing in which Basturk netted his first international goal, Hakan Sukur boosted his all-time tally to 35 with Okan and Arif (2) completing the scoring.

Turkey have a realistic chance of progressing to the second round from a group that includes World Cup novices Costa Rica and debutantes China. The Turkish media expect their team to beat both of these sides heaping yet more pressure on Senol Gunes, who is, after all, only the second coach of a Turkish World Cup team.

---

### ★ THE LOWDOWN

**Population:** 66.4 million

**Capital:** Ankara

**Leader:** Bulent Ecevit

**Life Expectancy:** Male: 69 yrs
Female: 73 yrs

>> Turkey became a republic in 1923. Its founding father was Mohammed Kamal, who adopted the name Ataturk.

>> Turkey is home to Mount Ararat, the legendary landing place of Noah's Ark.

>> Besides being renowned for Turkish delight, belly dancing and raki (an aniseed flavoured alcoholic drink), Turkish carpets are also world famous. It can take two women over 2 years to make a decent sized one – so careful with those shoes!

- ★ **ASSOCIATION:** Turkiye Futbol Federasyonou
- ★ **JOINED FIFA:** 1923
- ★ **JOINED UEFA:** 1962
- ★ **PLAYERS:** 64,600
- ★ **CLUBS:** 230
- ★ **WEBSITE:** www.tff.org
- ★ **HONOURS:** None.

*Johan Mjallby brings down Hakan Unsal while he's still singing the Turkish National Anthem.*

## ★ ROAD TO QUALIFICATION

**Sep 00 Moldova** (h) > (w) **2-0**
Okan 45, Emre 75

**Oct 00 Sweden** (a) > (d) 1-1
Havatacu 90

**Oct 00 Azerbaijan** (a) > (w) 0-1
Hakan Sukur 73

**Mar 01 Slovakia** (h) > (d) **1-1**
Hakan Sukur 53 pen

**Mar 01 Macedonia** (a) > (w) **1-2**
Mitrevski 68 og, Umit Davala 70

**Jun 01 Azerbaijan** (h) > (w) **3-0**
Tayfun 2, Oktay 27, Hakan Sukur 33

**Jun 01 Macedonia** (h) > (d) **3-3**
Alpay 43, 58, 70

**Sep 01 Slovakia** (a) > (w) **0-1**
Hakan Sukur 34

**Sep 01 Sweden** (h) > (l) **1-2**
Hakan Sukur 51

**Oct 01 Moldova** (a) > (w) **0-3**
Emre 8, Nihat 78, Mansiz 82

**Nov 01 Austria** (a) > (w) **0-1** Okan 60

**Nov 01 Austria** (h) > (w) **5-0** (agg **6-0**)
Basturk 24, Hakan Sukur 31, Okan 45,
Arif 70, 84

## ★ FINAL GROUP TABLE

| Team | P | W | D | L | F | A | Pts |
|------|---|---|---|---|---|---|-----|
| Sweden | 10 | 8 | 2 | 0 | 20 | 3 | 26 |
| **Turkey** | **10** | **6** | **3** | **1** | **18** | **8** | **21** |
| Slovakia | 10 | 5 | 2 | 3 | 16 | 9 | 17 |
| Macedonia | 10 | 1 | 4 | 5 | 11 | 18 | 7 |
| Moldova | 10 | 1 | 3 | 6 | 6 | 20 | 6 |
| Azerbaijan | 10 | 1 | 2 | 7 | 4 | 17 | 5 |

## ★ RECENT RESULTS

**Feb 02 Ecuador** (h) > (l) **0-1**

**Mar 00 South Korea** (h) > (d) 0-0

## DID YOU KNOW?

**Turkey are back in the World Cup for the first time in 48 years and Senol Gunes is only their second ever World Cup coach.**

A serious ankle injury to Aston Villa defender Alpay makes the player doubtful for the World Cup and his probable absence will have a serious effect on Turkey's defensive capabilities. Alpay has been ever present on the left of a back three which includes Emre Asik and Umit Ozat, but Alpay's understudy, Hakan Unsal, has been hovering in the wings and is ready to shine. An exciting midfield, which emphasises attack, mixes the new talent of Yiliray Basturk with the experienced Abdullah, Okan and Tugay, experience which may help to cover any weaknesses at the back. Turkey, though, still rely on goals from Hakan Sukur. In Hasan Sas he has a perfect foil, a player whose movement is an integral part of Turkish attacking play, and who creates the space and chances for marksman Hakan Sukur.

# PROBABLE FORMATION 3-4-1-2

RUSTU

EMRE ASIK — HAKAN UNSAL

UMIT OZAT

UMIT DAVALA — OKAN — TUGAY — BASTURK

ABDULLAH

HAKAN SUKUR — HASAN SAS

## ★ MEN THAT MATTER!

### YILDIRAY BASTURK

Age>> 23

Club>> Bayer Leverkusen

Basturk is a German-born Turkish international playmaker who became the youngest captain in the Bundesliga with Bochum. He later joined Leverkusen for £4 million and has impressed every time he's played for Turkey.

### HAKAN SUKUR

Age>> 30

Club>> Parma

Turkey's main striker whose goals have been the reason Turkey have qualified for their first World Cup and two European Championships. Confirmed his status as a top striker in Serie A with Parma.

### TUGAY KERIMOGLU

Age>> 31

Club>> Blackburn Rovers

Tugay is Turkey's midfield anchor, a reliable, inventive and experienced player. He has been a consistent performer in the English Premiership with Blackburn.

## ★ PROBABLE SQUAD          ★ QUALIFICATION RECORD

| NAME | POSITION | CLUB ? | APS/GOALS | GAMES | MINS | Y/C | R/C | GOALS |
|------|----------|--------|-----------|-------|------|-----|-----|-------|
| Metin Aktas | Goalkeeper | Trabzonspor, Turkey | 2/0 | 0 | 0 | 0 | 0 | 0 |
| Omer Catkic | Goalkeeper | Gaziantepspor, Turkey | 3/0 | 0 | 0 | 0 | 0 | 0 |
| Rustu Recber | Goalkeeper | Fenerbahce, Turkey | 62/0 | 12 | 1080 | 0 | 0 | 0 |
| Fatih Akyel | Defender | Fenerbahce, Turkey | 33/0 | 9 | 610 | 1 | 0 | 0 |
| Emre Asik | Defender | Galatasaray, Turkey | 13/2 | 1 | 90 | 0 | 0 | 0 |
| Umit Bozkurt | Defender | Galatasaray, Turkey | 2/0 | 2 | 180 | 0 | 0 | 0 |
| Bulent Korkmaz | Defender | Galatasaray, Turkey | 65/2 | 7 | 569 | 2 | 0 | 0 |
| Umit Ozat | Defender | Fenerbahce, Turkey | 10/0 | 7 | 594 | 1 | 0 | 0 |
| Mehmet Polat | Defender | Gaziantepspor, Turkey | 4/0 | 1 | 90 | 0 | 0 | 0 |
| Ogun Temizkanoglu | Defender | Fenerbahce, Turkey | 74/5 | 6 | 482 | 2 | 0 | 0 |
| Emre Belozoglu | Midfielder | Internazionale, Italy | 9/1 | 7 | 570 | 3 | 0 | 1 |
| Okan Buruk | Midfielder | Internazionale, Italy | 25/4 | 8 | 585 | 2 | 0 | 3 |
| Umit Davala | Midfielder | Milan, Italy | 20/1 | 6 | 540 | 0 | 0 | 1 |
| Abdullah Ercan | Midfielder | Fenerbahce, Turkey | 67/0 | 9 | 730 | 0 | 0 | 0 |
| Tayfur Havutcu | Midfielder | Besiktas, Turkey | 37/6 | 6 | 333 | 0 | 0 | 1 |
| Tugay Kerimoglu | Midfielder | Blackburn, England | 66/2 | 5 | 450 | 1 | 0 | 0 |
| Tayfun Korkut | Midfielder | Real Sociedad, Spain | 36/1 | 6 | 212 | 0 | 0 | 1 |
| Ergun Penbe | Midfielder | Galatasaray, Turkey | 18/0 | 8 | 316 | 0 | 0 | 0 |
| Hakan Unsal | Midfielder | Blackburn, England | 22/0 | 4 | 360 | 0 | 0 | 0 |
| Basturk Yildiray | Midfielder | Bayer Leverkusen, Germany | 11/1 | 7 | 309 | 0 | 0 | 1 |
| Arif Erdem | Forward | Galatasaray, Turkey | 48/8 | 10 | 513 | 0 | 0 | 2 |
| Hasan Sas | Forward | Galatasaray, Turkey | 12/0 | 11 | 709 | 1 | 0 | 0 |
| Hakan Sukur | Forward | Parma, Italy | 70/34 | 11 | 990 | 1 | 0 | 6 |

**KEY:** APPS/GOALS = International Appearances/Goals; GAMES=Qualification Games played; MINS=Minutes played; Y/C= Yellow cards R/C=Red cards

# HISTORY AT THE WORLD CUP

1930 1934 1938 1950 1954 1958 1962 1966 1970 1974 1978 1982 1986 1990 1994 1998

**1954 >** Turkey qualify for the World Cup by the drawing of lots after three games with Spain.

**1950 >** Turkey thrash Syria 7-0 to qualify but then withdraw from the competition.

**1958 >** Turkey refuse to play Israel in qualifying and withdraw from the World Cup.

**1970 >** Turkey lose all four qualifying matches to USSR and Northern Ireland.

## ★ WORLD CUP HISTORY

| | |
|---|---|
| **1930** >> Did Not Enter | **1970** >> Did Not Qualify |
| **1934** >> Did Not Enter | **1974** >> Did Not Qualify |
| **1938** >> Did Not Enter | **1978** >> Did Not Qualify |
| **1950** >> Withdrew | **1982** >> Did Not Qualify |
| **1954** >> First Round | **1986** >> Did Not Qualify |
| **1958** >> Did Not Enter | **1990** >> Did Not Qualify |
| **1962** >> Did Not Qualify | **1994** >> Did Not Qualify |
| **1966** >> Did Not Qualify | **1998** >> Did Not Qualify |

## ★ WORLD CUP RECORDS, STORIES AND WEIRDNESS

**TOP SCORER** >> Turkey's best international goalscorer is Hakan Sükür with 16 to date.

**WORLD CUP PERFORMANCE** >> Turkey have played a total of 87 matches (including qualifying) winning 28, drawing 12 and losing 47.

# GROUP D

| OPPONENT | DATE | UK TIME | VENUE |
|----------|------|---------|-------|
| Portugal | **5 June** | **10.00** | **Suwon, Korea** |
| South Korea | **10 June** | **07.30** | **Daegu, Korea** |
| Poland | **14 June** | **12.30** | **Daejeon, Korea** |

## *"they will play for honour"*

# UNITED STATES

Events of September 11 have had a profound effect on America and the nation's footballers are by no means immune. On the day the USA played their crucial qualifying match against Jamaica at the Foxboro Stadium in Boston, the US bombing of Afghanistan began. "We knew we were at war so it was pretty emotional during the national anthem, but after that we just focused on the game," admitted forward Joe Max-Moore.

And America's footballers needed to focus on the game – after three dreadful performances (losing, in the process, to Mexico, Honduras and Costa Rica), a victory over Jamaica was crucial to the country's World Cup qualifying hopes. The USA got off to an ideal start when Moore scored after just four minutes with a diving header from Claudio Reyna's free-kick. Ten minutes later Jamaica equalised through Jamie Lawrence, but the USA were dominating the game. Frustratingly, they seemed incapable of creating meaningful chances when, in the 81st minute, teenage star Landon Donovan was brought down in the penalty area. Moore stepped up to send the goalkeeper the wrong way for a 2-1 win which, combined with Honduras's shock defeat by Trinidad & Tobago, meant the USA had qualified for the World Cup on a day of high emotion.

With all they've been through the USA will be a more united squad than they were four years ago when internal disputes between players and staff badly affected the squad and led to the USA finishing with the worst record of the 32 teams at France 98.

After the huge disappointment of the last World Cup, the USA brought in new manager Bruce Arena, America's most successful club and college coach who has won an international cap as a goalkeeper.

So far their Japan/Korea preparations have been good. The USA won the 2002 Gold Cup beating Costa Rica 2-0 in the final in Pasadena. The goals came from Josh Wolff, who missed most of the qualifiers through injury and defender Jeff Agoos, who was ever present throughout the qualifying campaign.

Success at the Gold Cup was helped enormously by a 35-day pre-tournament training camp and coach Bruce Arena hopes to reproduce the camp ahead of the World Cup.

Eight years after hosting the World Cup, America has an estimated 18 million soccer players, but the game can still only be considered a minority sport in the US. There are only ten professional teams in the Major Soccer League after two teams recently went out of business. The Gold Cup attracted an average crowd of 18,500 (compared to the 90,000 spectators who watched the USA women's soccer stars win the World Cup Final in Pasadena, California). Indeed, at home matches against Mexico and Honduras, away support outnumbered the home side's fans – leading to the observation that it was easier for the US to play Mexico in Mexico City rather than Los Angeles.

America goes into the World Cup Finals with justifiable ambition. Under coach Arena they have become a side that can win matches – as the third ever win over Mexico during the qualifiers demonstrated.

★ **ASSOCIATION:** United States Soccer Federation

★ **JOINED FIFA:** 1913

★ **JOINED FOOTBALL CONFEDERATION:** 1961

★ **PLAYERS:** 1,411,500

★ **CLUBS:** 7,000

★ **WEBSITE:** www.us-soccer.com

★ **HONOURS:** CONCACAF Gold Cup – 1991, 2002

## ★ ROAD TO QUALIFICATION

Jul 00 **Guatemala** (a) > (d) 1-**1** Razov 45

Jul 00 **Costa Rica** (a) > (l) 2-**1** Stewart 65

Aug 00 **Barbados** (h) > (w) **7**-0
Pope 14, McBride 28, Moore 45, 82, O'Brien 46, Ramos 72, Stewart 74

Sep 00 **Guatemala** (h) > (w) **1**-0
McBride 72

Oct 00 **Costa Rica** (h) > (d) **0**-0

Nov 00 **Barbados** (a) > (w) 0-**4**
Mathis 63, Stewart 73, Jones 77, Razov 90

Feb 01 **Mexico** (h) > (w) **2**-0
Wolff 47, Stewart 87

Mar 01 **Honduras** (a) > (w) 1-**2**
Stewart 32, Mathis 87

Apr 01 **Costa Rica** (h) > (w) **1**-0 Wolff 69

Jun 01 **Jamaica** (a) > (d) 0-**0**

Jun 01 **Trinidad & Tobago** (h) > (w) **2**-0
Razov 2, Stewart 20

Jun 01 **Mexico** (a) > (l) 1-0

Sep 01 **Honduras** (h) > (l) 2-3
Stewart 7, 83

Sep 01 **Costa Rica** (a) > (l) 2-**0**

Oct 01 **Jamaica** (h) > (w) **2**-1
Moore 3, 80

Nov 01 **Trinidad & Tobago** (a) > (d) 0-**0**

## ★ FINAL GROUP TABLE

| Team | P | W | D | L | F | A | Pts |
|---|---|---|---|---|---|---|---|
| Costa Rica | 10 | 7 | 2 | 1 | 17 | 7 | 23 |
| Mexico | 10 | 5 | 2 | 3 | 16 | 9 | 17 |
| United States | 10 | 5 | 2 | 3 | 11 | 8 | 17 |
| Honduras | 10 | 4 | 2 | 4 | 17 | 17 | 14 |
| Jamaica | 10 | 2 | 2 | 6 | 7 | 14 | 8 |
| Trinidad & Tob | 10 | 1 | 2 | 7 | 5 | 18 | 5 |

## ★ SEMI-FINAL GROUP TABLE

| Team | P | W | D | L | F | A | Pts |
|---|---|---|---|---|---|---|---|
| United States | 6 | 3 | 2 | 1 | 14 | 3 | 11 |
| Costa Rica | 6 | 3 | 1 | 2 | 9 | 6 | 10 |
| Guatemala | 6 | 3 | 1 | 2 | 9 | 6 | 10 |
| Barbados | 6 | 1 | 0 | 5 | 3 | 20 | 3 |

## ★ RECENT RESULTS

Feb 02 **Italy** (a) > (l) **1**-0

Mar 02 **Honduras** (h) > (w) **4**-0
Mathis 14, 59, Donovan 44, 67

Mar 02 **Ecuador** (h) > (w) **1**-0 Lewis 21

Mar 02 **Germany** (a) > (l) 4-**2** Mathis 17,71

Apr 02 **Mexico** (h) > (w) **1**-0 Mathis 65

*Captain America remembers he's left the gas on.*

## DID YOU KNOW?

When the USA famously beat England 1-0 at the 1950 World Cup, Haiti-born Larry Gaetjens scored the historic winning goal.

**Captain Claudio Reyna is still** the USA's key player in a side that, in recent years, has switched from 3-5-2 to 4-4-2. Reyna remains the heart of midfield from which so many American moves begin. The whole system is designed to supply America's twin strike force of Joe Max-Moore and new wonder boy Landon Donovan through Reyna's superb passing which release an attacking midfield of Chris Armas, John O'Brien and Ernie Stewart. Moore is an established member of the side while Landon, a relative newcomer, has made himself an automatic first choice. No mean feat considering the highly rated Josh Wolff is waiting in the wings. Reyna must also deal with the less spectacular but vital defensive work in front of a back four headed by Jeff Agoos. Who will start in goal? It is difficult to choose between Brad Friedel and Kasey Keller.

## PROBABLE FORMATION 4-4-2

FRIEDEL

HEJDUK — JONES

POPE — AGOOS

ARMAS — O'BRIEN — REYNA — STEWART

DONOVAN — MOORE

### ★ MEN THAT MATTER!

#### CLAUDIO REYNA

Age>> 28

Club>> Sunderland

Regarded as America's best player, he missed USA 94 through injury and was considered a big danger at France 98 and marked out of games. He is America's most expensive player at £4.5 million.

#### LANDON DONOVAN

Age>> 21

Club>> San Jose Earthquakes

Landon Donovan is America's latest bright young soccer star. He has gelled superbly alongside Joe Max-Moore in attack. The MLS signed him back for £145,000 after an unhappy spell with Bayer Leverkusen.

#### JOE-MAX MOORE

Age>> Everton

Club>> 31

Long serving forward who has been given a boost with the arrival of Landon Donovan. Moore was a squad member at USA 94 and played in midfield at France 98.

### ★ PROBABLE SQUAD    ★ QUALIFICATION RECORD

| NAME | POSITION | CLUB | APS/GOALS | GAMES | MINS | Y/C | R/C | GOALS |
|------|----------|------|-----------|-------|------|-----|-----|-------|
| **Brad Friedel** | Goalkeeper | Blackburn, England | 73/0 | 6 | 540 | 1 | 0 | 0 |
| **Tim Howard** | Goalkeeper | MetroStars, USA | 0/0 | 0 | 0 | 0 | 0 | 0 |
| **Kasey Keller** | Goalkeeper | Tottenham, England | 56/0 | 8 | 720 | 0 | 0 | 0 |
| **Jeff Agoos** | Defender | San Jose Earthquakes, USA | 125/4 | 12 | 1080 | 0 | 0 | 0 |
| **Gregg Berhalter** | Defender | Crystal Palace, England | 22/0 | 7 | 454 | 1 | 0 | 0 |
| **Steve Cherundolo** | Defender | Hannover 96, Germany | 9/0 | 7 | 606 | 1 | 0 | 0 |
| **Frankie Hejduk** | Defender | Bayer Leverkusen, Germany | 36/5 | 2 | 29 | 0 | 0 | 0 |
| **Carlos Llamosa** | Defender | New England Revolution, USA | 25/0 | 9 | 653 | 3 | 0 | 0 |
| **Eddie Pope** | Defender | DC United, USA | 44/4 | 9 | 764 | 0 | 0 | 1 |
| **David Regis** | Defender | Metz, France | 24/0 | 12 | 1067 | 2 | 0 | 0 |
| **Tony Sanneh** | Defender | Hertha Berlin, Germany | 27/1 | 14 | 1205 | 1 | 0 | 0 |
| **Greg Vanney** | Defender | Bastia, France | 12/0 | 4 | 249 | 1 | 0 | 0 |
| **Chris Armas** | Midfielder | Chicago Fire, USA | 43/2 | 14 | 1216 | 2 | 0 | 0 |
| **Cobi Jones** | Midfielder | Los Angeles Galaxy, USA | 151/14 | 13 | 767 | 0 | 0 | 1 |
| **Jovan Kirovski** | Midfielder | Crystal Palace, England | 53/7 | 8 | 562 | 0 | 0 | 0 |
| **Eddie Lewis** | Midfielder | Fulham, England | - | 6 | 301 | 0 | 1 | 0 |
| **John O'Brien** | Midfielder | Ajax, Holland | 12/1 | 6 | 337 | 0 | 0 | 1 |
| **Claudio Reyna** | Midfielder | Sunderland, England | 85/8 | 9 | 711 | 2 | 0 | 0 |
| **Earnie Stewart** | Midfielder | NAC Breda, Holland | 75/15 | 15 | 1301 | 4 | 0 | 8 |
| **Landon Donovan** | Forward | San Jose Earthquakes, United States | 15/2 | 4 | 273 | 0 | 0 | 0 |
| **Brian McBride** | Forward | Columbus Crew, United States | 57/18 | 5 | 293 | 0 | 0 | 2 |
| **Joe-Max Moore** | Forward | Everton, England | 93/24 | 12 | 784 | 1 | 0 | 4 |
| **Josh Wolff** | Forward | Chicago Fire, United States | 14/4 | 5 | 259 | 1 | 0 | 2 |

**KEY:** APPS/GOALS = International Appearances/Goals; GAMES=Qualification Games played; MINS=Minutes played; Y/C= Yellow cards R/C=Red cards

# HISTORY AT THE WORLD CUP

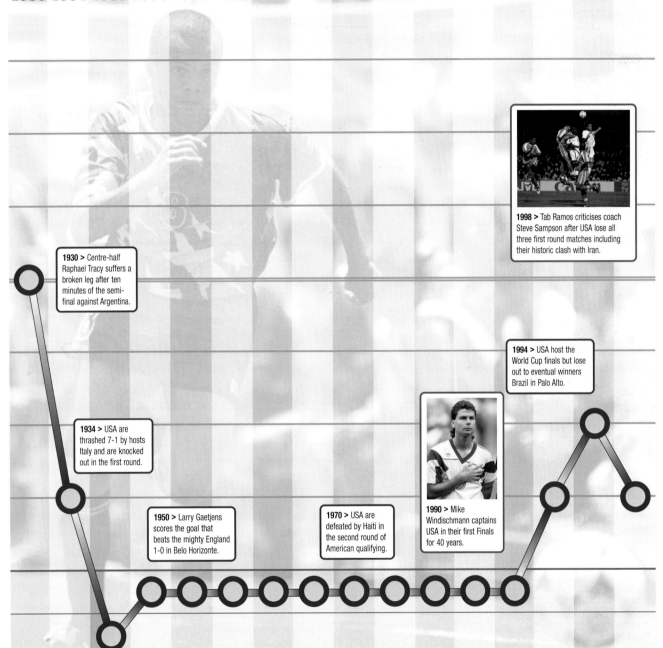

**1998 >** Tab Ramos criticises coach Steve Sampson after USA lose all three first round matches including their historic clash with Iran.

**1930 >** Centre-half Raphael Tracy suffers a broken leg after ten minutes of the semi-final against Argentina.

**1994 >** USA host the World Cup finals but lose out to eventual winners Brazil in Palo Alto.

**1934 >** USA are thrashed 7-1 by hosts Italy and are knocked out in the first round.

**1950 >** Larry Gaetjens scores the goal that beats the mighty England 1-0 in Belo Horizonte.

**1970 >** USA are defeated by Haiti in the second round of American qualifying.

**1990 >** Mike Windischmann captains USA in their first Finals for 40 years.

## ★ WORLD CUP HISTORY

| | |
|---|---|
| 1930 >> Fourth Place | 1970 >> Did Not Qualify |
| 1934 >> First Round | 1974 >> Did Not Qualify |
| 1938 >> Did Not Enter | 1978 >> Did Not Qualify |
| 1950 >> Did Not Qualify | 1982 >> Did Not Qualify |
| 1954 >> Did Not Qualify | 1986 >> Did Not Qualify |
| 1958 >> Did Not Qualify | 1990 >> First Round |
| 1962 >> Did Not Qualify | 1994 >> Second Round |
| 1966 >> Did Not Qualify | 1998 >> First Round |

## ★ WORLD CUP RECORDS, STORIES AND WEIRDNESS

**FIRST PLAYER TO SCORE A HAT-TRICK**>> American Bert Patenaude scored the first ever World Cup hat-trick against Paraguay in 1930.

**UNLIKELIEST RESULT**>> When news about the USA's 1-0 defeat of England reached England, people thought it was a misprint in the newspaper. England, with legends Billy Wright and Tom Finney in the side, wasted lots of chances and couldn't prevent the American part-timers from winning.

| OPPONENT | DATE | UK TIME | VENUE |
|----------|------|---------|-------|
| Denmark | **1 June** | 10.00 | **Ulsan, Korea** |
| France | **6 June** | 12.30 | **Busan, Korea** |
| Senegal | **11 June** | 07.30 | **Suwon, Korea** |

## "defence is everything"

# URUGUAY

Uruguay took the longest journey of all to the Finals, playing a staggering 20 qualifying games over 21 months to become the 32nd and last team to book their place – their first appearance at the World Cup since Italia '90.

For Uruguay it's been a tough, long haul made especially difficult by the problems of recalling players from their European clubs and aggravated by the country's leading club, Nacional, refusing to release its players too! In the end, Nacional reluctance to play the national squad game, withholding their players for a sixth time, caused coach Daniel Passarella, and former Argentine international, to quit midway through the qualifiers.

His successor was assistant Victor Pua. It was a natural transition causing the minimum of disruption to the squad and style of play. Pua continued with Passarella's ultra defensive approach making Uruguay very difficult to beat. Uruguay are a team that know how to defend a slender lead, but this also means that they're not at all suited to chasing games.

So the first goal in any Uruguayan international is vitally important and this factor has contributed to the team's inconsistent results. They beat Brazil at home with a first half Federicio Magallanes penalty but were also beaten 2-0 by South America's worst team, Venezuela. The Venezuelan defeat effectively ended their hopes of automatic qualification and Uruguay were left to battle for a play-off place with Colombia in the last round of matches.

Uruguay, with a two-point advantage, needed to beat South America's in form team and group winners Argentina to be certain of qualification. In turn, Colombia had to win away to Paraguay and see Uruguay lose. Dario Silva, who has been a revelation in attack, gave Uruguay the lead after 19 minutes. It was only Uruguay's 19th goal in 18 matches. However, just before the break Claudio Lopez equalised for Argentina. Meanwhile, Colombia had torn apart a lacklustre Paraguayan side and led 4-0. This meant a goal for either Argentina or Colombia would knock out Uruguay. Fortunately, the scores remained unchanged and Uruguay had earned a two-legged play off with Australia.

In the away first leg Uruguay lost 1-0. Now the normally goal-shy Uruguayans would have to score at least twice to qualify. In Centenario, Dario Silva provided the equaliser after 14 minutes. Chances were few and far between but the match was decided, ironically, by a Nacional player, Richard Morales, who scored twice for a 3-0 win – the first time in 14 months Uruguay had scored three goals in a game.

Uruguay probably won't be the most exciting team to watch at the Finals, although striker Dario Silva is one to watch. Their game is all about stopping the opposition scoring. Captain Paolo Montero marshals one of the best defences in international football – they conceded just 13 goals in qualifying, less than any other side on the South American continent.

## ★ THE LOWDOWN

**Population:** 3.3 million

**Capital:** Montevideo

**Leader:** Jorge Batlle

**Life Expectancy:** Male: 72 yrs Female: 79 yrs

>> Freezing temperatures are almost unknown in Uruguay.

>> Three-quarters of the country is grassland used for cattle and sheep grazing.

>> The biggest industries in the country are food processing and textiles.

- ★ **ASSOCIATION:** Asociacion Uruguaya de Futbol
- ★ **JOINED FIFA:** 1923
- ★ **JOINED CONEMBOL:** 1916
- ★ **PLAYERS:** 134,400
- ★ **CLUBS:** 1,091
- ★ **WEBSITE:** www.auf.org.uy
- ★ **HONOURS:** World Cup 19/50; Copa America 1916/17/ 20/23/24/26/42/56/59/67/83/87/95; Olympics – 1924/28.

Pablo Garcia hears the patter of Australian Mark Viduka's tiny feet approaching.

## ★ ROAD TO QUALIFICATION

Mar 00 **Bolivia** (a) > (w) **1**-0 Garcia 26

Apr 00 **Paraguay** (a) > (l) 1-**0**

Jun 00 **Chile** (h) > (w) **2**-1
Silva 34, Ortero Larzabal 42

Jun 00 **Brazil** (a) > (d) 1-**1** Silva 6

Jul 00 **Venezuela** (h) > (w) **3**-1
Olivera, Nic 30, 90, Rodriguez 53

Jul 00 **Peru** (h) > (d) **0**-0

Aug 00 **Colombia** (a) > (l) 1-**0**

Sep 00 **Ecuador** (h) > (w) **4**-0
Magallanes 15, Silva 37, Olivera, Nic 55,
Cedres Vera 87

Oct 00 **Argentina** (a) > (l) 2-**1** Ayala 48 og

Nov 00 **Bolivia** (a) > (d) 0-**0**

Mar 01 **Paraguay** (h) > (l) 0-**1**

Apr 01 **Chile** (a) > (w) 0-**1** Munoz 12 og

Jun 01 **Brazil** (h) > (w) **1**-0
Magallanes 33 pen

Aug 01 **Venezuela** (a) > (l) 2-**0**

Sep 01 **Peru** (a) > (w) 0-**2**
Silva 11, Recoba 45

Oct 01 **Colombia** (h) > (d) **1**-1
Magallanes 34 pen

Nov 01 **Ecuador** (a) > (d) **1**-1
Olivera, Nic 34 pen

Nov 01 **Argentina** (h) > (d) **1**-1 Silva 19

Nov 01 **Australia** (a) > (l) 1-**0**

Nov 01 **Australia** (h) > (w) **3**-0 (agg 3-0)
Silva 14, Morales 70, 90

## ★ FINAL GROUP TABLE

| Team | P | W | D | L | F | A | Pts |
|---|---|---|---|---|---|---|---|
| Argentina | 18 | 13 | 4 | 1 | 42 | 15 | 43 |
| Ecuador | 18 | 9 | 4 | 5 | 23 | 20 | 31 |
| Brazil | 18 | 9 | 3 | 6 | 31 | 17 | 30 |
| Paraguay | 18 | 9 | 3 | 6 | 29 | 23 | 30 |
| **Uruguay** | **18** | **7** | **6** | **5** | **19** | **13** | **27** |
| Colombia | 18 | 7 | 6 | 5 | 20 | 15 | 27 |
| Bolivia | 18 | 4 | 6 | 8 | 21 | 33 | 18 |
| Peru | 18 | 4 | 4 | 10 | 14 | 25 | 16 |
| Venezuela | 18 | 5 | 1 | 12 | 18 | 44 | 16 |
| Chile | 18 | 3 | 3 | 12 | 15 | 27 | 12 |

## ★ RECENT RESULTS

Feb 02 **South Korea** (h) > (w) **2**-1
Abreu 6, 54

Mar 02 **Saudi Arabia** (a) > (l) 3-**2**
Forlan 4, O'Neill 58

## DID YOU KNOW?

The only World Cup winners never to have defended their title are Uruguay who, after their 1930 triumph, refused to travel to Europe in 1934.

Great at defending, not so good at scoring goals – that, in short, sums up Uruguay. A solid defence has been the key to their success. Their preferred 3-4-2-1 formation can easily switch to a 5-4-1 when defending a lead and in Fabian Carini, Uruguay have one of South America's most reliable goalkeepers. He is well protected by the three central defenders – Lembo, Montero and Rodriguez – and if the need arises both Tais and Guigou can be pulled back from the flanks, while De Los Santos and Garcia can also form another formidable layer of defence. Frederico Magallenes, the team's penalty taker, and Alvaro Recoba, are the only two midfielders with an attacking brief in support of Dario Silva – who has proved to be an excellent lone striker taking the few chances that come his way. Once Silva has scored, Uruguay will invariably shut up shop.

# PROBABLE FORMATION  3-4-2-1

CARINI

LEMBO    RODRIGUEZ

MONTERO

TAIS    DE LOS SANTOS    GARCIA    GUIGOU

MAGALLANES    RECOBA

SILVA

## ★ MEN THAT MATTER!

### DARIO SILVA

Age>> 29
Club>> Malaga
Dario Silva has been a revelation for Uruguay. Cast as the lone striker in a defence-minded team, he scored crucial World Cup qualification goals.

### FABIAN CARINI

Age>> 21
Club>> Juventus
Young goalkeeper who played in all but one of the qualifiers and the main reason Uruguay had the best defensive record of South America. Deservedly assumed the mantel as Uruguay's number one.

### PABLO GARCIA

Age>> 25
Club>> Venezia
When Pablo Garcia was absent for two games the midfielder was sorely missed — Uruguay were awful. He is an influential player playing in front of the back four instigating many of Uruguay's moves.

## ★ PROBABLE SQUAD ★ QUALIFICATION RECORD

| NAME | POSITION | CLUB | APS/GOALS | GAMES | MINS | Y/C | R/C | GOALS |
|---|---|---|---|---|---|---|---|---|
| Fabian Carini | Goalkeeper | Juventus, Italy | 32/0 | 18 | 1620 | 4 | 0 | 0 |
| Adrian Berbia | Goalkeeper | Penarol, Uruguay | 0/0 | 0 | 0 | 0 | 0 | 0 |
| Gustavo Munua | Goalkeeper | Nacional, Uruguay | 7/0 | 1 | 90 | 0 | 0 | 0 |
| Alejandro Lembo | Defender | Nacional, Uruguay | 28/1 | 16 | 1365 | 2 | 0 | 0 |
| Gustavo Mendez | Defender | Cagliari, Italy | 42/0 | 8 | 720 | 6 | 1 | 0 |
| Paolo Montero | Defender | Juventus, Italy | 45/3 | 12 | 1071 | 5 | 0 | 0 |
| Dario Rodriguez | Defender | Penarol, Uruguay | 18/2 | 11 | 990 | 4 | 0 | 0 |
| Gonzalo Sorondo | Defender | Internazionale, Italy | 15/0 | 8 | 638 | 1 | 0 | 0 |
| Washington Tais | Defender | Real Betis, Spain | 19/0 | 9 | 783 | 0 | 0 | 0 |
| Pablo Garcia | Midfielder | Venezia, Italy | 33/1 | 17 | 1521 | 4 | 0 | 1 |
| Guill'mo Giacomazzi | Midfielder | Lecce, Italy | 6/0 | 5 | 115 | 1 | 0 | 0 |
| Gianni Guigou | Midfielder | Roma, Italy | 32/0 | 17 | 1352 | 1 | 0 | 0 |
| Nicolas Olivera | Midfielder | Sevilla, Spain | 22/8 | 13 | 1006 | 3 | 0 | 4 |
| Diego Perez | Midfielder | Defensor, Uruguay | 8/0 | 2 | 8 | 0 | 0 | 0 |
| Gonzalo D L Santos | Midfielder | Valencia, Spain | 25/0 | 9 | 810 | 2 | 1 | 0 |
| Gustavo Varela | Midfielder | Nacional, Uruguay | 5/0 | 3 | 193 | 0 | 0 | 0 |
| Sebastian Abreu | Forward | Cruz Azul, Mexico | 9/4 | 2 | 47 | 0 | 0 | 0 |
| Federico Magallanes | Forward | Venezia, Italy | 22/4 | 11 | 689 | 3 | 0 | 4 |
| Richard Morales | Forward | Nacional, Uruguay | 9/3 | 2 | 51 | 1 | 0 | 2 |
| Alvaro Recoba | Forward | Internazionale, Italy | 40/8 | 17 | 1349 | 1 | 0 | 1 |
| Mario Regueiro | Forward | Racing Santander, Spain | 10/0 | 8 | 305 | 1 | 0 | 0 |
| Dario Silva | Forward | Malaga, Spain | 36/12 | 8 | 613 | 1 | 1 | 4 |
| Javier Chevanton | Forward | Lecce, Italy | 4/1 | 3 | 187 | 0 | 0 | 0 |

KEY: APPS/GOALS = International Appearances/Goals; GAMES=Qualification Games played; MINS=Minutes played; Y/C= Yellow cards R/C=Red cards